From *Publishers Weekly*

"What are the attributes of a successful explorer? Why do some perish while others survive to tell their tales? Paton (*Lewis and Clark: Doctors in the Wilderness*) attempts to uncover the answers in this book, documenting the high and low moments of ... prominent 18th- and 19th-century adventurers and investigating the recurring obstacles that all explorers who lead their comrades into the unknown must tackle. Instead of focusing on celebrity explorers, Paton selects a well-thought-out cross-section of famous seekers (Lewis and Clark; John Wesley Powell), shadowy adventurers (Zeb Pike), businessmen (Samuel Hearne; Alexander Mackenzie) and infamous voyagers (William Bligh). Each chapter gives a primer on an expedition's personnel, goals, tragedies and accomplishments. The missions ... demonstrate that the success of each undertaking usually depends not on grand physical achievements but on the smallest details. While Paton's extensive forays into what the explorers ate (whatever they could) and who they met (natives) aren't surprising, the author excels in detailing the characteristics of survivors and leaders. His work has elements of an accessible textbook and an informative field manual."

More Praise for *Adventuring with Boldness*

"With *Adventuring with Boldness*, Bruce C. Paton, author of *Lewis and Clark: Doctors in the Wilderness*, has generated another fascinating chronicle of courage and daring. He recounts the feats of Bligh, who amazingly navigated his small boat 4,000 miles across the Pacific; of Hearne, Mackenzie, Franklin, and Rae, who probed the Canadian Arctic and found portions of the Northwest Passage by land; of Lewis and Clark, Frémont, and Pike, who helped open the American West; and of Powell, first through the Grand Canyon. With detailed analyses, Paton explores how all but Franklin survived, the way they dealt with hunger, starvation, even cannibalism; how they coped with bitter cold or searing heat, the diseases and injuries they faced; their contacts with natives; and the qualities that made them successful."
—James A. Wilkerson, M.D., editor of
Medicine for Mountaineering and
Hypothermia, Frostbite, and Other Cold Injuries

D1714567

"What does a retired cardiac surgeon and mountain wanderer do to sustain an adventurous life? Well, Bruce Paton has chosen to put his scholarly talents to use in chronicling the journeys of ten explorers, predominantly of the North American West. Each of his vignettes is alive with humanity, and once these tales are told, Paton uses his analytical skills to examine what makes these leaders tick. For those of us who savor adventure in a comfortable chair, *Adventuring with Boldness* is a captivating journey."

—Thomas Hornbein, M.D., author of
Everest: The West Ridge

Adventuring
with **Boldness**

The Triumph of the Explorers

Bruce C. Paton, M.D.

Fulcrum Publishing
Golden, Colorado

Library of Congress Cataloging-in-Publication Data

Paton, Bruce C.
  Adventuring with boldness : the triumph of the explorers / Bruce C. Paton.
    p. cm.
  Includes bibliographical references and index.
  ISBN 1-55591-517-5 (pbk.)
  1. Explorers—Biography. 2. Discoveries in geography. I. Title.
  G200.P32 2006
  910.92'2—dc22

                                        2006002638

ISBN-13: 978-1-55591-517-9
ISBN-10: 1-55591-517-5

Printed in the United States of America
0 9 8 7 6 5 4 3 2 1

Editorial: Bob Baron, Katie Raymond
Cover design: Jack Lenzo
Interior design: Patty Maher

Fulcrum Publishing
16100 Table Mountain Parkway, Suite 300
Golden, Colorado 80403
(800) 992-2908 • (303) 277-1623
www.fulcrumbooks.com

Contents

Introduction

The century between 1770 and 1870 saw an extraordinary series of explorations that opened North America to a wave of emigration and occupation. At the start of this period, the Mississippi River was the limit of western land exploration, except for limited exploration as far as the Missouri. A narrow strip of country along the West Coast had been opened from the sea, and a few communities, mostly settled by the Spanish or the Russians, were scattered along the shoreline. In Canada, the fur trade drove the expansion west, and the success of this trade was one of the forces that persuaded President Thomas Jefferson to launch Meriwether Lewis's and William Clark's expedition toward the West Coast.

After Alexander Mackenzie reached the Pacific in 1793, and Lewis and Clark pushed through the Rockies to the mouth of the Columbia in 1805, geographical and psychological barriers had been broken. The floodgates had been opened. Within forty years, long lines of wagons were crossing the prairies, but there were environmental prices to pay, apart from the lives lost and bones whitening along the wagon routes. By the time the century ended, beaver had been almost exterminated and the herds of bison that darkened the prairies when Lewis passed by had been almost exterminated. Within that same time frame, half a continent that had lain untouched by the white man's incessant drive to occupy the land would be changed forever: gold had been discovered and extractive industries were leading the mad rush for riches and a railroad across the continent carried people in comfort and at a speed unimagined by the Corps of Discovery.

During the past few years, and especially during the years of the bicentennial of the Corps of Discovery's expedition, the story of Lewis and Clark has been celebrated in a profusion of books, conferences, films, and television programs. Without in any way detracting from the achievements of these great American heroes, it is important to realize that during the same period, there were many other amazing explorers whose adventures were every bit as dramatic, and some of them more harrowing, than those of Lewis and Clark. All of the explorers whose exploits are discussed in this book made incredible voyages, surmounting daunting circumstances. All had to deal with problems of food and starvation, disease, encounters with indigenous people—sometimes friendly, sometimes hostile—and, above all, they all had to solve the problems of leadership.

All the explorers made their journeys by land or on rivers within North America, except for William Bligh. His journey, with eighteen men in a twenty-three-foot boat traveling 4,000 miles across the Pacific without the loss of a single life, is beyond the limits of our modern experience. This was an achievement that involved all the problems mentioned above and which occurred during the period under examination. It could not be ignored.

Most of the explorers wrote journals during their journeys, or soon thereafter, and many of these accounts have been reedited in modern times, making access to their personal feelings readily accessible. The availability of these accounts was, admittedly, one of the reasons for choosing this particular set of heroes.

I have not attempted to make comparisons between the various expeditions. It is impossible to say that one adventure was "better" than another. Some achieved their hoped-for objectives; some failed. But all expanded our understanding of, and admiration for, the human spirit. If two words could describe their collective essential spirit, it would be "undefeatable determination."

In the intervening years, many other men and women have accomplished similar feats of endurance and determination. We know most about those whose stories have been passed from generation to generation. Yet there have been millions of indigenous people of every nation who have achieved equal feats of endurance whose stories will never be told. Many of them accompanied the men whose stories are told here: the Indians who saved Samuel Hearne and John Franklin, the guides and hunters who went with John Charles Frémont and Alexander Mackenzie. And these people— many of whom were women—could not retire to the comforts of Montreal, London, and Washington. They turned around to face the harshness of the wilderness once more. They deserve to be remembered.

The problems these explorers faced were common to all of them but were solved in many different ways. Their styles of leadership varied from quietly persuasive to brutally tough. Yet they all led according to their personal standards and social backgrounds. As we look at the current world leaders, we see the same traits and motives, both good and bad. Nothing has changed.

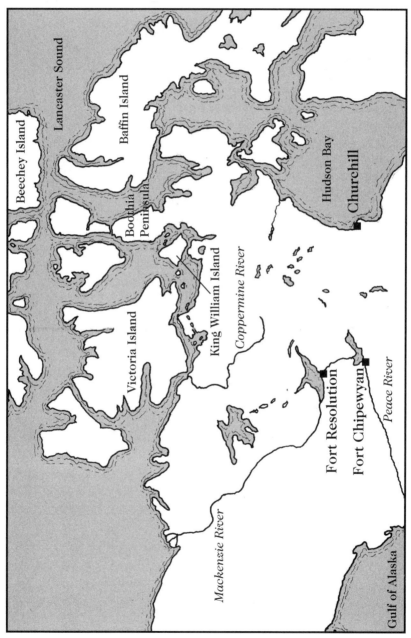

The Arctic

Beechey Island

Lancaster Sound

Baffin Island

Boothia Peninsula

Victoria Island

King William Island

Coppermine River

Hudson Bay

Churchill

Fort Resolution

Fort Chipewyan

Peace River

Mackenzie River

Gulf of Alaska

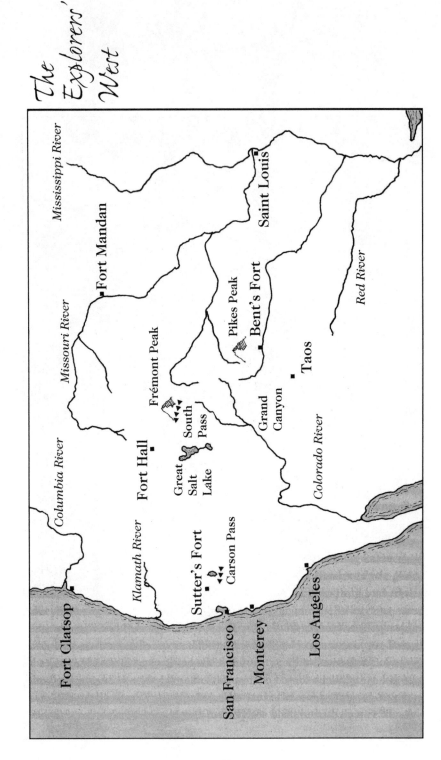

The Explorers' West

Mississippi River

Fort Mandan

Missouri River

Columbia River

Fort Clatsop

Klamath River

Fort Hall

Frémont Peak

South Pass

Great Salt Lake

Sutter's Fort

Carson Pass

San Francisco

Monterey

Los Angeles

Colorado River

Grand Canyon

Taos

Pikes Peak

Bent's Fort

Saint Louis

Red River

Part One

1
William Bligh
(1754–1817)

Beast or Hero?

Difficulties are just things to be overcome, after all.

—*Ernest Shackleton*

Lieutenant William Bligh of the Royal Navy—frequently but wrongly called "Captain," for he had not yet been promoted to that rank—stood on a spit of sandy land in the Great Barrier Reef screaming bloody murder at his exhausted men lying around him. Set adrift by mutineers from his ship HMS *Bounty*, they had just landed on a bleak island after sailing 3,000 miles across the Pacific in an open boat. Bligh was scrawny thin, disheveled and bearded, and dressed in tattered fragments of clothing his servant had saved from the ship.

"You damned scoundrel. Fight me, you damned reptile," he shouted as he waved a cutlass and threatened to kill William Purcell, one of the crew, challenging him to a fight. Bligh barely had enough strength to wield the cutlass, let alone deal a lethal blow. John Fryer, the former master of the *Bounty* and one of Bligh's irreconcilable rivals, called on the rest of the crew to arrest their captain. "Arrest him, arrest him!" he urged. The crisis died down. No one was hurt, or arrested, but Bligh realized that his behavior had divided the crew into two groups: those for and those against him.

Bligh's achievement in bringing his men across the Pacific to this point was a remarkable victory over seemingly impossible circumstances. Everyone was alive, but the stress of the voyage was beginning to tell, and a mutiny was brewing. All the men were hungry and ill, and many of them hated their leader and believed that when they reached England, he should be blown to his death from the mouth of a cannon.

HMS *Bounty* had sailed from Portsmouth on December 23, 1787, bound for Tahiti, where she was to take on a cargo of breadfruit in the West Indies to be used as a cheap food for the slaves. Bligh had already visited Tahiti with Captain James Cook and was an expert navigator and cartographer. The voyage was to be part commercial and part exploratory, to chart a new route back from the east through the Torres Strait. Little did Lieutenant Bligh imagine the circumstances under which he would sail back through the Torres Strait.

HMS *Bounty* was a small ship manned by a small crew. She was eighty-five feet, one and one-half inches long, and only twenty-four feet across. Because she was rated as a cutter, she could not have a captain as commander. Bligh was the only commissioned officer on board, and as a lieutenant, he was paid only four shillings a day. He was a stickler for cleanliness and discipline, but, by the standards of the day, sentenced his men to relatively few floggings. His idea of a perfect voyage was one without scurvy or deaths from disease, and with no floggings.

Soon after setting sail from Portsmouth, one man was swept overboard, and ferocious storms forced Bligh to turn around and head for the Cape of Good Hope. One man, at Fryer's insistence, was punished with two dozen lashes, but the health of the crew was good. Bligh reported from Capetown, "I am happy and satisfyed in my little ship and we are now fit to go round half a score of worlds." After leaving Capetown, they sailed to Tasmania, where the first sign of trouble appeared.

Bligh went ashore to supervise the cutting of wood and found the carpenter, Purcell, sawing billets that were too large. When Bligh ordered Purcell to make them smaller, Purcell accused the captain of coming ashore just to find fault. This blatant insubordination could have led to a court martial, but Bligh could not afford to lose a good, hardworking crewman. Purcell was a warrant officer and could not be flogged, and Bligh could only order Purcell back to the ship, where he received no food until he agreed to work. The rest of the crew was ordered not to assist him. While peace seemed to be restored, a lasting hatred had been born between Purcell and Bligh.

Before the *Bounty* reached Tahiti, one man, James Valentine, died from an infection after being bled by the surgeon. With one man having been flogged and the death of Valentine, Bligh's perfect voyage was already ruined.

The *Bounty* reached Tahiti after a voyage of 28,086 miles and stayed at anchor offshore from October 24, 1788, until April 5, 1789. During this time, William Peckover directed the collection of breadfruit, while many other members of the crew enjoyed the generous hospitality of the Tahitians.

Although the place was idyllic, discipline was breaking down. Bligh was disgusted by the freedom with which the women offered their sexual favors; and venereal diseases, which had not been a problem before landing, began to appear. One man had to be flogged, then two more. Men were tattooed according to the local customs, mostly on their buttocks, and many became attached to a woman and her family.

The historic mutiny—the subject of films and books in which Bligh has been vilified as an unmitigated sadist—started after the breadfruit had been grown and collected and the ship had sailed from Tahiti. Bligh was woken from sleep by Fletcher Christian, the master's mate, and hauled above decks in his nightshirt, naked from the waist down and with his hands tied behind his back. Within two hours, he, along with eighteen other men, were cast adrift in an open boat twenty-three feet long and six feet wide with a freeboard of nine inches, faced with a voyage of 4,000 miles, across largely unknown seas, to the nearest port from which they might find a ship to return them to England.

Soon after being set adrift, the small boat approached the island of Tofoa. The men were badly in need of water and food, and Bligh reluctantly let some of them ashore. The natives were suspicious and did not believe the story that the men came from a larger ship that had sunk. While the men were getting cocoa nuts, the natives captured John Norton and, after a scuffle, murdered him. The death of Norton persuaded Bligh not to let the men land on any other island, even though they became desperate for food. He was convinced that all the natives were aggressive and would kill them if they landed.

Humans can survive for several weeks without food, but only for a few days without water. Almost constant rainstorms and gales brought them water, and water meant survival. They had started with 150 pounds of bread, 6 quarts of rum, 6 bottles of wine, 30 pounds of pork, 28 gallons of water, and the few cocoa nuts they had picked up in Tofoa—slim pickings for eighteen men for a journey calculated to take at least forty days: just an ounce or two of bread per day and barely a sliver of pork. A couple of birds were unfortunate enough to land on the rigging and were killed and sliced into bloody morsels. Even the fish in the stomachs of the birds were welcome additions to the men's diet.

The men were soaked and in constant discomfort. There were eighteen men in a boat designed to hold ten on short trips between the main ship and a nearby shore. The transom was only nine inches above the water. It was almost impossible to lie down and sleep; only because of a system of eight-hour watches was it possible for some men to curl up and sleep. The men who were awake spent most of their time bailing to keep the boat afloat.

Bligh made a weighing machine from two halves of a cocoa nut and some twine and controlled the distribution of the food. He divided it with meticulous, but ruthless, care, and never gave in to the pleadings of the starving men. He had calculated how much each man could have per day, and, by God, he was going to stick with that plan, no matter what. Some men thought that Bligh was keeping extra food for himself, although later, under oath, the same men denied this accusation.

They used a traditional British naval method to divide up extra food. One person cut up the food into small, equal pieces. He then asked another person, whose back was turned away, "Who shall have this?" That man then called out the name of a recipient, not being able to see the size or delicacy of the morsel. On occasion, Bligh gave extra food to someone who was particularly weak or sick. When a booby was killed, its blood was given to three of the men to try to strengthen them.

Fryer, the master of the *Bounty*, thought that he was every bit as good as Bligh and resented that he was not included in the decisions about navigation, food, and the continuing problems that cropped up every day. He was, in fact, a competent navigator, and Bligh's task might have been made easier if he had consulted with him, especially as Bligh was afraid that if something happened to him, the men would not know how to navigate to the nearest land.

As the journey progressed, the medical problems increased. Constipation combined with cramping—from lack of food and dehydration—made a bowel movement impossible for most of the men. Some men lost sensation in their legs, which also became swollen. They shivered with cold and, paradoxically, soaked their clothes in seawater to increase their body heat, as the water was warmer than the air.

One night, Fryer squeezed into the narrow space of the bow; peering into the darkness, he thought he could hear the sound of waves breaking on rocks. "Do you hear it? The sound of breaking waves," he asked Robert Tinkler, a seventeen-year-old midshipman. They held their breath and listened again. Yes. There was no doubt. Land! They woke the others, lowered the sail, and turned the helm to avoid running aground. As the light grew stronger, they saw waves crashing on unseen reefs. They spent more than a day navigating through the reefs before they could land on a sandy island. It was small, uninhabited, but had some vegetation, and there was wood for a cooking fire—if they could find anything to cook. The rocks were thick with oysters, and oyster stew was the best food they had eaten in a long time. Even better, there was space to lie down and sleep, although they must have still felt the rocking of the boat, the ghosts of ocean movement still embedded in their brains. They named their haven Restoration Island.

They were all pathetically weak and could barely walk on the beach, and the group was seriously divided into those who supported Bligh, and those who held him responsible for all their troubles.

Bligh had sailed up the Great Barrier Reef before, while serving on the *Endeavour* with Captain Cook, so he was well aware of the infinite navigational twists and turns that made the route so dangerous. The *Endeavour*, a much larger ship with many sails and a healthy crew, had come to grief on a hidden reef. Now, trying hard to remember the old charts, and true to his calling as a navigator and cartographer, Bligh went to the highest point on the island to take compass readings, jotting down notes and descriptions of the visible landmarks.

Finding land and extra food saved their lives. By digging in the sand, they even found brackish water. This might have been a place to stay awhile, rest, and recuperate. But that was not what Bligh had in mind.

They had seen signs of aborigines—ruined huts and other artifacts—and feared an attack. Bligh felt they had to keep moving. So with full water casks, fern roots as vegetables, and the remains of oyster stew, they pushed off again.

As they were leaving, they heard a shout from the nearby mainland and saw a party of naked natives, yelling and gesturing. They did not know if they were being invited to come ashore or being threatened. They did not turn aside to investigate because they assumed that all aborigines were cannibals.

At their next stop, Sunday Island, the smoldering tensions between Bligh and the men burst into flames. Purcell, the carpenter, whom Bligh hated, refused to put oysters he had harvested into the communal pot. Bligh, screaming at the man and calling him a scoundrel, raised a cutlass and made a pathetic attempt to start a fight. He was so weak, he could hardly raise the sword. But this was the opportunity that Fryer had been waiting for. "Cole!" he shouted to the boatswain, "Arrest him!" pointing at Bligh. Cole did not move. Bligh shouted back, "If I had not been with you, you would all have perished by now. And that man [pointing at Purcell] said he was as good a man as I am." Purcell's accusation, claiming to be as good as his captain, was highly incendiary, especially to a senior officer and a man of Bligh's temperament. The flame died down. Bligh threw down his cutlass and stormed away.

More serious problems were to come. Six men lay prostrated with weakness, doubled up by bowel cramps and dehydration. David Nelson, the botanist, was obviously dying. The men had asked Nelson if certain berries were edible, and, without really looking at them, he had assured the men they were safe. Perhaps Nelson had been wrong. Perhaps the berries poisoned the men.

Some of the men lit a fire to cook their dinner. The flames set the surrounding brush on fire, and Bligh became furious with Fryer for signaling their presence to every aborigine for miles around. When Bligh had left, Fryer sarcastically called out in a loud voice to the imaginary Indians, inviting them to come and join them.

The situation both sickened and infuriated Bligh. Could they not see that their salvation lay with him? How could the men be so ungrateful for all the leadership, the self-sacrifice, the hours awake at the helm, guiding them almost to within sight of safety? He was determined that no matter how ungrateful these miserable slugs of men might be, he would get them safely to Timor. If they hated him—well, to hell with them. He had his duty to perform.

On June 3, the launch turned the corner around the northern tip of Cape York, and they headed due west through the Torres Strait. Once again, Bligh had memories of Cook's chart and added to them his own detailed observations.

Bligh, now confident of success, increased the men's rations by a minuscule amount. But the skies became dark, storm clouds gathered, and rain battered the men. The tiny scraps of extra food made very little difference to their comfort. They caught a fish and divided the carcass according to the "who shall have this?" tradition. Bligh received the fish's liver, and within hours he was doubled up with abdominal cramps, leaning over the side of the launch retching and vomiting. He had never felt worse. He could no longer steer the boat, but still took notes on how sick the other men looked. "Sir," said Cole, in gentle jest, "if you saw yourself you would think we were doing fine."

June 12, 1789, 3:00 A.M. Timor in sight. Within hours, they could see cultivated terrain and new fields, but there were few signs of life. Bligh knew that if they could reach the port of Coupang (now spelled Kupang), they would find Dutch hospitality and helping hands.

Neither Bligh nor Fryer knew how to reach Coupang and a shouting match flared between them over the correct direction to take. Peckover, who had visited Timor on a previous expedition, said that Fryer was correct.

Timor is a long flake of land, oriented from southwest to northeast, 300 miles long, and not more than fifty miles across. A narrow strait separates Timor from Roti off the extreme southeast tip of the main island. Was the shape they could see Timor or Roti? While landing on Roti might have brought temporary safety, Coupang, the center of Dutch power, was on Timor.

There was one last argument over food. As they sailed along the coast, Fryer wanted to go ashore to search for food. Bligh refused but then relented. Farther down the coast, they spotted a cottage, and Bligh ordered Cole and Peckover to land to ask for directions. The locals were friendly, gave them food, and offered to guide them to Coupang. After another night of sailing close to the coast, they sailed into the harbor at Coupang, a makeshift Union Jack fluttering from their masthead. The first person to greet them spoke perfect English.

They were received with compassion and amazement—with compassion because the effects of their privations were obvious: sunken eyes, lips split by the sun, straggly beards, ribs like washboards, and legs like sticks; with amazement because no one could imagine how they had survived the storms, the sun, native attacks, intestinal diseases—all on a small piece of bread and a few mouthfuls of water every day.

The governor gave them a house and servants. With new clothes, good food, and a barber to shave them, they began to look like respectable humans again. But the ending was not perfect. Nelson, one of the few men who Bligh genuinely liked, died on July 20, barely a month after reaching safety.

But was it really safety? During the few weeks between their stay in Coupang and living in Batavia waiting for a ship home, seven of the men died from malaria and other fevers. West Africa may have been known as "The White Man's Grave," but the Dutch East Indies were every bit as fatal.

In Coupang, Bligh was concerned that he might catch a fever and die before reaching England. He wrote to his wife about the voyage out, the mutiny, and the details of their extraordinary voyage. "Thus happily ended through the assistance of divine providence without accident a Voyage of the most extraordinary nature that ever happened in the world let it be taken in its extent, duration, or so much want of the necessities of life." With what anguish he must have written the final words, "Know then, my dear Betsy, I have lost the *Bounty*."

In Timor, Bligh bought a ship, the *Resource*, to sail them to Surabaya and on to Batavia. The weeks in Surabaya were hell, despite the beauty of the place and its people. His men became insolent and drunk on the local wine. Only one man remained sober and loyal to Bligh. Once again, Bligh, white with fury, confronted his men, bayonet in hand. A hearing before the governor ensued, the men accusing Bligh of heinous offences and cruelty. But in court, when asked for their testimony, their complaints melted away, and they became abjectly contrite.

When they reached Batavia, Bligh immediately caught a fever and had to leave the city to recover. He was terrified that he might die before arriving home. He and two others found passage on the *Vlydte*, sailing for Holland. On March 14, 1790, Bligh arrived in England, landing where his voyage had started, at the great naval base of Portsmouth.

2
Samuel Hearne
(1745–1792)
First to the Coppermine

There is nothing impossible to him who will try.

—Alexander the Great

In the spring of 1757, a fifty-gun frigate of the Royal Navy, HMS *Antelope*, was flying before the wind in the English Channel in hot pursuit of a French frigate, the *Aquilon*. The *Antelope*'s captain, Samuel Hood, who as Lord Hood would one day become the most famous admiral of his time, was pacing the quarterdeck, shouting commands, ordering the sails to be trimmed to gain maximum speed, preparing the guns to be fired, and ordering the marines to be ready to board. The French ship could not escape and ran aground on an unseen reef. Her fate was sealed as the *Antelope* closed in, guns blazing, demolishing her rigging, bringing the mast crashing to the deck, and smashing great holes in her decks.

Standing off to one side, exhilarated, terrified, and waiting for orders, stood a twelve-year-old boy who had been in the navy for only four months. Samuel Hearne, receiving his baptism of fire, was lucky to come out of the encounter alive. Luck would be with him during his seven years before the mast, on four different ships but always under the command of Captain Hood. He saw the decks run red with blood, had seen friends killed beside him, witnessed floggings for trivial offences; watched as men twitched in their death throes, hanging from the yard arm, or were flogged "round the fleet," receiving twenty-five lashes alongside every ship in port. Yet his experience was not all blood and guts. He learned to navigate, to set and manage sails, and to use the heavy cannons. He was promoted to quarter-master's mate and was discharged with honor—indeed, with regret—by his captain, who thought he would make a fine naval officer. But he had seen enough. His inquisitive mind, filled with the nonconformist ideas of Voltaire, was not suitable for a life in the navy, with its cruel, rigid, and frequently unjust discipline. As he stepped off the deck of the *Vestal*, the last of the ships on which he had served with Hood, his mind turned toward a broader future. He did not know exactly what that future would be as he stepped onto a post chaise and headed for London. All he knew was that the navy was not for him.

Hearne's father, also named Samuel, was an important man, the secretary to the London Bridge Water Works, which supplied water from the Thames to most of London. The water carried the germs, chemicals, garbage, and sewage of the river directly into the homes through wooden pipes. But as this was an era in which sterility and bacteria were not understood, the rich people to whom the water was supplied accepted it with gratitude. The cholera pandemic of 1832 had not yet struck Europe or America, but other intestinal diseases were common.

Hearne was born in the shadow of London Bridge. His father died from a fever when Hearne was only five years old, perhaps from the very water that he supplied to the city, and the family moved out of London to Beaminster, a small, charming village southwest of the city. There Hearne was able to attend the Tucker Free School, where he received a good but stultifying education. The school had to send two boys to sea every year and, despite the misgivings of his mother, Samuel insisted on being one of them. His mother had social connections with the Hood family of nearby Netherbury, and through them was able to get an assurance from Captain Hood that he would take on the boy as a midshipman young gentleman. So, early in 1757, the small boy, dressed in his new naval uniform of white trousers and blue jacket, reported for duty on the deck of HMS *Torbay*, which was bobbing quietly at anchor in the huge harbor of Portsmouth.

The Seven Years War had begun in 1756, and Hearne served out his time during a period of warfare. The Treaty of Paris, in 1763, which ended the war, was also an opportune moment for Hearne to leave the navy. His first intention was to join the merchant marine, where the pay was better, the discipline not as harsh, and the possibilities for travel greater.

Hearne's opportunities were great. He could join a ship going to India. He could stay closer to home, crewing on a ship sailing up and down the coast. He could think of joining a company, such as the East Indian Company that held a royal monopoly, in which the chances of promotion for a young man were good. Hearne worked out of London for three years, increasing his knowledge of the sea and burnishing his nautical skills.

About this time, his mother remarried a prosperous businessman, relieving Hearne of any concern for her welfare. Always inquisitive, he became enthralled by the philosophy of Voltaire, an enchantment that would stay with him for the rest of his life. Voltaire's sometimes cynical look at the world and questioning of established thought and doctrine appealed to him, and his description of Admiral John Byng's execution in *Candide*, *"pour encourager les autres,"* fit with his own view of the injustice of the event. Voltaire's views on religion and superstition molded Hearne's and must have undercut the teaching he had received from his strict, nonconformist parents.

In February 1766, Hearne learned that the Hudson's Bay Company was looking for a mariner to command a whaling vessel. He was disappointed that the company could not offer him a captaincy, but he was willing to accept the position of first mate in the hope that his experience and skill would soon get him the position he sought. Hearne sailed from London on a company ship, stopping in Stromness in the Orkney Islands to take on fresh water, then over the North Atlantic to the Hudson Bay and the mouth of the Churchill River, where the Prince of Wales Fort had been built. The fort was a square with high ramparts on which protective guns were mounted. The buildings inside the square housed the staff and a substantial gate guarded the entrance and controlled the traffic of Indians coming into the fort.

Hearne soon went south to York Factory, at the southern tip of the Bay, to prepare his sloop and to experience his first winter ashore. (The terms "fort" and "factory" were interchangeable.) The men in the company posts had a limited social life. Many of them had little education and equally little interest in the indigenous people or the natural history of the surrounding country. Alcohol was readily available and drunkenness the order of the day. Hearne did not drink, but spent his time learning about the local people, studying their way of life and their languages, and hunting and fishing. The Cree and Chipewyan were the main hunting groups, but there were many subgroups, the Déné, Slaves, and the Esquimaux (the spelling of the time), a totally separate racial group that was frequently at war with the Indians.

The greatest source of stress within the forts, especially during the winter, was the absence of women. The Hudson's Bay Company had a strict rule against the men taking "country wives," but turned a blind eye to women visiting the forts, so long as they did not stay overnight. The rules that applied to the men did not apply to the men who governed the forts. Moses Norton, the governor of Prince of Wales Fort at Churchill, where Hearne spent several years, was notorious for having several Indian girls to serve his needs while at the same time raging against any man who tried to have a wife of his own. He became pathologically angry with any man he suspected of making a pass at one of his wives and rumor had it that he had poisoned wives he suspected of cheating on him. Hearne came to hate Norton, not only for the cruel way he dominated his women, but for his two-faced attitude toward others who enjoyed the company of women.

The forts acted as trading posts to which the Indians brought their furs every spring. Once a year, a ship arrived from England, loaded with trade goods that were exchanged for the furs. The currency of the fur trade was the "made beaver," a cured and trimmed pelt. The trade to Europe was large and profitable. About 30,000 to 50,000 skins were exported from Prince of Wales Fort every year, and the total export of pelts from the continent to Europe was in the hundreds of thousands per year—an unsustainable number. The profit margin was huge. A musket that cost £5 might be sold to an Indian for sable furs worth £300 on the London market. No wonder the investors in Fenchurch Street guarded their monopoly and resented the Scots of the North West Company and their French voyageurs when they muscled in on the trade.

Hearne, as first mate of the company sloop, was not restricted during the summer months to the fort, but had duties sailing up the coast. One of his first voyages was to hunt for black whales. The eight-man crews had hearty appetites, eating beef, pork, fish, geese, and bread, and swilling down the food with liberal draughts of beer. The company hoped to turn black whale fishing into a useful trade, but it did not take Hearne long to realize that there was little money to be made out of this trade, as the whales were few in number and difficult to hunt. During one of these voyages, Hearne carved his name on a rock, a relic of his presence that remains to this day: "S^L. Hearne ye July 1, 1767."

Hearne spent several years at Prince of Wales Fort, increasing his language skills and becoming adept in wilderness travel and hunting. Andrew Graham, the master of the fort at Severn River, was a knowledgeable naturalist and stimulated Hearne's latent interest in the wildlife of the area. Hearne maintained this interest throughout his years in the Arctic, writing evocative descriptions of the birds and animals and being constantly on the lookout for new observations. Many years later, he dissected the testicles of a Canada goose to demonstrate a theory about why some of them were larger than others. (He found that the larger geese had smaller testicles and, therefore, could not reproduce. The theory was wrong, but the observation was accurate.)

Of all the Indians Hearne met, none played a greater part in his life than a Chipewyan chief. Matonabee had been born at Churchill to a Déné man and a Métis woman. He was tall, strong, an impressive and commanding figure. He spoke English as well as native tongues, and was extremely influential with the local tribes. Norton had hired him to help with the fur trade and act as mediator between the company traders and the Indians. In the course of his duties, Matonabee brought in two Déné Indians who had a rough map and samples of copper they said had come from the Far Off Metal River—the Coppermine River. The findings and the map intrigued Norton, who immediately sensed the potential for a copper mine bringing in great wealth for the company and, presumably, for himself. He realized that there was only one man capable of making the long voyage to seek out the fabled river of copper, and that man was Hearne. He had already served the company for three years. He was strong, determined, inquisitive, and could speak native languages and travel without a retinue of company help. As Hearne wrote many years later, "I was pitched on as the proper person to conduct the expedition." Hearne perhaps had two motives in accepting the challenge: to make a great exploratory voyage and to get away from Norton, whom he had come, increasingly, to despise.

Other members of the company had traveled far west. In 1690, Henry Kelsey had explored as far west as the Great Plains, and in 1754, Anthony Henday had ventured to the country of the Blackfoot and perhaps as far as the Rocky Mountains. But no one had gone both west and north, with the added possibility of finding the elusive Northwest Passage. Few white men had been brave enough to cross the Barrens, the bleakest, least inhabited part of the continent. In 1716, William Stuart had spent a winter there accompanied by Thanadelthur, a famous Indian woman, but little was known of his voyage or his findings. The area, which is mostly treeless, sits atop the Canadian Shield, a vast glacier-eroded granite relic of the Ice Age. It is bounded to the north by the coast, to the east by the shores of the Hudson Bay, and to the south by the oblique tree line twisting north and west to the mouth of the Mackenzie River delta. It is filled with countless lakes and rivers and is still an area where few people live, although mineral wealth and hydroelectric power have brought both riches and environmental destruction.

The concept that a fortune might be made from a copper mine was understandable but naïve and founded on ignorance. No one knew how the ore might be extracted, except that the Indians had brought large pieces of almost pure ore. Perhaps the board members sitting in London thought that it would only be necessary to shovel the ore into a boat. A sea passage had not been found around the north of the continent; it must have been obvious that ships bringing the ore to England would have a voyage of several years to and from an imagined port on the Arctic Ocean. Nevertheless, both Hearne and Norton, with encouragement from London, thought the endeavor to be worthwhile.

Hearne was promised a "gratuity proportionable to the trouble and fatigue." It was fortunate for Hearne that the promised gratuity was not based on the amount of copper found or the feasibility of extracting the ore. If that had been the promise, Hearne would have been seriously disappointed with his reward, as would have been the bewigged and powdered members of the board.

Hearne was twenty-four years old, strong and lean, an expert winter traveler on snowshoes, a competent hunter, and supremely self-confident that he could embark on a voyage into an area of more than 1 million square miles without any maps. He was to be met in the spring by Matonabee, who said he knew the route, had visited the area, and had found copper there. He chose two Déné guides, one of whom, Coneequese, said he had been near the copper-bearing river. After receiving detailed orders from Norton, he set out on November 6, 1769.

From the start, the journey did not go well. Hearne had to pull a sled full of food that one of the Indians left behind. It soon became obvious that the Déné chief was testing Hearne in the belief that white men could not stand the privations of winter travel in the Barrens. Food ran short, and they had to turn south into the woods, looking for game to eat. The chief suggested to Hearne that they return to the Fort, but Hearne refused. When the Indians began to steal food and belongings and indicate that they were going to turn south to their own hunting grounds, Hearne had no option but to turn back. He reentered the gates of the fort one month after first leaving with such high expectations.

The disappointment did not discourage Hearne. He tried to persuade Norton that women should be included in the group because of the important tasks they performed and the loads they carried. Norton denied the request, suggesting instead that he should take some junior Hudson's Bay Company men. Hearne did not want to do this and decided to travel as the only white man in the group. This was a revolutionary suggestion, but Norton agreed. On February 23, 1770, Hearne passed through the gates of the fort again, heading west.

The party consisted of three Déné hunters and their families and two Crees. Progress was good at first. Deer were plentiful so food was easy to obtain. Hearne lived in a moose-hide tent and was well protected from the weather that he described as "so remarkably boisterous and changeable, that we were frequently obliged to stay two or three nights in the same camp." The supply of food was either a feast or a famine. At first, the Indians killed more than they needed, leaving behind considerable supplies of meat. Then for several days there would be "a severe want of provisions ... but we seldom went to bed entirely supperless." But by March 8, they had no food, not even a ptarmigan. They found a place where fish were abundant and the guide suggested that they stay there for the rest of the winter and continue when spring arrived. On April 1, like a cruel April Fool's Day joke, the fish disappeared. For three days, Hearne lived on tobacco smoke and drinks of water. The guide, a "steady man," went hunting until he returned with the blood and remains of a caribou with which they made soup.

By mid-May, they were eating migrating birds, but the weather became so warm that their snowshoes and sleds were no longer of any use and Hearne had to shoulder a heavy, cumbersome load, including his quadrant and its tripod. Once more, the caribou had moved away and they had no food. Hearne again sought consolation from his pipe and water. Rain fell and made fires impossible to light. Although they shot a musk ox, the Indians did not like raw meat. For many days, they were reduced to eating berries and scraps of leather, and Hearne noticed the Indians examining their clothes to see what parts could be spared as food. Severe constipation was one of the worst complications of prolonged fasting, and Hearne described the agony of attempting a bowel movement "so dreadful that none but those who have experienced it can have an adequate idea of its effect."

As June progressed, they were heading deeper and deeper into the treeless Barrens and came across Indians spearing caribou as they migrated across the rivers. They met another large band of Indians on their way to trade at the Prince of Wales Fort, led by "Captain" Keelshies who volunteered to take messages to the Fort asking for more powder, shot, and tobacco. He also told Hearne that a small canoe would be essential for crossing the rivers they would encounter.

As they moved north and west, they came to a huge lake, Dubwant, its freshwater proving to Hearne that they were still a long way from the ocean. They were, in fact, about 1,000 miles of grueling tundra travel from their target and the chief said that there was not enough time to reach the Coppermine during this season. Another incident affected Hearne's decision. A gust of wind blew over the quadrant used for measuring latitude. The instrument was useless and much of the purpose of the expedition, therefore, blew away in the same gust of wind. Hearne had no choice but to return to Prince of Wales Fort to repair his quadrant. They were, at the time, more than 500 miles from their base.

As August passed into September, the temperature fell. Winter was near. The supply of food remained satisfactory, but Hearne suffered from the cold because he did not have the right clothing. The chief guide, however, had a fur suit and felt no discomfort.

The weather quickly turned bad, and on September 20, when Hearne was, as he wrote, "in a forlorn state," Matonabee appeared providentially out of the forest. Within minutes, he had ordered his wives to make a warm suit of otter skins for Hearne and dispatched other wives (he had six and was to acquire more later) many miles to find wood suitable for snowshoes. The Déné chief who had been the guide was pushed aside as a man of no importance. Matonabee was now in charge.

As they made their way back to Prince of Wales Fort, Matonabee offered to guide Hearne to the Far Off Metal River, if he still wanted to go, but under one condition: they must bring women. Women cooked, made the tents and snowshoes, carried heavier loads than the men, relieved the men of other duties so that they could hunt, and afforded comfort at night. And, as Hearne wrote, "Women can be maintained at trifling expense, for, as they always cook, the very licking of their fingers in scarce times is sufficient for their sustenance." Hearne did not have to be persuaded.

They arrived back at the fort on November 25 having been away eight months and twenty-two days. They had accomplished nothing. Hearne immediately announced to Norton that he was leaving again as soon as he could assemble the necessary supplies and repair his quadrant. They departed on December 7. Once again, Hearne was the only white man in the party, but this time he was accompanied by women, one of whom was, presumably, his "wife."

The group comprised Chipewyan Indians, a tribe for whom Hearne developed both respect and scorn. They were impervious to hardship, easygoing, and accepted life as it came to them. But they could be cruel, with little compassion for members of other tribes or those in misfortune, and were to show these character traits on more than one occasion.

They traveled across bare, rocky ground with little to eat. Eventually, on the twenty-seventh of December, they killed some caribou and ate to their heart's content. Christmas Day had been the dullest Hearne had ever celebrated; he was far from home, with strangers to whom the festival had no meaning. The only gift was to see fresh caribou tracks with their promise of food.

Large areas of the Barrens were incapable of supporting human life, except during very short periods in the summer. There were no trees for firewood, only moss that was frequently wet. Game was scarce in the open areas because even the animals sought shelter and food in the few clumps of trees. The cold was bitter, and modern measurements show that the average temperature in January is twenty degrees below zero. The lakes were frozen, and the few lakes deep enough not to freeze to the bottom often did not support fish. Because of the intense cold, the men traveled as quickly as possible and one day covered fourteen miles in two hours—a good speed for a marathon runner on a city street. The unfortunate, heavily laden women, bringing up the rear, took much longer.

Hearne's comments on the women were not always complimentary. He did not think them beautiful, except for some of the younger girls, and wrote that the average Chipewyan man, if asked to give a definition of feminine beauty, would have described a broad, flat face, small eyes, high cheekbones, black tattoo lines across the cheeks, and breasts hanging down to the belt.

The weeks of travel passed and by April the sun reflecting off the snow was so hot that walking became difficult and hauling a sled was exhausting. But they were now moving north instead of west and came to a lake that drained into Lake Athabasca. This was a favorite collecting spot for

Indians, as it was a good place to make kayaks and fish were plentiful. Hearne was amazed at the skill of the Indians in making kayaks, snowshoes, and other items. They needed only a hatchet, a knife, and an awl. "Yet they are so dexterous that everything they make is executed with a neatness not to be excelled by the most expert mechanic assisted with every tool he could wish." Their tents were made from caribou skin with the hair attached, and to carry their belongings, they made long bags of skin that could be dragged behind them and were "as slippery as an otter" when pulled over the snow.

The Indian chief Captain Keelshies, who had gone to Prince of Wales Fort, met them and delivered letters and a keg of rum—no doubt a welcome addition, although Matonabee, who had a liking for Spanish wine, did not drink spirits. But Matonabee may have needed some cheering up, because two of his wives had deserted him to return to a former husband. Matonabee regarded this as a great insult, especially as they had departed in front of Hearne, making him lose much face. He threatened to leave the expedition, but Hearne was able to persuade him to stay. Matters were not improved when a more powerful man took another of Matonabee's wives and challenged him to a fight to get her back, a fight that Matonabee knew he could not win. (If a man wanted another man's wife, he could challenge him to a wrestling match. If he won, the lady was his. If he lost, his reputation was greatly diminished.)

As they moved north, Hearne became aware that women and children were being left behind, and that the men were lightening their loads as though preparing for rapid travel. He found that they intended to attack the Eskimos who lived at the mouth of the Coppermine. Although he tried hard, there was nothing he could say to dissuade them from making the attack that to Hearne seemed vicious and ridiculous, especially as Matonabee had previously made a friendly visit to the same Eskimos.

There had always been antagonism between the Eskimo and Indian tribes. The Eskimos, who were miserably poor, were terrified of the Indians. The only worthwhile items the Indians could steal were copper pots. Even the Eskimo women were not acceptable prizes. The Indians thought Hearne was cowardly and that his reason for protesting their plan was that he did not want to fight. Eventually, being the only white among a large group of Indians on whom he depended for life itself, he agreed to stand by them.

According to Hearne, the Indians otherwise regarded him as a "perfect human being, except in the color of my hair and my eyes." They also thought that his skin looked like meat that had been sodden in water until all the blood had been extracted. Hardly a flattering description!

On July 3, they walked ten miles through a driving snowstorm and sheltered in the lee of a large rock. They were crossing the Stony Mountains where, through the passage of countless generations of Indians, there were clear paths. The rigors of the trail set against the few advantages to be gained from attacking the Eskimos made some of the Indians desert and return to their women and children. Hearne did not criticize them because the rain was incessant and they had no shelter except under rocks. Their clothes were constantly wet and the moss for making fires was soaked with water. Only with difficulty could they light their pipes.

As the weather improved, they were able to walk sixty miles in two days. The heat dried their clothes but brought out plagues of mosquitoes that were "uncommonly numerous, and their stings almost insufferable."

They finally reached the Coppermine River about forty miles from the sea. They were successful in killing several caribou, which they roasted over open fires. Hearne found Indian food fascinating. One of the most popular dishes was very similar to the *boudin blanc* made by Pierre Cruzatte on the Meriwether Lewis and William Clark expedition: a mixture of chopped meat, blood, and fat encased in a stomach and roasted over the fire. Another dish, the half-digested contents of a caribou's stomach boiled to the consistency of porridge, sounds less appealing to modern tastes, but Hearne thought that "were it not for prejudice, it might be eaten by those who have the nicest palates."

As soon as Hearne saw the Coppermine, he knew that it was useless for navigation by anything except low draft canoes and kayaks. There was no hope that larger vessels, necessary for carrying the ore, could ever get upstream to a mine. Having discovered this, he might well have turned around. But two factors drove him on. First, he wanted to reach the ocean; second, he was—albeit unwillingly—part of a war party intent on slaughter.

The attack on the Eskimos took place in the middle of the night. The Indians went through an elaborate ritual of painting their faces and their shields, and as the dim twilight of the midsummer night approached, they crept closer and closer to their victims, until they were only 200 yards from the Eskimo camp. The Indians wanted Hearne to stay behind, out of sight, but he was unwilling to do this in case some of the Eskimos escaped, found him alone, and killed him. So he insisted on going forward with the attackers but said that he would not take part in the murders.

The attack was swift, vicious, and lethal. The Indians rushed in, screaming war cries, shooting, stabbing, and slashing the Eskimos as they tried to escape. "And so began the bloody slaughter while I stood neuter in the rear." Men, women, and children ran naked from their tents and were struck down without mercy. One unfortunate girl, about eighteen years old, already badly wounded, rushed to Hearne and wrapped herself around his legs, seeking safety. She was impaled by a spear and "wriggled like an eel." Hearne, knowing that nothing could save her, asked one of the Indians to put her out of her misery. Lifting his spear high, he plunged it into her heart. "Though much exhausted by pain and loss of blood, she made several efforts to ward off this friendly blow." This ghastly scene haunted Hearne for the rest of his life.

After everyone had been killed, the Indians plundered the tents for copper pots and tools, paltry trophies of the massacre. Hearne called the place Bloody Falls.

When the killing was over, Matonabee calmly announced that now Hearne could continue his survey. He went to the mouth of the river and confirmed that shoals, shallow water, and rocks made the approach to the river totally unfit for large ships. The group turned back and visited the "copper mine," which Hearne found to be a rocky hill with few traces of copper, of no commercial value. The largest piece of ore weighed about four pounds.

The year was 1771. The trip had been commercially worthless in one sense, but Hearne had clarified the geography of the Northwest in a way that no white man had done before. He was the first white man to reach the Arctic Ocean by land, and no other would pass this way until George Back paused at the Bloody Falls in 1821 and sketched the whitening bones and skulls of those who had been killed fifty years before.

The homeward journey started in a rush. The men were anxious to return to their wives and families, and they proceeded at such a pace that Hearne's feet became swollen and bloody. Gravel in his moccasins ground into his skin, and every footstep marked the ground with blood.

They started home around July 25 and eventually reached Prince of Wales Fort on June 29, 1772, eleven months later. They traveled throughout the winter, pausing at times when they met another tribe or to spend time hunting for food. As always, there were days of plenty and days of starvation. Matonabee acquired and lost more wives. He was fond of strong women capable of carrying heavy loads, and Hearne wrote that most of them would make good grenadiers.

One day, in the middle of the winter, they noticed some strange snowshoe prints and followed the trail until they came on a solitary girl sitting outside a small shelter. She was a Dogrib Indian who had been taken prisoner by the Athabascans and then escaped and attempted to make her way home. For seven winter months, she had lived by herself in the forest, catching rabbits for food and making their skins into clothing. Hearne was amazed at the calm and efficient way she had made use of the natural material around her, and despite the fact that she had only two very rudimentary tools, she had been able to make attractive and functional clothes. She had started a fire by striking stones together and, afraid that she might not be able to start another, had kept it burning all winter. "The singularity of her circumstances, the comeliness of her person, and her proven accomplishments, occasioned a strong contest between several of the Indians of my party as to who should have her for a wife. The poor girl was actually won and lost at wrestling by half a score of different men that same evening." The girl's reaction to being rescued was not recorded and perhaps she was not entirely pleased at exchanging the quiet solitude of the forest for the arduous duties of a wife.

One other incident infuriated Hearne. They came upon some poor Indians living deep in the forest. The area where they lived was well stocked with fish and game, and they had no need to trade. The Indians with Hearne immediately stole all the furs they had stored for future use and captured one of the young women. "This," wrote Hearne, "served to increase my indignation and dislike ... because it was committed on a set of harmless creatures whose general manner of life renders them the most secluded from society of any of the human race." Once more, Hearne could do nothing but fume at injustices he could not stop.

When they finally marched through the gates of Prince of Wales Fort to the booming of a welcoming cannon, it had been two years and seven months since Hearne had first set out to reach the Coppermine River, and eighteen months and twenty-three days since the start of his third expedition. During those months, he had traveled between 3,500 and 5,000 miles. He did not return laden with copper, or even furs, but he had opened the door to the far Northwest and had accomplished a journey that no one would ever repeat.

Later, he became the first member of the Hudson's Bay Company to set up an inland trading post at Cumberland House, not far from Lake Winnipeg, to compete with the North West Company. He was appointed governor of Prince of Wales Fort and married Mary Norton, the lovely daughter of Moses, after her detestable father died in agony from peritonitis, scream ing abuse at those around him. It was a union of true love that gave Hearne great happiness.

The American revolutionary war reached out to the far north in 1782 when the French captured the fort at Churchill. Hearne knew that the fort was indefensible for two reasons: there was no internal water supply and the battlements were too narrow to permit the cannons to recoil after they were fired. The fort was given up without a shot and without the loss of life. Some days later, York Factory surrendered in a similar manner. Hearne, who was taken prisoner, was allowed to keep his diaries and persuaded the courteous French leader Jean François de Galaup, Comte de La Pérouse to allow him to try and sail back to England. He succeeded in sailing across the North Atlantic to England with thirty-two other men in a tiny open boat, arriving with all his men alive and well. In return, the English government released an equal number of French prisoners. He returned to Churchill in 1783 to find a situation of utter devastation: his beloved Mary had died of starvation and Matonabee had committed suicide in a fit of despair.

The Indian population had been decimated by a smallpox epidemic from 1781 to 1782, bringing home the painful truth expressed by Charles Darwin: "Wherever the European has trod, death seems to pursue the aboriginal." Trade was in tatters. The few remaining Indians were starving, from lack of trade, disease, and because of a mysterious disappearance of the animals that sustained them. Hearne was faced with a daunting task. The fort was rebuilt on a better site, the Indians slowly began trading again, and the epidemic gradually petered out as the victims died and the survivors gained immunity.

Hearne remained in charge of the fort until 1787, when he retired to England. He died from dropsy, due either to congestive heart failure or kidney failure, in 1792, at age forty-seven.

3

Alexander Mackenzie
(1762–1820)

First to the Pacific

*The toil of our navigation was incessant, and often-times extreme;
and in our progress over land, we had no protection
from the severity of the elements.*

—*Alexander Mackenzie*

The outer Hebrides lie in a gentle curve off the northwest coast of Scotland: a chain of islands, low lying and mostly treeless, that form a buttress against the thrust and heave of the Atlantic swells. Lewis, the most northerly and the largest of the islands, has on its northeast shore a bay, Broad Bay, in which is tucked the town of Stornoway.

In the second half of the eighteenth century, Stornoway was a small collection of stone houses with peat roofs, most of them with only two rooms—one on either side of the low front door—called a "but and ben," with the people living on one side and animals on the other. The wealthier citizens lived in more substantial houses with two stories and slate roofs and it was in one of these, in the middle of town, that in 1762 Isabella MacIver Mackenzie gave birth to her fourth child, Alexander. Her husband, Kenneth, was well known, a loyal supporter of King George III and a member of the Stornoway Company of Volunteers.

This was a time of turmoil in Scotland. The landlords and clan chiefs displaced the people from the land to raise sheep. Thousands of Scots sailed to America and Canada, and in later years to Australia and New Zealand. Isabella already had a brother with a successful business in New York, so, after she died, Kenneth, Alexander, and an aunt joined the hundreds leaving their windswept homes to cross the Atlantic to the New World.

Alexander's family did not stay long in New York but moved north to the Mohawk valley. Both his father and uncle joined the Loyalist army, and in 1779 young Alexander was sent with his aunt to live in the greater safety of Montreal, for the flames of revolution were already sweeping the country and the cause of King George III was increasingly unpopular. Alexander's father died in the army, possibly from scurvy.

The young Alexander came to America already well versed in mathematics, Latin, and grammar. Thus it was possible for him to enter the employment of Gregory and McLeod—later part of the North West Company—a promising business in the fur trade, when he was only sixteen years old. Within five years his obvious talents as a hardworking, reliable man who had quickly picked up the intricacies of the competitive fur trade resulted in him being sent to Detroit.

Detroit was then an important frontier town in the network of North West Company forts that stretched from Montreal to Lake Athabasca, 4,000 miles away. In the spring, dozens of large freight canoes, *canots de maître*, thirty-six to forty feet long, five feet wide, and capable of carrying seventy ninety-pound packages of trade goods, set out from Lachine, near Montreal. Over the next weeks, they paddled up the Ottawa River to Georgian Bay, along the north shores of Lakes Huron and Superior, to Grand Portage.

Grand Portage was the bustling, prosperous exchange point where the trade goods were packed into smaller *canots du nord*, twenty-four feet long and capable of transporting a one-and-a-half-ton load. The smaller canoes bore the traders to the various posts, where they would spend the long, cold winters bargaining with the Indians for furs. The following May, when the ice broke on the rivers of the north, the canoes were loaded up with packages of furs and returned to Grand Portage.

The voyageurs who paddled these canoes were French Canadian, while the traders, the bourgeois, were mostly Scottish. These two nations controlled virtually all the highly profitable business of the trade. The well-educated Scots ran the business (and made the money) and the illiterate French provided the muscle that propelled the canoes over phenomenal distances at amazing speeds.

The voyageurs were a wild, proud, and sometimes undisciplined crowd, dressed in distinctive clothes finished off with a red sash around the waist. Their hats were decorated with feathers and fox's tails and as they toiled they sang with a cadence to match the rhythm of their strokes. They usually took forty-five strokes per minute, continuing from before dawn to sunset with only short breaks. The men who paddled the "express" canoes stroked at sixty dips per minute and, at eight knots, hurried their bosses back to Montreal.

There were about 2,000 paddlers divided into classes depending on experience and responsibility. The lowest men on the ladder were those in the middle of the canoe and paddled mindlessly. The next higher were the bowmen, followed by the steersmen. The guides, or leaders, who had served for many years and knew every twist and rapid in the rivers, were the most important and the best paid. There were probably fewer than forty of them.

Like any fraternity, the voyageurs had their own initiation ceremonies. At the highest point of the voyage to the far north, where the drainages went north and west instead of to the southeast, the novitiates would kneel before the guide and be blessed with a branch dipped in the river to the north. The newly blessed *homme du nord* would then swear allegiance to the code of honor of the voyageurs and promise, among other vows, never to kiss another voyageur's wife without his permission.

The vast and intricate matrix of rivers and lakes that made the transportation system possible was broken by hundreds of portages. At each portage, the canoe was unloaded and the men each carried loads of 180 pounds and the canoes around the rapid. Like all the great load carriers of the world, the men used a tumpline to support the load. A circle of rope and cloth was looped across the forehead and fell backward over the shoulders and around the package. After one package had been lodged in the loop on the man's back, another package was placed on top of the first. Although the usual load was 180 pounds, there were stories of men carrying 450 pounds, and one man was supposed to have carried 500 pounds, without interruption, for eighteen hours! The portages varied from fifty yards to many miles. Methy Portage was by far the most strenuous. It separated the Mackenzie River Basin from the Churchill River, leading to the Hudson Bay, and was twelve miles long, with a vertical carry of 600 feet. That the view from the top was fantastic must have been of little consolation to the men after they had struggled up the ascent.

The North West Company came on the scene long after the Hudson's Bay Company and was their great rival. The North West Company worked on an entirely different system from the Hudson's Bay Company. The Hudson's Bay Company had a series of trading posts along the shores of the Hudson Bay and expected the Indians to bring the furs to them. The North West Company, the descendant of the early French traders who had moved west along the line of the Great Lakes, could not do that. To reach the rich fur country of the far north and west, their traders traveled thousands of miles into the center of the continent, traded directly with the Indians, and brought the furs back to Montreal. As the beaver and other animals were killed off, posts were established farther and farther west, finally ending up at the mouth of the Columbia river in one direction and the mouth of the Mackenzie River to the north. If the factor of Fort Good Hope at the mouth of the Mackenzie River sent a message back to Montreal, he would not receive the answer for two years. This, then, was the vast, competitive, adventurous, and sometimes brutal system into which Mackenzie plunged, little knowing that he would extend its boundaries to the Arctic and Pacific Oceans.

Mackenzie must have impressed his employers after he had worked in Detroit, because, without any solicitation on his part, he was made a partner in the firm, on the one condition that he would go to the Indian country of Saskatchewan within a year. Alexander readily agreed to this condition, for fortunes were being made in the field. So, in the spring of 1785, he moved to Grand Portage. His companions were John Gregory, John Finlay, and his cousin Roderick Mackenzie. He went farther northwest, to Isle-à-la Crosse, to take charge of the district known as the English River—actually the headwaters of the Churchill River that ran northeast to the Hudson Bay, an area technically under the control of the Hudson's Bay Company.

The life of a fur trader was tough, uncomfortable, dangerous, and isolated; there was little companionship except for that of the boisterous voyageurs. Many of the traders, including Mackenzie, took Indian wives. There were many advantages in having a "country wife": she acted as an interpreter and go-between with the local tribes, cooked, made clothes, and offered companionship. Mackenzie had a long relationship with his "country wife," Catt, and continued to support her and their children after he retired to Scotland. At the time of her death in 1804, her obituary stated that she was the wife of Sir Alexander Mackenzie, although they had never married legally.

The backcountry was by no means uninhabited. Numerous Indian tribes had been hunting and surviving off the land for thousands of years but had become increasingly dependent on European traders for supplies of guns, ammunition, and rum. The French had been dealing with the Indians for 200 years and were not interested in acquiring more territory but wanted to find new trading areas. As the French moved west, they learned the Indian's languages, married their women, and established those good relations so necessary for trade. This attitude was different from that of the later American mountain men. The British and French regarded the Indians as trading partners; fighting the Indians could only ruin trade. The Americans, who did their own trapping, saw the Indians as rivals to be eliminated. The Indians reciprocated and reacted to the mountain men as intruders, often attacking and killing them.

The Cree and Chipewyan Indians hated making the long, arduous voyage across the Barren Lands and down the rivers to the Hudson Bay. They had to travel in the winter, in time to deliver the furs to the ships that arrived in the spring. They often starved along the way, or met rivals who stole their furs. This discontent gave the North West Company traders the opportunity to intercept some of the Crees and persuade them to trade with them and avoid the tedious journey to the Hudson Bay.

As the North West Company cut into their business, the Hudson's Bay Company revised their policy of waiting for the Indians to bring them furs. They built trading forts in the middle of the country, often within sight of the North West Company posts. Cumberland House was the first of these new posts, a fine-sounding name for a collection of log cabins set up by Samuel Hearne in 1774.

When Mackenzie moved out west, he never took his eye off the commercial ball. But under a shell of commercialism lay an increasing desire to explore the unknown regions of the vast Canadian west and extend the interests of Britain.

The search for a northwest passage by sea had been going on for centuries. The trade possibilities in the exotic Far East had excited the imaginations of generations of traders and government officials alike. The first organized trip to try to find the elusive passage was led by John Cabot in 1495. When the first ship commissioned by the founders of the Hudson's Bay Company sailed in 1668, the captain was instructed to keep an eye open for the passage to the South Seas. Britain's East India Company already had a monopoly on trade with India and also with China—a monopoly similar to that of the Hudson's Bay Company, protected by a royal charter. But the trade routes to the east were long and dangerous. A ship sailing from England to China around the Cape of Good Hope and across the Pacific was committed to a journey of several years. The route to the west from England, around Cape Horn, was equally long and dangerous. If a shorter route could be found around the north of Canada, the advantages to trade, especially British trade, would be enormous. The alternative to a sea route was a navigable river route across the continent.

Captain James Cook had whetted the appetites of geographers by sailing up Cook Inlet near what is now Anchorage, Alaska, and postulating that the inlet was the mouth of a great river flowing out of the northwest of the American continent. He had tried to sail north into the Bering Strait but had been turned back by a sea of ice. The route that existed only in the minds of geographers was even given a name, the Straits of Anian.

The fur traders who had ventured into the interior of the continent had heard rumors from the Indians of rivers flowing west to the sea. Peter Pond picked up these rumors. Pond was an adventurous man who, in his day, had traveled farther west than any other white man. He was born in Connecticut in 1739 and, after serving in the army of King George III, moved to Canada and entered the fur trade. He came to the far west before Mackenzie and had a reputation as a ruthless, bad-tempered adventurer who was rumored to have killed at least two trading rivals.

Pond spent three winters trading with the Indians in Athabasca, spoke their language, and was familiar with their legends about great rivers. In addition to being a good trader, he was also an explorer who opened up a vast new area for trapping by finding the Methy Portage, the door to territory untouched by previous traders. The Cree and Chipewyan Indians who occupied this territory were happy to trade with Pond rather than go to the Hudson Bay.

A new source of almost unlimited wealth had been found, for the beaver pelts from this cold northern land were thicker and more luxuriant than those from farther east. In the spring of 1779, Pond came out of the Athabascan wilderness with two loads of the finest pelts, scoffing that he had taken the trade from under the noses of the Hudson's Bay Company.

This was an era in which everyone made maps, whether they had explored new territory or had just listened to rumors and traveler's tales. Sometimes the maps were accurate, but frequently they included information that was speculation camouflaged as truth. Pond made a map for the Congress of the United States in 1785 that included a river going north and joining with Cook's river, and he thought it would take only six days from Fort Chipewyan to reach the West Coast. Authorities in Montreal and London became intrigued by his ideas, and one supporter, Judge Ogden of Montreal, went as far as to say, "There was an easy communication, and an advantageous commerce may be carried on by Posts established on Lakes Slave, Arabaska, Pelican &c &c, and to deliver the fruits of their commerce at the mouth of the Cook's River, to be then carried to China." The same letter included remarks that "another man by the name of Mackenzie" had received orders from Pond to go down the river and travel to Unalaska, Kamchatka, and thence to England through Russia. Mackenzie was anticipated to arrive in London within a year.

Pond and Mackenzie spent the winter of 1787–1788 together in Athabasca as Mackenzie had been sent to succeed Pond as overseer of that post. Although Mackenzie had good reasons to dislike Pond, they tolerated each other and undoubtedly discussed the prospect of exploring the rivers to the north and west of the Great Slave Lake. At the end of the winter, when Mackenzie returned to Grand Portage, he was apparently given the go-ahead to explore the route outlined by Pond. For whatever reasons, Mackenzie never credited Pond for his ideas and knowledge.

Many attempts had been made by Pond to get the British government to finance a search for the river to the Pacific, but the slowness of communications between the Canadian interior and London and the inertia of the British government combined to delay any official decision until after news had reached London that Mackenzie had already explored the river and found that it ended in the Arctic Ocean, not the Pacific.

By late in the summer of 1788, Mackenzie was making his preparations for an exploratory voyage. The government did not sponsor his trip, but his partners in Montreal realized what he was planning. He was an independent man who was willing to go his own way, but always with the thought of improving the business of the company. The benefits to his company would be enormous if he found the magical river to the Pacific. But was his primary motive in exploring the river an innate urge to explore or an effort to increase the business of his company and, thereby, his own personal wealth?

Mackenzie always said that he could do nothing without the help of the Indians, and one of the most experienced Indian wilderness leaders, the English Chief, approached him and offered his help. The English Chief, also known as Nestabeck, was a flamboyant Chipewyan leader who had traveled with Hearne and Matonabee to the mouth of the Coppermine River in 1771. Mackenzie thought Nestabeck knew more about survival in the wilderness than any other man. While he admired him, he never regarded him as a close friend as Hearne had Matonabee.

Mackenzie's plan was to cross Lake Athabasca, travel north along the Slave River to the Great Slave Lake, and find the outlet of the river to the north along the northern shore of that lake. Beyond that point, he had no idea where the river would lead him.

He embarked from Fort Chipewyan on June 3, 1789. Mackenzie and Laurent Leroux, who had already built a fort on the Great Slave Lake, were in one canoe. The plan was that Leroux would accompany Mackenzie beyond the Great Slave Lake, then take his own party northwest to trade with the Indians while Mackenzie traveled farther north along the great river. Their knowledge of what to expect was based entirely on Indian reports, and those were secondhand, at best.

The rest of the crew consisted of four Canadians, two of whom had Indian wives, and a German, John Steinbruck, whose presence on the crew remains a mystery. The English Chief with two of his wives and two young Indians employed as hunters occupied a third canoe. A fourth canoe carried trade goods to be used by Leroux in his negotiations with the Indians.

Little did they know it, but the true Mackenzie River, starting from the Great Slave Lake, winds its way 1,120 miles to the Arctic Ocean. Both the final destination and the length of the river were unknown as they set off up the Slave River. On the third day, a canoe was lost, but the crew came to no harm. Mackenzie wrote in his journal, "Men and Indians much fatigued." The weather became colder and rain and mosquitoes added to their trials. Finding the outlet from the Great Slave Lake proved to be more difficult than anticipated. The Redknife Indian guide, who was supposed to know the way, had not been in the area for eight years and was so useless that the English Chief wanted to shoot him. When they finally found the outlet, on June 29, they moved into country for which they had no guide.

Along the way, they encountered Slave and Dogrib Indians who could only be persuaded to come near with gifts. But they gave little information about what to expect farther downstream, except to say that Mackenzie and his men would all be old and gray before they returned from the mouth of the river, and they could expect to encounter monsters and impassable falls.

The English Chief and his companions believed what they had been told, and it was with difficulty that Mackenzie persuaded them to continue.

One of the Indians agreed to come along as a guide, but later, some of the others deserted, fearing death and starvation. Four canoes continued. The Indians were afraid of the river, but had underestimated the skill of the Canadians in navigating their canoes through the rapids.

By July 10, they were ten miles east of the Rockies and Mackenzie realized the river was heading north, not west, and would not lead him to the Pacific. The river became a braided northern stream, and Mackenzie could only get his men to continue by telling them that they would proceed no longer than seven days before turning back. He was afraid that if they continued longer, they would not be able to get back to Fort Chipewyan before winter set in. Only two days later, they came to an island from which they could see the ocean. Mackenzie took a reading of latitude and found, to his surprise, that he was 67°47' north; much farther north than he had expected. The sea was frozen in most places, but they saw beluga whales. They knew that this river would not end in Cook's River.

Despite the disappointment, Mackenzie had explored new country that would, in time, become one of the great fur trading areas of the continent. In 1820, John Franklin explored the river and, using better instruments, confirmed that Mackenzie's calculation of the longitude and latitude of the river mouth was off by only seven miles. Mackenzie called it the River of Disappointment or the Grand River and believed that he had reached the Hyperborean Sea—the Sea Beyond the North Wind. Only later was the river named the Mackenzie.

Mackenzie had experienced enough of the wilderness and decided to return to England, not only for a rest, but to learn more about navigation, astronomy, and the measurement of longitude and latitude. He had more exploration in mind and wanted to be better prepared scientifically. A great river to the west still remained to be found.

After Mackenzie returned from England, he made his way back to Fort Chipewyan and was soon planning another voyage to explore a route to the West Coast. Finlay had already established a trading fort farther west, 550 miles up the Peace River.

In October 1792, Mackenzie left Fort Chipewyan and started up the Peace River. At Finlay's Fort, he recruited some more men and picked up nine gallons of rum. They then paddled to the fork of the Peace and Smoky Rivers and built good winter quarters. There were five buildings for the Canadian voyageurs and a separate house for Mackenzie. An eighteen-foot palisade and a three-foot deep ditch surrounded and protected the buildings.

In the spring of 1793, most of the voyageurs went back to Rainy Lake, carrying the furs collected during a profitable winter. Mackenzie wrote to his cousin Roderick, telling him of his intention to go to the West Coast and implying that he might go even farther. He knew that if he could find his way through Russia to China, the profits would be enormous. He told Roderick that he was taking Russian money with him for trading with the empress. Whether he seriously thought that he could complete such a voyage is not clear, for later in the summer he wrote in his diary that he was concerned that he would not be able to get to the coast and back to Fort Chipewyan before winter set in.

In preparation for the voyage, Mackenzie had his men build a canoe twenty-five feet long, large enough to carry ten men, two Indian hunters, and a ton and a half of supplies and equipment. He complained that he was having difficulty in recruiting men to accompany him, which is not surprising, for they were about to enter country for which there were no maps and about which there was only the sketchiest of knowledge that came from a collection of stories from Indians who had never themselves been across the mountains and only knew rumors of rivers leading to a large lake where the water could not be drunk. They did not know if they would meet friendly or aggressive Indians, if there would be enough game for food, or if the rivers were passable. They did not even know how far it was from Fort Fork, as they called their compound, to the coast. That year, Captain Robert Gray, an American trader, had found the mouth of the Columbia River and fixed its longitude and latitude, but Mackenzie did not know this vital information. Had he known it, he would not later have mistaken the river he was on for the Columbia.

Mackinzie knew that if he were successful, he would achieve great fame. But if he failed, he thought he would be no worse off than he already was. Also, he did not know why any man in his right mind would subject himself to the rigors and discomforts of life in a remote trading post, far from the comforts of the city.

In May 1793, Mackenzie gathered his men together: Alex Mackay, a twenty-two-year-old Scot, who became his right-hand man; six Canadians; two Indian hunters; and a large dog, just called "our dog." As soon as they left Fort Fork, they found the Peace River had a formidable current and was full of rapids that sometimes required the canoe to be constantly unloaded and reloaded. Within a few days, they came close to the Rockies and had to make an exhausting nine-mile portage round the Peace River Canyon, a stretch of the river that was totally impassable in a flimsy birch-bark canoe.

At one point, they were lost in the middle of a thick forest and Mackenzie sent his men to find an escape route. They returned fatigued and near mutiny, but after a meal of "wild rice sweetened with sugar and their usual regale of rum," their spirits rose and they agreed to continue. This pattern of despondency and near mutiny, followed by the distribution of rum and a good speech from their leader, occurred several times during the weeks ahead. On one occasion, it took nearly a whole keg of rum to reestablish their resolve. These were not soldiers, disciplined by the Articles of War and liable to be flogged for disobedience. They were feisty, independent men who had to be persuaded, not ordered. They were used to great privation, hours of hauling and paddling canoes in foul weather, and carrying heavy loads across rough portages. They might complain, but when challenged, they would not give up.

The Peace River is the only river that crosses the Continental Divide. Within a few years, it would become the regular route to the west, but to these pioneers it gave nothing but trouble until they came to a fork in a large valley. One fork went north (the Finlay River) and the other went south (the Parsnip). Which to follow? Mackenzie's instinct was to take the northern route, but an old Indian had told him that it would not lead to the west, and he should take the southern fork. He believed the Indian and they went south. The route was difficult and involved "inexpressible toil," but they soon met with other Indians, the Sekani, who gave them valuable information and talked about another people they had traded with who had gone to the "Stinking Lake."

On June 12, they made a short portage of only 817 steps and found a river going to the west. They had crossed the Continental Divide. (This easy traverse of the Continental Divide would deceive Thomas Jefferson and others into thinking that the divide would be equally narrow far to the south.) But their difficulties had not ended. On a particularly severe rapid, the canoe crashed into the rocks and the men ended up floating down the rapid, hanging on in desperation to a sinking canoe. In the disaster, they lost all the bullets for their guns and were left with only some powder and shot. Undaunted, they made a new canoe, thirty feet long, to carry them, their remaining supplies, and extra bark for repairs.

On June 17, they had been traveling for thirty days and had covered 400 miles. They met a large river, believing it to be the Columbia, but they were the first white men to see the Fraser River.

Many miles later, they stopped to talk to some natives who told them that the river had impassable rapids. Once again, Mackenzie was faced with a hard decision. One Indian told him to go back upstream, abandon their canoe, and go overland. Mackenzie reluctantly decided to turn back and portage across country till they found another river and a tribe that might help them. They turned back, but not before one of the Indians asked Mackenzie, "I thought white men knew everything. How is it that you do not know the way to the sea?" Mackenzie, wishing to maintain the myth that white men knew everything, replied that while white men did know everything, in general, they sometimes needed help with the details.

They backtracked eighty miles, left their canoe, hefted their loads, and headed off through the forests. Although no white men had been this way before, Mackenzie noted that there were well-worn trails, even over the rocks, where generations of passing feet had worn steps. His men were exhausted but were persuaded again to keep going, as the thought of turning back was too painful to bear.

Suddenly, they found themselves in a new culture. The houses were permanent and made of trimmed planks. The mountains ahead were awe inspiring, covered with snow, and the path crossed a 6,000-foot-high pass. The natives were not surprised to see them, probably because their guides had sent word ahead of their coming, and greeted them with great hospitality. Mackenzie called this the Friendly Village. The chief provided them with food, guides, and canoes to carry them downstream. Their guides navigated the rapids with effortless ease, impressing Mackenzie that their canoe skills were far superior to those of the Canadians, whom he had always regarded as masters of the river.

Farther downstream, the natives met them with suspicion and overt hostility. The chief had a magnificent canoe, decorated with the teeth of sea otters, forty-five feet long, and capable of carrying forty people. The next village came to be known as Rascal's Village, because of the aggressive way they were treated. They were now on an inlet of the Pacific, but Mackenzie wanted to reach the sea. They never saw the open ocean but stopped in a fjord, the Bella Coola. There was seaweed on the rocks, bald eagles flew overhead, and seals and sea otters watched them cautiously from a safe distance.

The natives were so aggressive that Mackenzie feared they would be attacked and retreated to a small island where they could defend themselves. No attack came. The natives had been talking about a recent visit by Macubah (Captain George Vancouver) and Bensins (Archibald Menzies, Vancouver's botanist), during which the ship's master, James Johnstone, forced his way into a building. The natives were fearful and lied to the chief, saying that Mackenzie's men had killed four of their villagers. Mackenzie was glad to retreat back upstream, but not before one of his men had painted on a rock the historic words "Alexander Mackenzie, from Canada, by land, the twenty-second of July, one thousand seven hundred and ninety-three."

The return journey was only slightly less arduous than the outward expedition. They had little to eat, rapids to fight, and portages to suffer. It was with great relief that they broke out of the mountains onto the eastern Plains where game abounded and they were able to gorge themselves on elk and buffalo.

The route to the sea proved to be filled with great danger, extreme toil, and few immediate rewards, except for achieving what had never been done before. On August 24, they reached Fort Fork, from which they had started out seventy-four days earlier. They had logged 1,200 miles, 940 on water and 260 backpacking. Perhaps they had not reached Russia, but they had completed a journey that no one, native or nonnative, had ever made. Mackenzie could have become a trader again, but during the winter months, he was full of self-doubt and a sense of failure. He had nightmares about people who had died (although no one died under his command) and could not summon up the energy to write a report of his voyage. Nowadays, he might have been diagnosed with posttraumatic stress. He traveled east in the spring, never to return to the wilderness. He was only thirty years old.

It is impossible for anyone to forecast their legacy. Alexander Mackenzie knew that he was trying to extend British influence, but he could have no idea of the importance of his travels, which were not received at the time with great praise from his fellow partners of the North West Company.

Mackenzie retired to Montreal, London, and the north of Scotland. He became an important, wealthy man, was knighted by the king, and, at age forty-eight, married Geddes Margaret Mackenzie (of no relation), age fourteen, had a happy family life, and fathered three children. They lived in the village of Avoch, north of Inverness, in Scotland. He died at age fifty-eight, his body worn down by the exertions of life in the backcountry. He was buried in the local churchyard, where his grave is still easily visited.

Alexander Mackenzie was the point man for the western expansion of Canada. By the time he died, British influence extended to the mouth of the Columbia River, holding back the Russians to the northwest and the Americans to the south. He achieved this without losing a companion or killing an enemy.

4

Meriwether Lewis
(1774–1809)
and William Clark
(1770–1838)

First Americans across the Continent

*Impossible is a word to be found only
in the dictionary of fools.*

—Napoleon Bonaparte

Meriwether Lewis was only nineteen years old when he first aspired to lead an expedition from the Mississippi to the West Coast. His hopes did not materialize, and perhaps that was just as well. He was too young, without the military experience he later had, and—most important of all—the Louisiana Purchase had neither been conceived nor made. When Lewis was nineteen, William Clark was twenty-three and had already seen active service in the militia for four years. Neither young man at that age thought for a moment that they would meet during military service, develop an admiration for each other, and join forces to lead the most important American force to explore the vast lands between the central rivers and the Pacific Ocean.

Lewis's father died during the Revolutionary War and his mother remarried. The family was influential in Albemarle County in Virginia and did not live far from Thomas Jefferson, already a towering figure in American politics. Clark was the younger brother of George Rogers Clark, a national war hero who had already been asked to lead an expedition to the west but had turned down the offer believing that the Indian nations might see the incursion as unduly invasive and react accordingly.

Lewis joined the army at the time of the Whiskey War and stayed on when others were discharged, becoming a captain in the First Infantry Regiment, part of the very small permanent army of the time. While drunk, he insulted a fellow officer and challenged him to a duel. He was court-martialed, acquitted, and transferred to the Chosen Rifle Company of the Fourth Sub-Legion and found himself under the command of a steady, popular officer, Captain William Clark. The association did not last long, for Clark resigned from the army to take care of family affairs. But the two men knew each other long enough to start a relationship that would result in a remarkable example of brotherhood and leadership.

Jefferson had dreamed for many years of organizing an expedition to explore the west. He had initiated an expedition supported by the American Philosophical Society and led by a French scientist, André Michaux. Michaux turned out to be a French spy and the expedition fell apart. Another attempt was to be made by John Ledyard, an adventurous young man from Connecticut who had sailed with Captain James Cook on his third, and fatal, expedition across the Pacific. Ledyard believed that he could cross Russia to its east coast, obtain passage to a Russian colony in America, and then walk across the continent. Catherine the Great had different ideas. She arrested Ledyard before he crossed Russia and evicted him to England. He died on an exploration of the Nile.

When Jefferson became president in 1800, he immediately acquired the power to plan for the expedition of his dreams. He appointed Lewis as his secretary, perhaps with this expedition in mind, and in January 1803 wrote a letter to Congress asking for funds to support an "intellectual" expedition up the Mississippi. The Congress granted him $2,500 planning money (worth around $50,000 in modern value). Everyone realized that the real objective of the expedition was to travel up the Missouri river to its origin, then cross the Rockies to the West Coast.

As soon as Congress approved the money, Jefferson appointed Lewis leader of the expedition and instructed him to make preparations. The next few months were hectic for the young captain. In March, he went to the arsenal at Harpers Ferry and selected rifles and ammunition and had gunpowder sealed in lead boxes that could be melted down and turned into bullets. He also designed the frame for a collapsible boat that he intended to use on the upper reaches of the Missouri. Jefferson became irritated with the time he spent at Harpers Ferry and sent him to Lancaster, where he consulted with Andrew Ellicot, a mathematician, learning to make astronomical observations. In May, Lewis moved to Philadelphia, where he bought a chronometer for calculating longitude. He also spent a day with Dr. Benjamin Rush, who had been asked by Jefferson to give advice and instructions to the young officer who was going to travel to the West Coast. Rush provided a series of questions about Indian health and habits (to which he never received a formal answer) and instructions on maintaining health, none of which were very helpful. The instructions contained no information about therapeutic bleeding, which Rush believed to be a mainstay of medical treatment. He may not have realized the vast extent of the journey that Lewis was about to undertake. He did, however, provide Lewis with a useful list of medicines to deal with pain, fevers, skin problems, and gastrointestinal disorders.

Lewis shopped for the medicine and other items in the markets of Philadelphia, using the money that Congress had provided. The lists of drugs, trade items, and other supplies have been passed down to us, providing a wonderful insight into the preparations: 47 medications, including surgical and dental instruments; and 51 different gifts for the Indians, including 288 small knives, 100 burning glasses for starting fires, 288 common brass thimbles, tobacco, fishing hooks, and 30 pounds of red, white, and yellow beads.

Back in Washington in June, Lewis received instructions from Jefferson to find a "practicable water communication across the continent, for the purpose of commerce." Jefferson wanted to open up the profitable fur trade that was dominated by French Canadian and British trappers. If a good trade route could be found, furs trapped by Americans east of the Rockies could be quickly brought to Saint Louis by boat. And if a suitable place could be found on the West Coast, furs trapped west of the Rockies could be sent to the coast, then, by American ships, to the great fur trading centers of China. Jefferson emphasized the importance of friendly dealings with the Indians: "In all your intercourse with the natives, treat them in the most friendly & conciliatory manner which their own conduct will permit." The last paragraph in the orders told Lewis what arrangements to make in case he should be injured, incapacitated, or killed. The details in Jefferson's orders showed the breadth of his vision and his enquiring nature. Every day on the trail, Lewis must have felt Jefferson looking over his shoulder.

There was still one important detail to be arranged: a second in command. Lewis was given the freedom to choose his deputy, and he turned immediately to his old commander, Clark. Lewis wrote to Clark detailing the purpose of the journey and inviting him "to participate with me in it's fatiegues, it's dangers and it's honors, believe me there is no man on earth with whom I should feel equal pleasure in sharing them as with yourself." He offered Clark a captain's commission, but the army made him a Second Lieutenant in the artillery. But throughout the voyage, Lewis and the men referred to Clark as "Captain."

On July 29, the mail brought Lewis a reply from Clark: " My Friend I do assure you that no man lives with whome I would prefer to undertake Such a Trip &c. as yourself." Lewis could go to Pittsburgh, the starting point, with all the assurance and confidence that he needed, the full support of his president, and the knowledge that his good friend would be by his side.

Clark, in Kentucky, began to select the "best young woodsmen and hunters in this part of the countrey." Meanwhile, in Pittsburgh, Lewis was struggling to have a fifty-five-foot keelboat built by an unreliable, drunken boat builder. Eventually, the boat was finished, and on August 31 he departed down the Ohio River.

The voyage down the Ohio was not easy. Within hours of starting, a visiting lady was nearly killed by a bystander trying out the powerful air gun that Lewis had brought. Fortunately, only her scalp was creased. The boat frequently ran aground and teams of oxen, for which Lewis had to pay exorbitant prices, hauled it into deeper water.

As he sailed down the river, Lewis wrote to Clark and Jefferson, reporting his progress. He had hoped that he would be able to start up the Missouri before winter set in. It soon became obvious that this would not be possible and Lewis became resigned to spending the winter somewhere near Saint Louis. He reached Clarksville and Louisville, situated on opposite sides of the Ohio, on October 15. As he stepped ashore, Clark, whom he had not seen for seven years, greeted him. A momentous occasion. They began to select men for the expedition. Clark had already gathered some and Lewis had found two men in Pittsburgh who would play a big part in their success: John Colter and George Shannon. Thus began the Corps of Volunteers for North Western Discovery.

Jefferson thought the group should be small, but Lewis and Clark recruited a larger group. The keelboat alone required twenty oarsmen, and by the time they chose the site for their winter camp, the group had grown to more than forty men.

Clark camped at the mouth of the Wood River in early December and immediately set about building cabins. During much of the winter, Lewis stayed in Saint Louis, talking with the Chouteaus, the city's most influential businessmen, who had been trading up the Missouri for many years, and buying supplies for his greatly enlarged group, while Clark trained and disciplined the men who were young, eager, rough, and tough. The strict rules of behavior that Clark set were not always to their liking. But when spring approached, the men were ready, the boats loaded, and, on May 14, 1804, the little fleet of one keelboat and two pirogues pushed off into history. Clark's first journal entry was brief and to the point: "Set out from Camp River a Dubois at 4 o'clock P.M. and proceded up the Missouris under sail to the first island ... men in high spirits."

Lewis joined the expedition a couple of days later at Saint Charles, a small French community. Before leaving, some of the Catholic engagés wanted to attend mass. It was the last religious service they would attend before returning to Saint Louis more than two years later. Religious observances were not part of Lewis's and Clark's routines.

The journey up the Missouri was one of toil, because they had to pull, row, sail, or push the keelboat upstream against a strong current, avoiding floating trees, sandbanks, and every hazard the river could provide. The weather was hot and one man suffered from heat stroke. The strength and endurance of these men is hard to imagine, but they were chosen because they were "used to hardship to a remarkable degree." They were soldiers and river men, inured to privation, men who did not have to be trained (as do modern soldiers) to accept the discomforts of life in the field; hardship had always been their way of life. In some ways, life on the river was better than they would have experienced in an army camp. Food was usually plentiful, especially when they encountered game in unnumbered herds. They ate five to nine pounds of meat a day and received occasional morale-building shots of grog. One of the boatmen, Pierre Cruzatte, played the fiddle, and after a tough day rewarded with a shot of whiskey, Cruzatte would play and the men would dance.

There was plenty of adventure as they passed through the territories of forty-nine Indian tribes. Many of the soldiers had probably been brought up to believe that the only good Indian was a dead Indian. But Jefferson had told their commanding officers to treat the Indians with politeness and circumspection.

One tribe, the Teton Sioux, the most powerful on the prairie, had been exacting tolls from the traders for many years, and when the expedition appeared, they expected to be suitably rewarded. For three tense days, Lewis and Clark negotiated with the chiefs, alternating between elaborate feasts of dog and offers of "tawny damsels" for the night and shouting matches, with bows strung on one side and rifles loaded on the other. Much of the confrontation was bluffing. So long as women and children were watching the scene, a bloody fight was unlikely. The Indians tried to extract more presents and sometimes the response was the contemptuous toss of a carrot of tobacco.

Lewis had a standard approach to all the Indian tribes along the Missouri. He told them they had a new Great Father in Washington who wanted them to live in peace, but, at the same time, he did not want them trading with the British. If they made peace and behaved well, the Great Father would send traders and they would receive all the benefits they wanted. The stump speech might be preceded by a parade of the soldiers in dress uniforms and a demonstration of the magic, noiseless air gun. The chiefs, selected by Lewis, received gifts and medals—large medals for important chiefs and smaller imprints for lesser chiefs. An occasional chief would complain that his gift was not appropriate to his position. Lewis was not always correct in his assessment of the social hierarchy.

Discipline was occasionally a problem. Even before they were well on their way, three men attended a farewell dance and on their return shouted abuse at the sergeant. One, John Collins, received fifty lashes. Alexander Willard fell asleep while on sentry duty and could have been condemned to death for one of the most serious offences a soldier could commit. He was lucky to get off with 100 lashes. Yet another pair, Collins, again, and Hugh Hall, were accused of stealing whiskey. They, too, received fifty to 100 lashes on their backs. Two men deserted, one of them a French engagé, and were hunted down by George Drouillard, the most skillful hunter in the corps. He returned with one man, Private Moses Reed, who confessed to desertion and stealing a rifle and ammunition. He was sentenced to run the gauntlet of his fellow soldiers four times, received almost 500 lashes, and was discharged from the permanent party.

It is hard for the modern reader to imagine what it must have been like for the punished soldier to return to duty the day after a lashing, pulling the boat while wading waist deep in water under a broiling sun. Yet the journal entries show no sympathy for the culprits. Although the justice seems harsh, the courts were composed of sergeants and other enlisted men. Their peers tried the offenders and ranks of men, through which they had to run, administered the punishment.

In August of that first summer, tragedy struck. Sergeant Charles Floyd fell seriously ill, "taken very bad all at once with a beliose chorlick." Over the next twenty-four hours, he developed severe abdominal pain with vomiting and diarrhea. Clark records that they treated him as best they could, but no details remain. He became progressively worse and Clark recorded, "Floyd died with a great deal of Composure, before his death he Said to me, 'I am going away I want you to write me a letter.'" He was buried with full military honors on a bluff overlooking the river. Patrick Gass was voted to replace him as sergeant and the Corps of Volunteers for North Western Discovery proceeded on. (The name Corps of Discovery was not coined until after the expedition.) Whether or not the men were saddened by the event, the purpose and strength of the expedition had not changed.

Not all was sadness. Lewis and Clark, and presumably the men, gazed with wonder on the beauty of the land and the amazing wildlife that filled the open prairie. And on a personal level, the men enjoyed their encounters with many of the Indians. The cultural habit of several tribes was to offer women to visiting men and the men took full advantage of this generosity. There was a price to pay: venereal disease. Visiting French and Canadian traders had infected the Indians over the years and some of the men of the corps were probably also carriers of sexually transmitted diseases.

As summer slipped into autumn, the journals recorded the southward flight of geese and swans. The Mandan Indians were friendly to white traders and setting up a winter fort near their community was the obvious decision. In late October, a good place was found for a winter fort, with large trees for logs and near the river for water. The fort was substantial, with a three-sided plan, walls eighteen feet high, and a large gate that could be locked with a bar. Lewis did not fear an attack by the Indians, but he did not want them wandering in and out of the fort night and day.

The winter at the Mandan Fort, close to the present site of Bismarck, North Dakota, was an important phase in the expedition. There was time for

Lewis and Clark to learn from the Indians about the terrain and the course of the river ahead of them. The men rested and fraternized enthusiastically with the Indians. The Indians traded corn and other crops for metal axes made by the blacksmith. The weather was bitterly cold at times, but although some of the men got minor frostbite, none lost any fingers, toes, or limbs. Sioux bands harassed them, stealing horses and meat, but there were no battles and no bloodshed.

Historically, the most interesting event of the winter was the birth of a child. Toussaint Charbonneau, half Indian and half French Canadian, a Métis, arrived at the fort and asked to be employed as an interpreter. He could speak several Indian languages and was accompanied by two wives. The older wife already had a two-year-old child, and the younger, about age sixteen, Sacagawea, was pregnant and due to deliver in February. Sacagawea was a Shoshone from the Rockies who had been captured by the neighboring Hidatsa tribe in a sortie a few years before. Lewis immediately saw the significance of having a Shoshone-speaking person in the group. He knew that the corps would need horses to carry them through the mountains and that the Shoshones could supply them. After some initial difficulties in coming to an agreement, Charbonneau and Sacagawea were signed on. (It is not known what happened to the other wife.)

Sacagawea went into labor in February. She had never given birth before and labor was prolonged and difficult. Someone remembered that there was an Indian tradition that if the rings from a rattlesnake's tail were given to a mother in labor, the birth would be accelerated. Fortunately, Lewis had a few rings that were ground up and given in water to Sacagawea. Within ten minutes, she gave birth to a boy, Baptiste Charbonneau, who would later become a favorite around camp, especially with Clark. Lewis, always the scientist, was impressed by the action of the rings but said in his journal that he thought the method needed more testing.

In March 1805, the ice on the river broke, migrating birds filled the sky, and the corps prepared to move on. Lewis wrote a report for the president and a long letter for his mother in which he rhapsodized about the beauty of the country and assured her of his health and the well being of his men. To the president, he wrote of the country, the possibilities for agriculture, and his hope that the Sioux could be persuaded to be peaceful without the need for war. He told of the knowledge he had acquired of the tribes they would meet and that he believed that most of them would be friendly. Specimens of 108 plants and numerous minerals and animals were packed and prepared. Four live magpies, a prairie dog, and a prairie grouse were caged as presents for the president.

When all was ready, the specimens and reports were loaded into the keelboat and the pirogues under the charge of Corporal Richard Warfington for return to Saint Louis. Only one magpie and the prairie dog survived the trip to Washington.

Clark wrote of the others, "All the party in high spirits ... possessing perfect harmony and good understanding towards each other." And Lewis, equally enthusiastic, wrote, "With such men I have every thing to hope, and but little to fear."

On the afternoon of April 7, 1805, Lewis, Clark, three sergeants, Clark's servant, York, twenty-two privates, two interpreters, Sacagawea, Baptiste, and Lewis's Newfoundland dog, Seaman, in six canoes and two piroques headed upstream. That night, Lewis wrote in his journal, "This little fleet altho' not quite so respectable as those of Columbus or Captain Cook, were still viewed by us with as much pleasure as those deservedly famous adventurers ever beheld theirs; and I daresay with quite as much anxiety for their safety and preservation. We are now about to penetrate a country at least two thousand miles in width, on which the foot of civilized man had never trodden." Heroic thoughts, tinged with a hint of concern for the unknown, they were a realistic expression of his inner feelings.

The next few weeks, until they reached the Great Falls of the Missouri, were surprisingly harmonious. Food was abundant. Their daily progress was good, despite some near-disastrous incidents. They saw no Indians, although the Indians undoubtedly saw them and spread the word of their progress through the bush telegraph. A critical decision had to be made at the junction of the Missouri and another stream. Which stream to follow? The men thought they should follow one; Lewis decided on the other. They followed their commander without dissent and he was correct. The other river was named the Marias.

June 13. Lewis and a couple of men had gone ahead of the others, anticipating the discovery of the Great Falls. To Lewis's delight, he heard the water and saw the spray "like a column of smoke" rising above the banks. To his amazement, he found five falls spread along eighteen miles. The surrounding Plains were thick with buffalo in a concentration greater than he had ever seen. He shot one for his dinner, and, distracted by watching the dying animal, failed to notice a grizzly bear about to charge him. There were no trees to climb for escape. He ran and jumped into the river. The bear followed, came to the shore, decided he had chased the intruder away, and turned away. A near thing!

When Lewis returned to camp, he found Sacagawea very ill with abdominal pain and with a weak, irregular pulse. He feared for her life and was also concerned that if she died, they would not have an interpreter when they met the Shoshones. He gave her water from a nearby mineral springs and she soon recovered. Her diagnosis is unknown, but, whatever the illness, it never recurred.

The portage around the falls was a tour de force. Carts were made for the canoes, with wheels sectioned from large cottonwood trees. The men, sweating, cursing, sunburned, bitten by mosquitoes and gnats, and stepping on prickly pears, hauled the carriages for a month. At the end of every day, they dropped, exhausted, into sleep. With a sense of relief they must have launched the canoes above the last of the falls on July 15.

The next necessity was to meet the Shoshones. Lewis went ahead with Drouillard and Private John Shields. The first contact was the sight of an Indian scout on a horse, silhouetted against the sky. Lewis laid down his gun and approached the man slowly, at the same time shouting out an Indian word that he thought meant "white man." He got within 200 yards when the scout turned his horse, gave it a whack, and galloped off through the willows. Contact had been made, but what would the scout report to his tribe?

Lewis climbed to the top of Lemhi Pass and saw before him an immense panorama of seemingly unending mountains. His heart sank, contemplating the distance they still had to go.

The next day, the small group encountered three Indians, one old woman, and two children. The old woman believed she was about to be killed, and the older child ran away. But Lewis handed the woman some gifts and reached out to her with his hand. She realized that he was a friend, not an enemy. The old woman called to the teenager to return and the group set off toward the Indian camp. Alerted by another Indian who had run back to the camp, a group of sixty warriors on horses charged toward them, ready for battle. The old woman said the strangers were friendly, and, once again, Lewis showed great courage and diplomacy: he laid down his arms and approached the Indians. The chief rode toward them and, having received assurances from the woman, greeted Lewis with a hug, rubbing his face against Lewis's—a greeting that Lewis thought was overdone when repeated by most of the group.

The Indians were suspicious of Lewis's story that there was a larger group bringing up the rear. But a couple of days later, Lewis and the Indians went to meet Clark and the others. They waited tensely. Lewis gave the chief, Cameawhait, his rifle, indicating that he could shoot him if he was leading him into a trap. Clark and the others arrived and the Shoshones were reassured and made even happier when Lewis had Drouillard shoot a deer for the near-starving tribe. When they arrived back at the Indian camp and settled in to smoke a pipe, Sacagawea recognized, to her amazement, that Cameawhait was her brother. The reunion was emotional; nothing better could have happened to the expedition. The Indians knew that they came in peace. Although they were poor and about to leave on their annual buffalo hunt on the Plains, they sold horses to Lewis and gave him a guide, Old Toby.

The march through the Bitterroots was a tough physical challenge. The snow was deep, fallen trees obstructed their way, Old Toby got lost, horses fell off the trail, and they ran out of food. They survived on a diet of grouse, portable soup (brought all the way from Phildelphia), and an occasional colt that they killed in desperation. When they finally emerged from the mountains into the land of the Nez Perce, they were in a sorry state. Tradition holds that the Nez Perce were going to kill them but were dissuaded by an old woman who had been befriended by kind white people. If the Indians did not kill them, the change in diet and possible poisoning with death camas accidentally included in the camas bread nearly did. Almost all the men were very sick and Lewis was barely strong enough to ride on a quiet horse. They recovered and made new canoes for the journey to the Columbia River.

They had entered a new culture. Buffalo no longer blackened the land and salmon was the mainstay of the diet. The men did not like the change. The Indians were different from those on the Plains. They fished, traded with neighboring tribes, lived in wooden houses, and dressed for a wet climate. The Indians on the coast had been trading with American and British sailors for many years and were disappointed when Lewis announced that he had not come to trade.

The canoe journey down the Columbia was swift and, at times, exciting. The rapids were rough and the heavy wooden canoes difficult to maneuver in the white water. But the river widened and became calm and, on November 5, Clark recorded in his journal, "Ocian in view! O! The joy!" What they saw was the broad estuary of the Columbia and several days passed before they truly saw the ocean and heard the waves crashing on the shore.

They camped in misery on the north shore of the river. Game was scarce. The campsite was on a rocky shore washed by waves and the weather was foul. This was no place to spend a winter. The Indians advised them that game was more plentiful on the south shore, and, after what has been described as the first vote in America that included a woman and a slave, they decided to move to the south shore. Lewis found a suitable place for a winter fort: on a small rise surrounded by huge trees, near water, but not on the shore, and close to, but not next-door to, the local Clatsop Indians. They built a good winter fort with rooms down two sides of an open area, surrounded by a high wall and closed by a gate. They occupied Fort Clatsop on Christmas Day 1805.

The winter was spent quietly. Of fifty-four days at Fort Clatsop, only twelve days were without rain and only three days were sunny. Despite that, and a plague of fleas, they managed well. The local Indians provided them with some food. Drouillard hunted elk assiduously. Indian girls, brought to the camp by an "old bawd," provided the men with the comfort they sought and the diseases they did not seek. A group was sent down the coast to distill salt from the sea and Clark and Sacagawea made a trip south to get whale meat from the Tillamook Indians. Lewis stayed close to camp and wrote lengthy descriptions of plants, birds, fish, the Indians, and their languages. One man, William Bratton, developed a severe back pain that incapacitated him for weeks; otherwise, the men remained remarkably healthy. But they dreamed of returning home and spending the next Christmas in comfort.

The corps left Fort Clatsop at 1:00 P.M. on March 23, 1806. The journey up the Columbia was harder than the swift journey down and the Indians infuriated Lewis by trying to steal at every opportunity. Lewis was a changed man on the return journey. His temper was short; he threatened to burn down a village and had a violent argument with an Indian over eating dog, which had become a favorite part of the soldiers' diet.

After reaching Nez Perce territory and regaining their horses that had been left there over the winter, they waited for several weeks because the deep snow in the mountains made travel impossible. During this time, Clark became the local doctor, treating eye infections and rheumatic pains. He was careful not to do anything that could cause harm. Bratton and an Indian chief were both cured of back problems in a sweat bath—Bratton of what might have been a slipped disk, and the Indian of a strange case of paraplegia.

Impatient to move on, they tried to cross the mountains but had to turn back. When the snow receded, Indian guides took them through the mountains in a few days. On the eastern slope, the corps divided into two groups. Lewis explored the Marias River, hoping to find that it went far north, because the Louisiana Purchase included all the land drained by the branches of the Missouri. Clark went south, then along the Yellowstone River to rejoin Lewis on the Missouri. His journey was without serious incidents, except for Indians stealing all their horses.

Lewis took Drouillard and Privates Joseph and Reuben Fields up the Marias, leaving the remainder of the group to make its way down the Missouri. They turned back after finding that the river flowed out of the Rockies, not from the Plains farther north. One day, going along a bluff above the Two Medicine River, Lewis spotted a group of eight Indians and about thirty horses. Piegan Blackfoot! The one group of Indians he did not want to meet because of their reputation for violence. A young Indian galloped toward them, halted a short distance away, and then galloped back to his group. The two groups approached each other cautiously. Drouillard indicated in sign language that they wanted to be friends. They camped together under three trees, two of which still stand today, 200 years later. During the evening, Lewis told the Indians where they had been and how they hoped to expand American influence.

Blackfoot tradition tells us that the young men had been on a horse-stealing foray and were returning home with their trophies. Lewis thought they were a war party.

In the morning, one of the Fields brothers found an Indian stealing his rifle. He shouted a warning and in the scuffle that followed stabbed the Indian to death. Within seconds, Lewis and his men had their rifles stolen and the Indians were starting to drive away the horses. The struggle was short but lethal. One Indian was dead and Lewis shot another with his pistol, leaving him for dead. (Blackfoot tradition says he survived.) The Indian youths fled north; Lewis and his men fled south toward the Missouri. They rode more than 100 miles in the next twenty-four hours, fully expecting to be pursued by a large Indian band. Miraculously, as they approached the Missouri, they heard a gunshot. Their own men on the river had arrived at exactly the same moment. The horses were abandoned. Lewis and his men jumped into the canoes and they did not stop for fifteen miles, where they camped on the opposite side of the river.

After this near escape, the men were like horses heading for the barn. The strong current carried them along for sixty, seventy miles a day. Only one near disaster marred the rest of the voyage. On August 11, Lewis and Cruzatte, who was blind in one eye and had poor vision in the other, went hunting for elk. One of them shot an elk that escaped into heavy willows. They both followed. Cruzatte, thinking he saw the animal, fired his gun. There was a loud scream from Lewis, "Damn you. You have shot me!" The ball went through his buttocks from left to right, finally lodging in his buckskin pants. No vital structures were hit, and the next day, when they joined with Clark, the wound was correctly dressed, with drains at both entrance and exit wounds. Healing was complete by the time they reached Saint Louis. But Lewis made no entries in his journal after the accident.

When they arrived at the Mandan village, Charbonneau, Sacagawea, and Colter left the expedition. Charbonneau did not think he could find employment in Saint Louis and Colter wanted to join two trappers returning to the wilderness. Clark offered to take Baptiste to Saint Louis and educate him, but Sacagawea thought he was still too young.

Days before arriving in Saint Louis, they met traders going upstream and learned that most people thought they had died. Jefferson never gave up hope. They arrived back in Saint Louis on September 22, 1806, to shouts and huzzahs from the welcoming crowd. Lewis's first duty was to write to his president: "It is with pleasure that I announce to you the safe arrival of myself and party at 12 o'clock today at this place with our papers and baggage. In obedience to your orders we have penetrated the continent of North America to the Pacific Ocean ... and have discovered the most practicable route which does exist across the continent. ... "

They had done their duty bravely, although, as history would prove, the route they had discovered was not the most practicable.

5
Zebulon Montgomery Pike
(1779–1813)

Explorer or Spy?

Exploration is really the essence
of the human spirit.

—Astronaut Frank Borman

Zebulon Montgomery Pike, depending on how you interpret his story, was a hero, a man of unbelievable endurance, a great explorer who commanded the loyalty of the men under him; or he was incompetent, impetuous, self-centered, naïve, a poor leader who led his men into unnecessary disaster, and possibly a spy. Despite the wildly differing opinions of his character and achievements, his only true memorial is a magnificent mountain in Colorado: Pikes Peak.

Zebulon Montgomery's father, also Zebulon Pike, was a captain in the continental army and, after independence, farmed in Pennsylvania. Farming was hard, and when the call came for the militia to fight the Indians, he joined up again.

On November 4, 1791, Zebulon Pike, then a captain in the Pennsylvania militia serving in Ohio, was involved in a vicious four-hour battle during which his mortally wounded commanding officer sat propped against a tree, his loaded pistol in his hand, ready to fight to the end, which was quick in coming. Hundreds of men died, as well as nearly 200 women of the camp. Captain Pike escaped by hanging on to the mane of a wounded horse on which a friend was riding.

One year later, Captain Pike joined the newly formed regular army, commanded by General Anthony Wayne of Whiskey War fame, and he and his wife were ordered to Cincinnati, along with their three daughters and one son. The commander of the camp was General James Wilkinson.

Zebulon Montgomery Pike, thirteen years old, soon became entranced by his father's flamboyant commanding officer. Little did he realize how closely his own life and career would be joined with that of Wilkinson, once described as "the most villainous character" in early American history.

After a tough youth with very little education, Zebulon joined the army in 1794, age fifteen, and never left the service to the day of his death in 1813. Soon after joining the army, Zebulon, or Zeb, as he became known, was sent down the Ohio River in charge of a barge full of supplies to join his father's regiment. A string of forts had been built throughout Ohio and along the river to protect white settlers from the Indians. Captain Pike's job was to inspect barges plying up and down the river and his son's job was to carry supplies from post to post along the Ohio and Mississippi rivers. Sometimes he was in charge of as many as twelve barges—a great responsibility for a teenager, but one that was grooming him for later adventures.

In November 1799, Zeb was promoted to first lieutenant in the First Infantry Regiment, and by 1801 was adjutant at Fort Wilkinsonville, where one of his fellow officers was Meriwether Lewis.

His duties took him to many military posts, one of which was near Sugar Grove, Kentucky, where he met and fell in love with his cousin Clarissa Brown. Brown's father was strongly opposed to a marriage, but the young couple was determined, eloped to Cincinnati, and were married.

Both parents objected to the marriage, but Zeb replied with charac-teristic independence, "I will willingly receive the advise of those my superior in rank or age, or connected with me by ponsanguinity (sic) but whilst I have the breath I will never be the slave of any man."

Pike was a demanding officer, drilling and training his men, both to relieve the monotony of camp life and to turn the rough volunteers into competent soldiers. He was conscientious, temperate in his ways, intolerant of drunkenness, a skilled outdoorsman, and an expert marksman. He had great powers of endurance and was indifferent to cold and discomfort. His education may have been poor, but he taught himself French, Spanish, and the elements of science. While other officers—probably including Lewis—caroused, Pike studied to improve himself.

Throughout his military career, Pike seems to have been oblivious to the weakness, perifidious nature, and treachery of General Wilkinson. The Spanish were paying Wilkinson for information about American military forces, while at the same time Wilkinson was planning an invasion of Spanish territory. Theodore Roosevelt, in his book *The Winning of the West*, said of Wilkinson, "He had no conscience and no scruples; and he had not the slightest idea of the meaning of the word honor." His motives were entirely self-centered. He sought power and wealth and was willing to use whatever means necessary to achieve those aims.

Why did Wilkinson choose Pike to lead two expeditions, both of which were conceived to benefit himself? Perhaps he recognized in Pike a young offi-cer, intensely loyal, perhaps somewhat naïve, but a man with drive, courage, endurance, and persistence enough to complete whatever task he was assigned.

Late in 1803, control of the Louisiana Territory passed from the French to the Americans. Both Wilkinson and Lewis witnessed the handover ceremony in Saint Louis early in 1804. It was a critical moment. Lewis, under the orders of President Thomas Jefferson, was about to leave on his epic voyage to the West Coast. Wilkinson was calculating how to advance his own future.

During the next two and a half years, Lewis was out of touch, except for the messages he sent back from the Mandan Fort in the spring of 1805. In the meantime, back in Saint Louis, Aaron Burr, on his way to New Orleans, was visiting Wilkinson, hatching a plot to invade New Mexico.

Wilkinson, without instructions from Jefferson—but later approved by the president—ordered an expedition to explore the upper reaches of the Mississippi and chose Lieutenant Pike to be the leader. The public reasons were to explore the northern limits of the Louisiana Purchase, reestablish American authority over the area, pinpoint sites for military forts, and establish peace between rival Indian tribes. The additional private reason was to find commercial opportunities for Wilkinson.

On June 24, 1805, Pike received orders to come to Saint Louis and leave with all possible speed to explore the upper Mississippi and return before the winter.

The preparations for the voyage were hectic. Pike found a place for his family to live near Saint Louis. A large keelboat and four month's supply of food, ammunition, presents for the Indians, tents, and camp equipment was collected in only two or three weeks, and Pike left on August 9. The

Optimistic Hopes, Shattered Dreams

Overoptimism is a persistent failing of military planning. Only seven years later—and on a much grander scale— Napoleon would invade Russia, hoping that the campaign would be finished by autumn. The retreat from Moscow in 1812 was the disastrous result.

A hundred and thirty years later, Hitler repeated the same mistake, invading Russia in June 1941 to be caught by the terrible winter of 1941–1942.

Later in World War II, after the rapid breakout by the Allies across France in July 1944, winter clothing was not sent to Europe. Everything would be over by Christmas— everything but the Battle of the Bulge, which took the Allies completely by surprise and caused thousands of frostbite casualties.

departure date was too late in the season for a long, upstream voyage expected to return before winter. Because Pike was ordered to return before the winter, he took no winter clothing.

The scientific instruments were cheap and inaccurate, but that hardly mattered because the expedition was not scientific, and Pike was no scientist.

Seventeen privates, two corporals, and one sergeant were selected from available troops. We do not know how they were selected, but Pike later described them as "damned rascels."

Wilkinson gave Pike his orders on July 30, 1805, less than a week before his departure. Although shorter than those given by Jefferson to Lewis, the orders had the same tone. "You will please to take the course of the river and calculate distances by time, noting the rivers, creeks, high-lands, prairies, islands, rapids, shoals, quarries, timber, water, soil, Indian villages and settlements, in a diary to comprehend reflections on the winds and weather." He was also to investigate Indian trade and look for a site for a military post between Saint Louis and Prairie du Chien. He was then to buy and mark out the ground where it could be built. His other duties included collecting animal, vegetable, and mineral specimens, distribute "trifling" presents to the Indians. He was to ascend the river until he reached its source and "return before the waters are frozen up."

Pike, then twenty-six years old, was convinced that this expedition would bring him fame, promotion, and, possibly, wealth. But this was not a voyage into unknown, unexplored territory and it is surprising that he thought he would achieve the rewards that he anticipated.

The voyage started favorably, with a good wind to fill the sails and decrease the need for rowing. But the weather turned bad and rain ruined some supplies. After three weeks, the keelboat encountered eleven miles of rapids, through which they were helped by an Indian agent, William Ewing, and Saux Indians. Above the rapids, they rested in Ewing's village and Pike had his first opportunity to give his stump speech to the local chiefs. He assured them that the Great White Father had ordered his young warriors to begin to "take them by the hand and make such inquiries as might afford the satisfaction required." The chiefs, already well acquainted with British and French Great White Fathers seemed pleased but probably kept their doubts to themselves.

The river passed through country long inhabited by many different bands of Indians and traders and filled with trading posts. Despite this, Pike, who had a tendency to exaggerate, claimed in his journal to be 1,500 miles from civilization.

The expedition proceeded up the river. Two men became lost while looking for some dogs, delaying the group for several days. Straying men were a common complication for many expeditions. Usually, the country through which the group was traveling was deep wilderness. The men had neither compasses nor maps and had to rely on basic wilderness skills for finding their way. In addition, they frequently set out on a day-long mission without food and ended up in trouble.

Prairie du Chien was a good place to stop for a rest. Half the young people in the town appeared to be Métis, but "the Indian trade occasioned them to commit acts at their wintering quarters which they would be thought guilty of in the civilized world ... almost one-half the inhabitants under twenty years of age have the blood of the Aborigines in their veins."

Within a few days, they met the Sioux, whom they hoped to convince to stop fighting. But their chief, Wabasha, realistically told Pike that most of them were either drunk or hungover and in no condition to negotiate. He suggested waiting a day before starting talks. Wabasha gave Pike a peace pipe to show to other chiefs; it was a cultural sign that he intended to keep his word. Pike made a long, rambling, and patronizing speech, but he bought 100,000 acres of land for $200. Pike thought the true value was at least $200,000, and, understandably, was very pleased with himself. Later, Wilkinson would complain that Pike had paid too much for the land. Fifteen years afterward, Fort Anthony was built on the site.

The expedition reached Lake Pepin, a huge expanse of water subject to sudden storms. Characteristically, Pike thought he knew better than the locals, set sail against their advice, and was soon caught in a life-threatening storm. Thunder, lightning, and demasting of his boats forced him to return to shore.

Early in October, the expedition had arrived at the present Twin Cities. Pike noticed what he thought was a white flag attached to a bush. He investigated and found it to be a burial cloth marking the corpses of three women and a child. At a different site, Pike took a red cloth from an Indian shrine dedicated to the Matcho Manitou. "But I took the liberty of invading the rights of his diabolical majesty by appropriating the articles ... to my own use." He was not sympathetic toward what he regarded as Indian superstitions.

The river became more difficult to navigate. The large boat was left behind and the men took to canoes that they had to pull through rough, freezing water. Ice on the pools in the morning presaged the coming of winter, but, despite his orders, Pike pushed ahead. He was determined to find the source of the Mississippi. Fortunately, game was abundant and food was not a problem.

By mid-October, there was snow on the ground. Two of the men fell sick. Sergeant Henry Kennerman had a massive gastric hemorrhage and Corporal Samuel Bradley bled profusely from his bladder. Pike was clearly concerned about the state of his men. "These circumstances," he later wrote, "convinced me that if I had no regard for my own health and constitution, I should have for these poor fellows who, to obey my orders, were killing themselves." Both men recovered, but Pike was forced to set up a winter camp. Returning to Saint Louis without completing his assignments was inconceivable. The men built a stockade thirty-six feet square, while Pike and the hunters laid in a supply of meat. When the stockade was finished, Pike wrote with astounding self-confidence, "I would have laughed at the attack of 800 or 1000 savages, if all of my party were within."

Pike always kept meticulous records of how far they traveled. The record of successive days in October read "twenty miles, three miles, sixteen miles, twelve and a half miles, twenty-nine miles." One day, he walked thirty-five miles while his men, pulling loads, went only five.

Pike wanted to reach Lake Leech, the supposed source of the Mississippi. So in addition to the canoes, the men built sleds, for, by now—December 10—snow lay deep on the frozen ground. The canoes were too low in the water and unstable. One filled with water, soaking valuable powder and ammunition. In an ill-advised attempt to dry the powder by heating it in a pot, an explosion nearly killed some of the men. Little powder was saved.

Some days later, Pike awoke to a shout from the sentry, "Will you let the lieutenant be burned to death?" The lieutenant's tent was not the only one on fire, and the party lost vital clothing and moccasins, and Pike could have been blown to death by kegs of powder in his tent.

Although conditions were harsh and progress slow, game was still abundant and Pike shot deer and buffalo to feed the party. Already the eleven men of the group accompanying Pike were suffering from the lack of winter clothes and moccasins. Pike was astonishingly unaffected by the cold and miserable conditions and usually walked several miles ahead of the men to light bonfires at which they could warm themselves. "Never did I undergo more fatigue, performing the duties of hunter, spy, guide, and commanding officer," he wrote later.

On every expedition, Christmas was always a special day. Pike's men received extra meat, flour, whiskey, and tobacco. A week later, they met a party of Indians and two traders, one English, the other French. They belonged to the North West Company, a trading company that Pike wanted to expel from American territory. But the traders had a comfortable post nearby at Cedar Lake, to which Pike was invited and where he and his corporal received welcome hospitality, expulsion did not seem to be a reasonable demand. Cuthbert Grant and his scouts had been watching Pike's group and were glad to find that they were peaceful Americans and not a war party. Pike was unhappy to see the Union Jack flying over the post, but he did not demand that it be removed.

Pike and Corporal John Boley (who had been as far as the Mandan Fort with Lewis and Clark) rejoined the rest of the group and, over the next week, pushed on, freezing their noses and feet, until they reached another of Grant's posts. Here everyone was invited into the warmth and comfort of a well-built log cabin. The experienced traders lived well, with warm cabins, good food, vegetables raised in their summer gardens, horses, and the comfort of their country wives. Despite the comforts, Pike wrote, "It appears to me that the wealth of nations would not induce me to remain secluded from the society of civilized mankind, surrounded by a savage and unproductive wilderness, without books or other sources of intellectual enjoyment, or being blessed with the cultivated and feeling mind of a civilized female companion."

A Chippewa offered to guide them to Leech Lake. Pike, the Chippewa, and one man traveled ahead of the others until they reached another of Grant's posts. The remaining men did not catch up for two days and then had to continue without rest. They met Indians from whom they tried to receive information, but who were usually not forthcoming until they were given whiskey. The river twisted and turned, but on February 1, in the early afternoon, they reached the shores of Lake Leech. "I will not attempt to describe my feeling on the accomplishment of my voyage, for this is the main source of the Mississippi."

Pike could not be blamed for his belief, one that had been held for years, but Lake Itasca, twenty-five miles away, is the actual source of the river. (The name "Itasca" is taken from the central letters of the Latin term *Veritas Capita*, the "True Head.")

The group crossed the lake to the trading post of another Scot, Hugh McGillis, whose house was also flying the Union Jack. They were received with great kindness, hot coffee, bread, and cheese. The rest of Pike's group did not straggle in for another six days, during which Pike enjoyed warmth, good food, and, to his surprise, a good library.

Pike was no diplomat. After receiving every kindness and help from McGillis, he wrote him a sharp note demanding that he pay duties on the furs traded and remove the Union Jack. To enforce the latter demand, Pike had one of his men shoot the flag down from the staff over the house. To his credit, McGillis, after a suitable delay to let his anger die down, and when he probably realized that Pike would soon be leaving, agreed to pay the duties. There is no evidence that duties were ever paid and it is likely that the Union Jack was run up the flagstaff as soon as Pike was out of sight.

Three weeks later, back at Grant's house, Pike was exhausted and had to rest. His feet were cut to ribbons by the bindings of his snowshoes and he needed treatment. The rest of the group caught up but were given no rest. The journey home had to proceed as quickly as possible.

When they reached the stockade, they found that Sergeant Kennerman had sold or given away most of the gifts and had eaten all the smoked venison that was going to be a present for General Wilkinson. Amazingly, Pike, instead of sentencing the sergeant to death or 100 lashes for theft and disobedience, merely reduced him in rank to private.

The river was still frozen; the boats and canoes were useless. A month passed before "break-up," but this delay allowed another pow wow with the Chippewa chiefs who gave Pike a peace pipe to take to the Sioux. The pipe was later delivered to Chief Wabasha—a nice gesture, but not one that maintained a long-term peace between the bands.

The river opened. The canoes were loaded and on April 30, 1806, while Lewis and Clark were still waiting west of the Rockies, Pike returned to Saint Louis.

The achievements of the voyage were slim. His one success, which was scoffed at by Wilkinson, was the purchase of a huge tract of land for only $200. But he was pleased: "We have returned thus far on our journey without the loss of a single man, and have hopes of soon being blessed with the society of our relatives and friends."

Pike returned to Saint Louis expecting a promotion, a rest, perhaps a reward, and, certainly, praise. Instead, he received new marching orders. While Pike had been on the Mississippi, Wilkinson had been plotting another expedition. Two months after returning to Saint Louis, Pike received orders to escort a party of Osage Indians back to their village in Kansas, then continue west to find the headwaters of the Arkansas and Red Rivers and return to Natchitoches in the Louisiana Territory.

This expedition would start by crossing land that was undoubtedly American, but Pike would move into territory where the dividing line between American and Spanish control was contested. If he strayed too far to the southwest, he would enter territory that was definitely Spanish and would run the risk of being taken prisoner. What Pike did not know was that Wilkinson, the double agent, had informed the Spanish that he would be coming their way, hinting—if not actually saying—that he should be captured. Wilkinson may have had an ulterior motive. If Pike were captured, he would almost certainly be taken to Santa Fe, perhaps even farther into Spanish territory, and might then be able to come home with a detailed report on the Spanish. By the time Pike returned in 1807, Wilkinson was taking part in the trial of Burr and was rapidly becoming a persona non grata.

Pike knew nothing of this when he received his orders from Wilkinson. Once again, there seem to have been public and private orders. The public orders ran through the usual litany of finding the headwaters of rivers, making observations, keeping records, and bringing back specimens. The private orders and suggestions told a different story. If Pike were captured, he should, apologetically, pretend to be lost and perhaps the Spanish would treat him well. Wilkinson wrote to Pike that he should be careful what he reported to the secretary of war after he returned. "To me," he wrote, "you may and must write fully and freely, giving a minute detail of everything worthy of note. In regards to your approximation to the Spanish settlements ... your conduct must be marked by such circumspection and direction as may prevent alarm or conflict, as you will be held responsible for the consequences. On this subject I refer you to your orders." Were those the public or the private orders? Historians still do not know.

The expedition set out on July 15, 1806, a party of eighteen, some of whom had been with Pike up the Mississippi. The group included Lieutenant Wilkinson, the son of the general and Dr. John H. Robinson, a volunteer doctor who was to play an interesting role in the ensuing adventure, one interpreter, and two new privates. Among the men was Private, formerly Sergeant, Kennerman, who had been demoted during the first expedition and promptly deserted on the second. He disappeared from history.

Two boats carried supplies and equipment, but, once again, because Pike did not think he would meet winter conditions, he took no winter clothing. There were also fifty-one Osage Indians being escorted back to their village.

As this strange group progressed, the soldiers rowing the boats and the Indians walking onshore, Pike and a couple of hunters were off on the prairie, hunting for the group, when they delivered the Indians back to their own people. There was much rejoicing, but when Pike and his men were to leave, the Indians said they could only supply four horses. The Indians finally sold them fifteen horses and provided guides. The river had become too shallow for boats and the expedition was now on foot and horse.

The prairies stretched endlessly in front of the advancing party. Later Pike would propose that this vast, open expanse would be a favorable buffer between the white and Indian civilizations, discouraging the expansion of white people beyond the Missouri river and giving the Indians a place in which to live in their own way.

While Pike was returning the Osages to their home and starting out across the prairie, more than 600 Spanish dragoons and militia had set out from Santa Fe to arrest Pike and his men. But they were too early for Pike's slow-moving group. When Pike arrived at a Pawnee settlement, he was told that the Spanish had recently been there and had departed to the northwest. The Pawnee chief said that he had been asked to dissuade Pike from going any farther, and, in fact, warned him that he would try to stop him. Once again, Pike, saying they were not women to be deterred by such threats, bypassed the village to avoid a fight, following the route of the Spanish. This was not difficult because 600 horses and an accompanying supply train made a trail wide enough for the greenest Boy Scout to follow.

Despite this, Pike lost the trail and had trouble in telling the direction in which the Spanish force was moving.

While at the Pawnee village, Pike wrote back to Wilkinson that there would be no difficulty for men with baggage wagons and artillery to march across the prairie and "I would pledge my life and what is infinitely dearer, my honor, for the successful march of a reasonable body of troops into the province of New Mexico." This letter would later be used as evidence that Pike was spying for Wilkinson.

The route the Spanish followed would later be part of the Santa Fe Trail, heading south. Eventually, Pike arrived at the Arkansas River, where by design Lieutenant Wilkinson left the group to make his way back to civilization. The journey did not prove to be as easy as anticipated. He set off with four soldiers in a bull boat made from willows and buffalo hides and one canoe. The river was shallow and freezing. It took him seventy-three days to reach Fort Arkansas, where his four companions immediately deserted.

Pike proceeded north along the Arkansas River with fifteen men. The abundance of game was a source of constant amazement. "I believe that there are buffalo, elk, and deer sufficient on the banks of the Arkansaw alone, if used without waste, to feed all the savages in the United States one century." But other areas seemed less attractive. "These vast Plains of the western hemisphere, may become in time equally celebrated as the sandy desarts of Africa; for I saw in my route, in various places, tracts of many leagues, where the wind had thrown up the sand, in all the fanciful forms of the ocean's rolling wave, and on which not a speck of vegetable matter existed." (He was probably describing the Great Sand Dunes.)

The weather became colder. The river was filled with blocks of ice and some of the men were frostbitten. Horses escaped and men had to spend nights out looking for them. Snow covered the grass and the horses had to be fed the bark of cottonwood trees. Finally, Pike called a halt so he could hunt for food. Half the horses had died, and because of the lack of winter clothes, the men were already feeling the bitter weather.

Somewhere near the present city of Pueblo, Colorado, the group halted and built a stockade. They had seen mountains ahead and Pike thought that while the men rested, he and a small party could climb a great peak they had spotted "like a small blue cloud" from far out on the prairie. The air was so clear and Pike, inexperienced at judging distances and heights, thought that he could reach the peak in a day. Three days later, they were only at the foot of the mountain, where they left all their food and extra clothing, such as it was. One day later, on Thanksgiving Day, standing in deep snow, they had only reached the top of Cheyenne Mountain and Pike believed that no man could ever climb to the summit. Half starved, wearing cotton overalls, without socks, and with their lives at risk from the cold, they turned downhill. When they finally reached the stockade, several days later, they found the rest of the party worse off than they were. Their food was finished, the horses were starving and being attacked by magpies pecking at their sores, and a storm was raging.

A less driven leader would have rested his men, gone hunting, restocked the larder, and made clothes and moccasins out of deer or buffalo hide. Not Pike. As soon as the storm had finished, they pushed north into the mountains, passed the mouth of the Royal Gorge, and made their way into the huge expanse of South Park, where they found a branch of the South Platte River. Pike, at last, realized that going farther north was not feasible, turned around, crossed the mountains through the Royal Gorge, and, to their surprise, found themselves back at the spot from which they had started.

The expedition was collapsing. The men were starving, they had to sleep on the frozen ground without blankets, their feet pointing toward a huge fire. On January 5, 1807, they had no alternative but to make their way South and build another stockade. Two men whose feet were frozen so badly that they could not travel were left behind, while Pike and the remaining thirteen men turned west through the Sangre de Cristo Mountains into the San Luis Valley. Pike was still looking for the origin of the Red River, although he must have known that the way to the Red River was due south and not west. (Humboldt's map, which he had with him, may have deceived him into thinking that the Red River arose farther north.)

The men were near mutiny and one said, "It is more than human nature could bear, to march three days without sustenance through snow three feet deep, to carry burdens fit only for horses." The complaint was probably justified, as they had been carrying seventy-pound loads through ghastly conditions. But Pike turned on the man, accused him of sedition, and threatened to shoot him should he ever utter such words again.

It is easy, in retrospect, and backed by modern knowledge of the geography, to accuse Pike of stupidity, poor leadership, lack of preparation, and bad decisions. Starvation and hypothermia both affect rational thinking and Pike may have been suffering from this deadly combination. Rational decisions would have been difficult to make.

Traversing the Sangre de Cristos is a long, tough hike, even in summer. It was a near miracle that they were able to make the passage in winter, through thigh-deep snow, in wet cotton clothes, with the wind sucking the heat out of their bodies. And they did not do it just once. Some of the men made the passage three times, going back to rescue their incapacitated friends who were starving and freezing, sheltered only by a flimsy stockade and unable to hunt because their feet were frozen. When the rescue group finally made its way back across the mountains, some of the men were still unable to travel, and in a desperate appeal to Pike's sense of compassion and honor, sent him bones from their frostbitten feet as a grim reminder of their plight.

Pike did not spare himself. His judgment may not have been good, but he was usually pushing ahead of his men, finding the route, hunting for food, and planning the next moves. He did not lack determination.

Worse was to come. By the middle of January, nine of the men had frostbitten feet and could go no farther. Fortunately, Pike was still mobile and able to shoot a buffalo. Along with Dr. Robinson, he loaded as much meat as he could carry and arrived at camp, dizzy with exhaustion. But the meat was a lifesaver for the men.

As the pathetic group struggled on, they passed the Great Sand Dunes, from which Pike could see a stream flowing south, about fifteen miles away. He thought this might be the upper reaches of the Red River. They found a suitable place to build another stockade. This one was more elaborate than the others. The walls, built of logs two feet in diameter, were twelve feet high. A water-filled moat several feet deep was built outside the wall and the small entrance could only be reached by crawling across a log. Pike boasted, as he had done up the Mississippi: "Thus fortified I should not have the least hesitation of putting 100 Spanish horse at defiance until the first or second night and we made our escape under cover of darkness—or made a sally and dispersed them when they were resting under full confidence of our being panic struck."

Pike sent some men to rescue the stricken members of the group, leaving only himself and four men in the stockade. At the same time, Dr. Robinson left to go to Santa Fe. Somehow he seemed to know exactly how to get there. He went south along the river, by himself, and was in Santa Fe within a few days. Did he know, and did Pike know, that the river beside which they were camping was the Rio Grande and not the Red River?

Pike and his men did not have long to wait before they had a visit from the Spanish. Robinson had obviously told the Spanish authorities that there was a small, weak group of Americans in a stockade on the Rio Grande. The first visitors were two men, but within a day or two, a group of dragoons arrived. There was no fight. Pike allowed the Spanish commander into the fort and agreed to go peacefully to Santa Fe if the Spanish would stay and rescue the remaining members of his group.

The Spanish governor in Santa Fe found Pike's story contradictory and unbelievable. In modern terms, Pike said—as he had been instructed to do by Wilkinson—"Gosh, I thought I was on the Red River. You mean this is the Rio Grande? I am awfully sorry and had no intention of straying into Spanish territory." Whether the Spanish believed him or not, they treated him with respect and kindness. He dined with the governor and was allowed the freedom of the city, such as it was. But he was then sent to Chihuahua to explain his position to a more senior governor. Finally, the Spanish authorities decided to allow Pike to return to the Louisiana territory. On the month-long journey, Pike was escorted by the same Spanish officer, Lieutenant Don Facundo Malgares, who had been sent to find them shortly after they set out from Saint Louis.

The Spanish authorities forbade Pike from taking any notes and they took all his diaries. (The diaries were found in Mexico City in 1907 and returned to the National Archives of the United States in 1910.) Pike, however, was an acute observer with a good memory and kept some notes concealed from the Spanish by hiding them in the barrels of his soldier's rifles.

After his return to Natchitoches on July 1, 1807, roughly eleven months since his departure from Saint Louis, Pike was able to give a detailed report on the Spanish territory through which he had passed, in addition to information about Santa Fe, Taos, Chihuahua, and other Mexican cities. His journals were published in 1810.

Pike returned to find himself in the middle of Burr's trial, at which Wilkinson was a prime witness. He was never formally accused of spying on behalf of Wilkinson or Burr, but over the years there has been suspicion that he was, if nothing more, an unwitting participant in their plans.

Pike was quickly promoted in the next few years to captain, major, colonel, and, finally, brigadier. It was as a brigadier commanding an attack on York (Toronto) in 1813 that he was killed. His troops made an amphibious assault across Lake Ontario and drove the Canadian troops before them. But the Canadians had planted explosives in an underground armory and exploded them when the American soldiers were over the site. Pike was mortally wounded by flying rocks and debris and died later the same day, a true war hero and the victor of one of the first American successes of the War of 1812.

6

John Wesley Powell
(1834–1902)

First Down the Grand Canyon

Never, never, never quit.

—*Winston Churchill*

John Wesley Powell was born March 24, 1834, in Mount Morris, New York, to immigrant parents from England. One of eight children, and the oldest son, he was named after the founder of the Methodist movement in England, John Wesley, and was brought up in a religious household where the Bible was regarded as the literal truth and the first chapter of Genesis explained the founding of the world, with no argument or dissension.

His parents, appropriately named Mary and Joseph, were pious churchgoing folks who settled in upper New York, where Joseph practiced his trade as a tailor but aspired to be a preacher. After four years, they moved to Jackson County, Ohio, before moving again to the tiny town of South Grove in Walworth County, Wisconsin. In Wisconsin, they started a small farm. Twelve-year-old Wes was responsible, along with his ten-year-old brother, Bram, for breaking the land, planting the crops, selling the wheat, and doing all the farm jobs, while his father traveled from church to church. This phase only lasted a few years. His family had strong abolitionist views, and after several acts of vandalism on their property, including cutting off their horse's tail, they moved again, to Wheaton, Illinois. Joseph soon became associated with the Illinois Institute, a nearby Wesleyan school that took students of every age from elementary to college level.

During all this moving, Wes had scratched together bits and pieces of an education from an eccentric but highly knowledgeable friend of the family in Ohio; by reading and teaching himself as he drove the wheat-laden wagon from the Wisconsin farm to market; by going to a secondary school, learning the elements of geography and mathematics; and then by using this limited experience to get a job as a teacher while still a teenager.

At the time of the 1850 census, Wes put down his job as "farmer," but in the census of 1860, he was recorded as "naturalist." During the intervening years, he had developed a passion for geology. Geography, geology, and the study of fossils and mollusks not only filled his mind, but changed his religious views, and he doubted the creationist teachings of his father.

He never stuck with any school or college for long. Either he ran out of money and had to take a job, or the school did not provide the scientific education that was his Holy Grail. He tried the Illinois Institute at Wheaton, where he could live with his parents. He moved to Oberlin College, where he found the emphasis on religion and the inadequacy of the scientific education a bad combination. He returned home after only five months.

During the summer months, between switching from one school to another, he explored the rivers of the Midwest. He floated down the navigable length of the Mississippi. He hiked across Wisconsin and sailed on the Ohio River, receiving an education not only in natural history, but in self-confidence. Unfortunately, he never kept a diary of his voyages and we can only guess at his adventures, the people he met, the storms he encountered, the food he ate, the near misses, and education in reading the currents and whirlpools of the rivers. All these experiences turned him into a real naturalist, able to look after himself in the wilderness. Rocks, fossils, and mollusks were his passion for the rest of his life.

He collected everything he could, and the top floor of the Powell house became a museum. He began to base his beliefs on the teachings of geology and scientific theories of the age and origins of the world. But more was going to change in Wesley's life than his religious views.

The country was in a turmoil over the division of the states and slavery. In 1861, as soon as Fort Sumter surrendered, Wesley volunteered for the army, little thinking that the war would last four years and change his life and health forever. Like young men everywhere (and in every age), he was swept up in the enthusiasm of his cause and blissfully ignorant of the horrors to come. He went to the library and read books on military engineering, hoping to become a builder of forts and defenses. He was eager for battle but soon found himself at Cape Girardeau on the banks of the Mississippi, developing plans for defending the city.

Powell's unit was visited by General John Frémont and he was commended for his plans. When General Ulysses Grant, who had replaced Frémont, made a tour of inspection, he thought the plans unnecessary and ordered Powell to be put in charge of a battery of artillery. Although he was only a captain, Wesley became friendly enough with the general to ask for leave to get married. Leave was granted and he hurried back to marry Emma Dean, who would follow him throughout the war.

Powell, in charge of Battery F of the Second Light Artillery of the Illinois Volunteers, was responsible for 132 soldiers, including his younger brother Walter, and six six-pounder guns. He drilled his men relentlessly so they would be prepared for battle.

On the March 14, 1862, Powell's unit finally went to war, near the small church of Shiloh. When the Confederate army attacked on Saturday, April 5, the Union army was not prepared. Powell and his men waited for orders and eventually he took events into his own hands, gathered up his battery, and headed for the battle.

For the first time, Powell saw the unimaginable horrors of war. The Confederate soldiers overran the Union placements and the battle swayed back and forth. After about six hours of fighting, Powell was hit in the right arm by a musket ball. He did not realize how badly he had been wounded until General Wallace came on the scene and gave up his own horse so that Powell could get attention. The general himself was killed a few minutes later.

Powell rode for several hours bemused, in shock, and in increasing pain. Finally, he arrived in Savannah, by boat, where Emma was waiting for him. His right arm was amputated the next day. Powell took three months to recuperate and he was sent home to Illinois to recruit new soldiers. He must have been a discouraging advertisement for the war. He had lost weight and was having great pain from his arm, but he always intended to return to his unit as soon as possible. For the rest of his life, Powell suffered pain, despite which he was able to achieve amazing goals.

Once again, Powell returned to service. By this time, he was a major, responsible for commanding 1,000 men and their guns. At the battle for Nashville, he stood with the commanding general overlooking the battle-field. After it was clear that the Confederate army had been defeated and the end of the war was in sight, Powell left the army in January 1865 and returned home to restart his life.

His younger brother Walter returned home a shadow of his former self, morose, and subject to fits of violence. The psychiatric damage done to Walter by the war and his imprisonment in a terrible prison camp would stay with him for the rest of his life. Two Powell sons had gone to war and both returned damaged, one with his dominant hand gone—for Wesley was right-handed—and the other with a tortured mind that would never heal.

In the four years between Powell's discharge from the army and the start of the great adventure down the Grand Canyon, the American West became the land of opportunity.

Thomas Jefferson had wanted Meriwether Lewis and William Clark to find a commercially practical way to the West, but this dream never became true until the steam engine, powering boats and trains, made the transportation of both people and goods fast and efficient. The transcontinental railroad completed Jefferson's dream. The telegraph made communication almost instantaneous. Transportation and communication were no longer limited to the speed of a horse.

Wesley Powell had to rebuild his life. He was thirty-one years old, married, without a job, and physically disabled. His only civilian experience was as a teacher—with very limited academic background and no college degree, except an honorary masters degree from a Wesleyan college.

He was fortunate to receive a professorship in science at Illinois Wesleyan University and his salary was helped by a government disability pension.

Powell threw himself into his duties with almost manic enthusiasm. He taught every subject from agricultural chemistry to botany and the history of geology to all students. He started a small museum and took the students on field trips. He was no stuffy, classroom-bound, absentminded professor. He was as restless as ever.

Within months of his appointment, he was seeking a better post at Illinois State Normal University, a college with a stronger scientific program. He pressured the state to appropriate money for a museum for the Illinois Natural History Society. To no one's surprise, he was appointed curator of the new museum and given a full professorship at Normal University. He only taught one course before becoming full-time curator at the museum in 1867.

His next move was to take a group of students to the Rocky Mountains. Powell was what would now be called a "schmoozer." He squeezed additional funds from various organizations and obtained a supply of military rations and a military escort through his former commanding general Ulysses Grant. He even required each participant to contribute $300.

His party of twelve, including Emma, headed from Council Bluffs, Iowa, to Colorado, traveling in mule-drawn wagons. Each member was armed with a rifle and a revolver, perhaps with good reason, for while crossing the Plains, they met Generals William Tecumseh Sherman and George Custer, both in pursuit of Indians.

They eventually reached Denver, a city in decline because of the collapse of gold mining, then headed south toward Pikes Peak (14,110 feet), which they climbed on July 27. They experienced all the effects of altitude—shortness of breath, headaches, difficulty sleeping—but this did not deter them from climbing another fourteener, Mount Lincoln (14,286 feet). They returned to Denver in September, their wagons filled with more than 6,000 mineral and biological specimens.

Wesley and Emma continued their journey, while the others returned home. During their extended trip west of Denver, they met Jack Sumner, trapper, outfitter, and would-be mountain man. During this visit, the topic of exploring the Colorado River from its origins to the Gulf of California appears to have been discussed. (Sumner's account of the conversation was written forty years later and may have been biased by later events.) Powell returned to Illinois, already planning a second, more extensive trip.

The next trip was to last for two summers. Powell returned again to General Grant for help, proposing a trip to explore the Colorado River. Within three weeks of the Congress granting approval for rations, Powell was on his way west. Except for Emma, the twenty-one members of the group were all greenhorns. Included in the party were three Protestant ministers, one seeking a cure in Colorado for a chronic sore throat!

This time, they did not ride the dusty emigrant trail but chugged west in comfort on the newly built train, all the way to Cheyenne, Wyoming. They headed south to Denver, trying to ride newly broken Mexican horses that stampeded at the drop of a ten-gallon hat.

By mid-July, their ambitious plans to explore the Colorado River changed. They headed west through the mining town of Central City and over Berthoud Pass (now the way to the ski resort of Winter Park), then made an exhausting climb over an 11,000-foot pass to camp in Middle Park, a broad, flat area of thousands of acres surrounded by mountains.

A small group, including Powell and Sumner, who had joined the expedition, took off to climb Longs Peak (named after Stephen Long). They chose a route from the west that is seldom climbed nowadays and, after some difficulty, succeeded in reaching the summit, amazed by the magnificent view that they saw across the Plains to the East.

Although Powell and his companions had no aggressive encounters with the Indians, there were rumors of trouble all around. Powell had a great interest in the Indians and their culture, but most of the others in the group had different views and regarded the Indians as stupid and inferior.

Hot Sulphur Springs, Colorado, where the expedition gathered, and which was Sumner's home, had been a historic watering place for the Ute Indians. But it was turned into a popular resort by William Byers. There Powell met Samuel Bowles, a well-known journalist, who wrote glowingly about the work that Powell was doing.

Powell and Emma stayed at the springs while directing the others to find their way over Gore Pass to the Yampa River. Walter Powell, the leader of the group left at Hot Sulphur Springs, sent some of the men back to Middle Park to get supplies, while Wesley Powell was climbing more mountains—including one that would later be called Mount Powell.

Early in October, the whole party was reunited and chose a sheltered spot on the White River to build a winter camp. The party built good, warm cabins and lived out the winter separated from the comforts of home and civilization but surrounded by the wonders of nature. Powell described the winter as "so very mild." The men remained healthy, their animals were well fed, and Emma occupied her time preserving bird skins, while Wesley compiled a Ute vocabulary and dreamed of his next great adventure: exploring the Grand Canyon.

The area surrounding the Grand Canyon was the last remaining big blank on the map of the United States—a blank labeled, simply, "unexplored." Powell had completed two trips to the West and had looked down on the Green River from its high surrounding cliffs—a view that softens all rivers, flattening the rapids into innocent-looking splashes. Viewed from water level, those benign splashes would take on a totally different character.

On May 24, 1869, just a few days after the Golden Spike had been driven into the Utah desert completing the transcontinental railroad, Powell and nine companions pushed off into the Green River, ten men in four boats built specially in Chicago and brought by train to Green River Station: the *Emma Dean*, *No Name*, *Kitty Clyde's Sister*, and *Maid of the Canyon*.

Powell's companions included his brother Walter; Jack Sumner; two brothers, Oramel and Seneca Howland; Billy Hawkins, as camp cook; Bill Dunn; George Bradley (who would keep a useful and insightful diary); Andy Hall, eighteen years old and eternally cheerful; and Frank Goodman, an Englishman seeking adventure. Only two received pay—Hawkins to cook, and Oramel Howland to draw maps. All regarded themselves as tough outdoorsmen, but their previous experiences in the wilderness varied considerably. None had ever rowed a boat on white water. As boatmen, they were completely, perhaps blissfully, ignorant. Not a single one, including Wesley Powell, would have been remotely considered for employment by a modern rafting company.

Ten men, four boats, and ten months' (7,000 pounds) supply of food started the voyage. It was a trip fueled by unwavering determination but conceived in ignorance, with the wrong boats, no river skills, led by an authoritarian, one-armed veteran who because of his disability could not row, portage, or line a boat down a rapid. One man left the expedition at the first opportunity and three left at the end, within twenty-four hours of safety, and were killed by Indians. The six who survived amazed both themselves and the country, for no one thought that it was possible to enter the Grand Canyon and come out alive. Only one man, Wesley Powell, would gain fame from the expedition—and, ultimately, political power—while the others slipped back into obscurity, some of them embittered.

Modern astronauts are chosen with meticulous, scientific care. They are physically and psychologically tested. Their skills are honed by years of training and, above all, they must be ultimate team players. Powell, however, chose a motley group of free-spirited mountain men, with no skills other than an ability to hunt, light a fire, and endure physical discomfort. They were certainly not team players—that was why they had chosen to be mountain men, unrestrained by the discipline of city life. In their diaries, they grumbled and complained, and in life, almost came to blows. Yet in times of danger, they went to each other's help without hesitation.

Within hours of the start, two boats had run aground on sandbars. At this stage, these incidents were jokes to be laughed off. But the men were quickly learning that handling these boats, built with a prominent keel that caught the current of the river, was not going to be easy in rough water. They were badly designed for white water, almost uncontrollable, heavy, and ponderous to portage, and difficult to lower by lines from the shore.

Powell's boat, the *Emma Dean*, was smaller and lighter than the three heavier freight boats. The plan was that Powell would lead, spot impending rapids, and signal the other boats to pull to shore so that the rapid could be overlooked and a plan devised for its passage. They soon found out that the system did not work, and for a very simple reason.

Modern white-water boatmen row facing downstream. They can see what is coming and can quickly turn their flat-bottomed boats to avoid rocks, holes, standing waves, and the many other hazards of the river. Powell's men rowed looking upstream, as though they were rowing across a quiet lake. This meant that they had to look over their shoulders in order to see upcoming rapids, and, more importantly, to see Powell's signals. Shouted signals were impossible to hear as the roar of the water drowned out all sound. Even signals shouted in desperation at the last moment could not be heard, or, if they were heard, the boats could not be maneuvered quickly enough to avoid disaster.

On the second day, Powell's boat and two others hit the same sand-bar. No damage was done, but rain was pouring down and the men were soaking wet. It took a roaring fire and hot coffee to revive everyone's spirits.

The upper reaches of the Green were relatively easy. The few rapids were not severe, but the men soon discovered that any portage carrying seven tons of food and equipment, as well as the heavy oak boats, was a miserable task. The rocks were sharp and slippery and their boots were not designed for this type of work.

Inexperienced as the men were, all rapids seemed bad. From the start of the expedition, a constant theme ran through the diaries, until on the last day it became a primal scream: "This is the worst rapid we have seen. It is quite impassable." When they finally passed into calm water, with the Canyon behind them, they must have looked back at some of the early rapids and wondered why they had thought them so bad, and wondered why they did not just run them, but portaged them laboriously, or strained to line the boats down the river.

Another recurring theme was that the hunters returned without finding—let alone shooting—any game. Canyon bottoms are not wildlife refuges. Bighorn sheep skipped along the cliffs far out of range and only in the flatter areas were there deer, geese, or ducks. Even the fishing was not good. Their hopes of feeding themselves off the land were dashed.

The course of the rivers could be divided into several well-defined stages: the upper Green, which was relatively benign; Brown's Park, a paradise of a resting place; Lodore Canyon, a succession of hard rapids, one after another; the junction with the Yampa, followed by a long section of quiet water; the fusion of the Grand and the Green, followed by Cataract Canyon, a wild, dangerous series of rapids, treated with the greatest respect even today; a gorgeous run down Glen Canyon, now under the waters of Lake Powell; the Grand Canyon itself, with its massive rapids ready to swallow the boats and drown the men and from which there was virtually no escape; and the final two days of travel beyond the canyon, when the land opened out and the sky changed from a narrow strip seen between towering cliffs to a broad and welcoming vault of blue.

Powell and his men were not the first white men to run the upper Green. In 1825, William Ashley, pioneer of the American free traders, accompanied by seven trappers, made an abortive attempt to navigate the river in buffalo-skin bull boats, getting as far as the junction of the Grand and Colorado Rivers. A quarter of a century later, Captain William Manly, tried to float the river all the way to the Pacific. His boat was smashed against a rock, and in a makeshift dugout made from logs, he miraculously reached the Uinta valley. There an Indian chief persuaded him, with dramatic sign language, that he would perish if he went farther down the river. The chief was describing the Grand Canyon. Manly proceeded overland.

The transition between Brown's Park, a quiet pastureland that once sheltered Butch Cassidy, and the Lodore Canyon is sudden and intimidating. The cliffs rise a couple of thousand feet and the roar of unseen rapids fills the air. The rapids came fast and furious. In his diary, Bradley wrote about "the wildest rapid yet seen"—a comment he would repeat many times in the next weeks. The *Emma Dean* pulled to shore, as did the *Maid of the Canyon*, but the *No Name* went barreling past, out of control, crashed into rock after rock, and broke in half. The Howland brothers and Goodman, the crew of the boat, hung on desperately, eventually landing on a rock in the middle of the river, stranded. Using the unloaded *Emma Dean*, Sumner rescued the men.

A ton of supplies had been lost—one-third of their total, including rifles, ammunition, and much of their food. At first, Powell thought that all three barometers, vital for his research, had also been lost. But the next day, when the boat had floated onto a sandbar, Sumner and Hall volunteered to explore the wreck. To their amazement, they found all three barometers undamaged—and a ten-gallon keg of whiskey! Powell, appropriately, named the rapid Disaster Falls.

What would happen next? How bad would the future rapids be? Could they survive without the food? Powell had a lot to worry about. The loss of another boat would end the expedition. Some of the men turned to divine help. Sumner, an earthier man, wrote that after taking a good drink of whiskey, they spent the rest of the day "as best suited."

They were not finished. Anxiety and uncertainty were Powell's constant companions. He was responsible for his men. As he had worried about the safety of those under him during the war, so did he worry about them on the river.

After Disaster Falls, the rapids seemed to be continuous. Portaging was often the safe but painfully slow course of action. A mile of river might involve a day of labor.

Powell had planned a scientific expedition. Often, while the men worked in camp, repairing boats or resting, he, sometimes with others, would take off with his geologist's hammer, exploring for fossils, unusual rocks, and clues to geologic history.

The men complained in their diaries. "He has chosen the worst possible campsite again." They fished and caught nothing. They hunted and returned empty-handed. Their clothes were constantly wet. Powell wrote: "Everything is wet and spoiling."

Bradley was religious and objected that they did not observe Sunday as a day of rest. They could not afford to. A day without progress was another day that diminished the food supply without a commensurate distance traveled.

Triplet Falls and Hell's Half Mile, nowadays run with scarcely a pause, slowed them even more. They portaged and let down their boats on lines. They hauled heavy loads over huge boulders. They slipped and fell, bruising their legs and cutting their feet. The hazards of the riverbank were as bad as those of the river itself.

On the river, a boat could be slammed broadside against a rock. If the planks were not smashed, the boat could tip, filling with water in seconds. Holes—those swirling whirlpools downstream from big boulders—could suck a man down to eternity. The current on a bend could pin a boat against the overhanging cliff. In some places, the cliffs were so smooth and the banks nonexistent that there was no alternative but to run the rapids.

Surgeons say, with gruesome humor, that "bleeding always stops." Powell could have said the same about the rapids: they always stopped—but not before another near disaster. While lining the boats down a rapid, the *Maid of the Canyon* pulled loose and was swept downstream and out of sight. Sumner and Hawkins, in the *Emma Dean*, raced down the river to catch the *Maid*. Like a wayward girl who changes her mind after running away from home, the boat was turning gently in an eddy a mile downstream, bruised, but floating and reparable. The next day, *Kitty Clyde's Sister* hit a rock and began to leak badly. More delays. More repairs.

The campsite that evening was nice—perhaps too nice. A fickle wind blew the flames from the campfire into a bush. Soon the whole camp was on fire. The only escape was to the boats. Some of the men's clothes were on fire. A rope mooring one of the boats burnt through and the boat floated away. The men jumped into the river to save it. Powell, who was high on a cliff above the camp and could not see the fire, looked down to see the three boats floating downstream. He must have thought he was being abandoned.

When everyone came back to camp, they found that most of their cooking and eating utensils had been destroyed. But to the men, the fire was more of a joke than a disaster.

On June 18, 1869, the expedition reached the junction of the Yampa and the Green. On the west bank, opposite the inflowing Yampa, the huge red face of Echo (Steamboat) Rock rose abruptly, 500 feet from the river, dwarfing the passing boats. On the east bank, between the rivers, was a quiet place to camp and recuperate. They could look back over one month and three days of travel, three near drownings, the loss of one boat, and a diminishing food supply.

The hunters killed a deer—a great but temporary improvement in their diet—and there was relief from the rapids when they entered the Uinta Valley. The river was smooth and fast, and with hard rowing, they covered sixty-three miles in a day.

Across the nation, wild rumors were circulating that the expedition had come to a disastrous end. William Riley told the *Omaha Republican* that nine of the ten members of the expedition had died and that only Sumner, whom he had met at Fort Bridger, had survived. He blamed Powell for impetuous leadership that killed all the men but one. But the story soon fell apart. The *Rocky Mountain News*, with which Oramel Howland was connected, found that no survivor from the expedition had walked into Fort Bridger. Another hoaxster entered the fray. John Risdon, claiming to be a second survivor, spread his story across the nation, complete with lurid details, conning the nation and collecting money from sympathetic listeners to his story. He said he had served under Powell in the army and gave a list of false names of other members of the expedition. His story was a pack of lies. The final nail in Risdon's coffin of falsehoods came when he claimed that Powell had died on May 16, but Emma had received a letter written by her husband on May 29. Risdon, the ultimate con man, who had several aliases, ended up in jail. Powell, on the other hand, was a national hero.

While the expedition was enjoying a temporary stop, Powell went to the nearby Indian Agency to buy food but was only able to buy 300 pounds of flour. At the same time, Goodman decided his adventure had come to an end and he left the group. Now there were nine men for three boats.

They started again on July 6 and soon found an island garden with beets, turnips, and potatoes. They ate the vegetables, including the potato greens, but they did not know that potato greens are toxic. Those who had eaten them rolled around in agony, clutching their bellies and puking. Fortunately, the poisoning was short-lived and no harm was done.

Desolation Canyon lived up to its name: the river was rough, the canyon walls high and, to most people, impossible to climb—but not to Powell and Bradley. They struggled to find a route up the cliff, and when Bradley reached the top, with Powell behind him, they reached an impasse.

One of the rules of rock climbing is, if possible, to have three points on the rock at all times: two hands, one foot; two feet, one hand. This leaves a fourth limb free to move: an arm to reach higher; a foot to find a new hold. Powell had three points on the cliff, his left arm and both feet, but he had no right arm; there was no fourth limb to move. They were 100 feet above the canyon, without a rope. In an act of genius and desperation, Bradley removed his long johns, in which he was climbing, lowered them to Powell, who, in one wild movement, let go with his left hand, leaned back, grabbed at the pants, and was pulled to safety.

What might have happened if Powell had fallen and been killed? The men would have continued, but would they have looked for an escape route out of the canyon? Would they have had the same judgment about which rapids to run and which to portage? The questions are unanswerable for Powell made all those decisions.

The entries in Sumner and Bradley's diaries became gloomier: "Worst run," "Wildest so far." The heat at the bottom of the canyon increased, making a ducking a relief. The *Emma Dean* crashed and another oar was lost; they had no spares. The *Emma Dean* tipped and Dunn was nearly drowned, while Powell—the only man with a life jacket—wrote that the swimming was quite easy. But fortune smiled. They ended up against a pile of driftwood from which they were able to make new oars. But in the accident, Powell lost 300 dollars, two guns, and a precious barometer. The finicky barometer readings were essential, not only to measure the heights of the cliffs they climbed, but also to tell how far they had descended on the river, giving them a clue to the distance they still had to go.

By July 14, they had, temporarily, come out of the canyons to a place where the river could be crossed. There were signs of Indians, but they had no desire to meet them. In 1853, Captain John Gunnison had been murdered here while surveying a route for the railroad.

The lack of food was becoming a serious problem. Their staples were beans and rice; the remaining flour was sour and much had to be thrown away.

A little bacon and a few dried apple's were the only variety available to them. They had started with enough food for ten months, but now, a little more than two months later, they were down to one pound of flour per man per day. Game and fish were scarce or uncatchable. Two beaver tails made good soup, and a nice change. But now, they had two fears: drowning and starving

The junction of the Green and Grand Rivers form the true Colorado River. Powell—in a ridiculous decision—wanted to spend three weeks here in order to wait for a solar eclipse. Fortunately, he was dissuaded.

Immediately after the junction, rapid followed rapid in quick and ferocious succession. The men portaged four rapids in three-quarters of a mile. At camp that night, they saw driftwood stuck thirty feet up the side of the canyon wall, showing how high the river could rise.

The boats needed to be repaired and caulked, so Powell made a difficult climb to the plateau to find resin. He found several pounds but had to cut off the useless right sleeve of his shirt to make a bag to carry it back to camp. Coming down, he was nearly swept away in a flash flood.

The next day, they went only one and a half miles and Bradley became increasingly impatient. But the hunters shot two sheep—"the greatest event of their trip," wrote the ever-practical Sumner. They feasted. Morale was high.

There was no respite. Bad rapids, portaging, and lining were the interminable sequence of events. Occasionally, their attention was drawn away from the tasks at hand. They spotted old Indian dwellings high on the cliffs and climbed to inspect them. The men wondered how the Indians could have survived in such dry and inhospitable conditions.

Entering Glen Canyon, they found a paradise of beauty: relatively calm water, ferns and waterfalls, willows and cottonwoods. They saw sheep but failed to shoot them. Near the Crossing of the Fathers, where Escalante and fourteen men had crossed the river in 1776, they shot a sheep and gained eighty pounds of meat, but for nine starving men, the meat did not last long. Farther downstream, at the future Lee's Ferry, the put-in place for most Grand Canyon boat tours of today, they once more had temporary relief but were about to begin the "Great Unknown." Beyond this point, no one had ever crossed the river: canyon walls were too high and steep. Nowadays, there are paths down the walls, but of these Powell and his men had no knowledge. They had gone 700 miles and some of the men were beginning to lose their nerve.

Powell was determined to observe the eclipse of the sun and made the men stop at a place where he could climb out to the plateau to make observations. He climbed thousands of feet carrying his instruments, but clouds obscured the sun and ruined his chances of making any observations. To make matters worse, he had to spend a cold night benighted halfway down the cliff.

August 8 was a good day: four portages, twenty-seven rapids, and thirteen miles covered. The canyon was beautiful, with springs streaming from the wall, gleaming like jewels. Greenery hung in veils from the dripping stones. Bradley described it as "the prettiest sight of the whole trip." Powell named the place Vasey's Paradise after a friend and botanist. More beauty followed in the immense cavern of Redwall Canyon.

Throughout the whole trip, Powell remained an ecstatic, enthusiastic observer. His diary, written post hoc, described the beauty of the scenery or the walks he took away from the river. "At two o'clock, we reach the mouth of the Colorado Chiquito. The stream enters through a canyon, on the scale quite as grand as the Colorado itself. It is a very small river and exceedingly muddy and salty. On my way back I killed two rattlesnakes, and find, on my arrival, that another has been killed just at camp."

The next day, while Bradley fretted in camp because he had no boots, Powell planned again to determine longitude and latitude and discovered another well-worn Indian trail where steps had been cut in the rock. "It was doubtless a path used by people anterior to the present Indian races." The men also discovered old pottery and petroglyphs.

Taking a measurement of latitude helped them to realize that they were due east of a Mormon settlement. So long as the river headed west, they were moving in the right direction. But their clothes were wearing out, food was low, and insects and blowing sand plagued them.

The canyon became narrower, the noise of unseen rapids louder. Sumner wrote, "We have finally encountered a stretch of water that made my hair curl." Powell agreed, "There is a descent of perhaps, 75 or 80 feet in a third of a mile, and the rushing waters break into great waves on the rocks, and lash themselves into a mad, white foam. ... We must run the rapid or abandon the river." The run was as wild as any they had taken—huge waves, whirlpools, projecting rocks, eddies, and all in a boat filled with water. The next rapid was even more difficult and required a dangerous lining down the right side of the canyon. They camped on a shelf fifty feet above the river.

From this point on downstream, the river presented greater challenges than any they had met before. Powell wrote, "And now we go on through this solemn mysterious way ... the boats are entirely unmanageable; no order in their running can be preserved."

Powell and Dunn got into a furious row. Dunn, through no fault of his own, ruined the watch essential for taking longitude measurements. Powell threatened him with a fine, and when one of the others said that Dunn had nearly drowned in trying to save the watch, Powell replied that his loss would have been of little account. Hawkins, the cook, refused to serve Powell his dinner, making him come and get it from the campfire like the others. Discipline threatened to fall apart completely, and after Powell had reprimanded Howland for losing some maps, Sumner told him, "The war is over. You can't come any damned military here." A near fatal fight ensued. Dunn said that if Powell had not been a cripple, he would have hit him. Walter, Powell's brother, got his gun, and Hall threatened to shoot Walter, but Walter backed off. Perhaps this release of steam and adrenaline was what was needed because Powell's authoritarian attitude began to mellow.

Now they were fighting for their lives. Only nine days' rations remained. The rain fell heavily day after day. They were caught in a "granite prison" from which there was only one escape: downstream. The *Emma Dean* flipped; the men were in the raging water, clinging to the boat. The *Maid of the Canyon* came to their rescue. They lost their oars. Their bedrolls were soaked. They could scarcely have been more miserable.

The granite ended and limestone, the sign of calmer water, reappeared. But the river turned due south, the wrong direction. Powell's thoughts were on the rocks and he speculated that the canyon must, at some time, have been dammed to a height of 1,200 to 1,500 feet. "What a conflict of water and fire must there have been here." That day, they had run thirty-five miles.

An Indian garden provided them with plenty of squash. "At supper we made unleavened bread, green squash sauce and strong coffee. We have been for a few days on half rations, but we have no stint of roast squash. ... A few days like this and we are out of prison."

The next day, Oramel Howland told Powell that he, his brother Seneca, and Dunn had decided to walk out. Powell went to his maps and worked out where they were and showed Howland that there was only a short distance to go. But Howland's mind was made up. Powell, sleepless, was himself in doubt. Should they all leave the river? Could they climb out? Could they survive the desert between the river and the nearest Mormon town? "To leave this exploration unfinished, to say that there is a part of the canyon which I cannot explore, having already almost accomplished it, is more than I am willing to acknowledge and I determined to go on."

Breakfast was "solemn as a funeral." The three men left, taking with them letters to loved ones and a copy of the diaries.

The *Emma Dean*, broken by the river, was abandoned. Powell unloaded his barometers, fossils, minerals, and rock specimens, obtained at such cost, and left them on the shore.

The remaining two boats, with six men, made it safely through the rapids. The men fired their guns to signal to those above that they were safe. They waited, but nobody came.

They made one last horrific run, but, at noon the next day, they emerged from the Grand Canyon into a broad valley. They were safe. The three men who walked out were never seen again.

The next day, they saw some Indians who ran away. The survivors must have been a fearful sight to the Indians, and they certainly surprised the Mormons they met a little later who had been warned to look out for water-logged shirts, broken boats, and perhaps a body or two.

Ninety-nine days after they had embarked, 1,000 miles downstream and 9,000 feet lower, six starving, half-naked, sun-blistered men, with food for barely three days, paddled out of the hell of the canyon. They had somehow survived 476 rapids and sixty-two portages, innumerable duckings, near-drownings, swamped boats, stove in planks, lost and abandoned food, rain, lightning, near disaster while climbing cliffs, and a crippling lack of game for food. The Mormons greeted them with astonishment, elation, and compassion, and they were soon feasting on bread, butter, and eggs.

Wesley and Walter Powell made their way back to civilization, Sumner and Bradley continued on down the river to Yuma, Arizona, and Hall and Hawkins rode the river all the way to the sea. Sumner remained embittered to the end of his life, believing he had not been properly rewarded for his efforts. He died in poverty. Bradley lived in California for the rest of his life. Hall was killed in 1882 while riding shotgun on a stagecoach. Hawkins farmed in Arizona until he died in 1919.

Powell made another trip down the canyon in 1871, but this time he went more as a surveyor than as an explorer. He saw that having filled in the gap on the map labeled "unexplored," it was now his duty to make detailed surveys of the land. On his second trip, he sought to find out how the Howland brothers had died. He was guided by Kaibab Indians and was greatly impressed by their intimate knowledge of the country. When he finally reached the Shivwit Paiute Indians, they did not hesitate to admit that they had killed the three men and said they had been led astray by "bad men" who convinced them that the white men had murdered a Hualapai Indian woman. Powell accepted their explanation as fully understandable and slept in their village that night, undisturbed and confident they would not harm him.

7
John Charles Frémont
(1813–1890)
The Pathfinder

Nothing his explorations required
was impossible for him to perform.

—Kit Carson

Anne Beverly Pryor was a young woman in Richmond, Virginia, who was married to an older man but fell in love with a romantic Frenchman, Charles Fremon, who taught dancing. The couple eloped in a blaze of scandal.

The unmarried couple had a difficult time making both ends meet, especially after the arrival of John Charles and a daughter. After Charles Fremon's father died, the couple, with their two children, moved in with his widow in Charleston, South Carolina. (They changed the family name from Fremon to Frémont shortly after they married.)

John Charles was born on January 21, 1813, an illegitimate child, a blot on his origins that would haunt him for the rest of his life. He was an eager schoolboy, bright and intelligent with a voracious appetite for knowledge and an aptitude for mathematics. In 1829, he received early admission to the College of Charleston, from which he was discharged two years later for "incorrigible negligence"—not a characteristic that would be obvious later, except for a tendency to neglect orders when they did not conform to his own plans. A couple of years later, he was appointed as teacher to the midshipmen aboard the U.S.S. *Natchez*.

In 1838, through the influence of an important Charleston citizen, Joel Poinsett, who was secretary of war, he was commissioned in the Corps of Topographical Engineers, a branch of the U.S. Army. He was assigned to accompany Joseph N. Nicollet, a well-known French scientist who had been commissioned to survey the area between the upper reaches of the Mississippi and Missouri Rivers.

This expedition taught Frémont surveying, scientific methods, botanical knowledge, and how to deal with Indians—all skills that would hold him in good stead in the coming years. The expedition surveyed more than 300 hitherto unknown rivers and lakes and produced a detailed map of a huge area.

Frémont went with Nicollet for a second voyage, this time up the Missouri in a steamboat, the *Antelope*. Having chugged slowly up the river, the party disembarked at Fort Pierre. They then set off across land, where Frémont had his first exciting experience of hunting buffalo at full gallop across the prairie—an experience that left him both exhausted and temporarily lost. It was about this time that, during a visit to the Yankton Sioux, he was offered a beautiful Indian girl as a wife (after Nicollet had declined the proffered gift). Frémont, who, later in life, was a notorious ladies man, also turned down the offer, explaining that he was going to be traveling. Other encounters with Indians were important in developing Frémont's friendly attitude toward them, although years later he would not hesitate to attack Indian tribes that antagonized him.

By the end of this expedition, Frémont was an experienced wilderness explorer and surveyor filled with the urge to explore the land toward the setting sun.

The First Expedition

While Nicollet and Frémont were working on the report of their second voyage, Senator Thomas Hart Benton, one of the most influential men in Washington, paid them a visit. Benton wanted Congress to support explorations that would lead to finding the "Road to India." He was enthralled by the data that Nicollett's expedition had collected and soon invited Frémont to his home. Benton's second daughter, Jessie, who was only sixteen, quickly became enamored with Frémont and the friendship blossomed into love.

Senator Benton and his wife were strongly opposed to any thoughts of marriage, taking into account Jessie's age and John's impecunious status as an army officer. They contrived to have John sent on a mission to the Ohio River, while Jessie was sent to a private school. Neither of these tricks worked, and when John returned, the couple first agreed to wait for a year but eloped, finding a Catholic priest who married them. The marriage was kept secret until they met with Jessie's parents and confessed. The senator was furious and, giving a "never darken these doors again" speech, expelled both of them from his home. But paternal love (combined with admiration for the young Frémont) made him relent and readmit the young couple to the their home.

When the Congress, pushed by Benton, decided to send a "survey" to take a detailed look at the Oregon Trail, Nicollet was chosen as chief of the project. But he was in bad health and Second Lieutenant John Frémont, newly married, was appointed in his place. This was the chance of a lifetime for Frémont, one that could place his name in the public eye and at the same time please his very influential father-in-law.

Frémont recruited Charles Preuss, a good artist and cartographer, to join the group. Preuss's maps were used for many years by later emigrants.

When Frémont reached Saint Louis, he acquired two members of the expedition who were obviously not going to play a major part in the survey: Henry Brant, a nineteen-year-old relative, and Randolph Benton, his wife's twelve-year-old brother. He then began seriously to collect men to take him west, including Lucien Maxwell as a hunter, nineteen engagés, and Basil LaJeunesse, who would become a close and trusted friend. En route up the Missouri River to the starting point, Frémont, almost casually, had a fateful meeting with a fellow passenger, Kit Carson. Carson, an experienced mountain man and guide and Indian fighter with an unequalled reputation, was out of a job. He was the guide Frémont needed, with his quiet composure and his vast knowledge and experience of the West. To look at, Carson was not impressive: small, slightly built but wiry, with sandy hair and a voice so quiet that Frémont had to listen carefully to hear him. He hired him, on the spot, at $100 per month.

The purpose of the journey was obscure, because anglos had crossed South Pass in 1812 and again in 1824, and in the intervening years unnumbered trappers had used the pass to reach the Green River valley. Benjamin Eulalie de Bonneville explored the route with wagons between 1832 and 1835, and Marcus and Narcissa Whitman, the first missionaries to the Nez Perce, had passed that way in 1836. But the first organized group, led by Dr. Elijah White, was only two or three weeks ahead of Frémont.

Frémont was to bring back detailed information of value to future emigrants but was not expected to make any genuine discoveries. His orders were to survey the land to the south of the Missouri and Platte Rivers, but he wanted to explore the Rocky Mountains. John James Abert, head of the Corps of Topographical Engineers, was not willing to go that far, despite promptings from Senator Benton, but did say, informally, that if a reconnaissance of the Rockies did not interfere with the main objectives, Frémont could explore the mountains. Abert did not realize that once Frémont was on his own, he could be a loose cannon, making his own plans and accepting the consequences of his actions.

The expedition left Chouteau's landing on June 10. The men were on horses, followed by eight mule-drawn carts with supplies, with Kit Carson in the lead. The group experienced the usual troubles. Their supply of coffee was dumped in the Platte—a disaster for the coffee-drinking voyageurs. Fortunately, they soon found another supply.

When they reached the branching of the Platte, Frémont went south and sent the others north to Fort Laramie. Within a couple of weeks, during which he was entertained by Baptiste Charbonneau, son of Sacagawea, he rejoined his companions at Fort Laramie to find them alarmed about rumors of Indian attacks along the route they proposed to take. Having come this far, Frémont was not about to be put off. He gave a rousing speech to his companions, implying that anyone who stayed behind was "chicken." Only one man left the group. For obvious reasons, Frémont left behind the two boys and ordered the older boy to wind the chronometer every day—a dull task for a young man dreaming about exploring the West.

The expedition left Fort Laramie and on July 29 the men ate their first buffalo, the dietary mainstay of trappers and travelers. Along the trail, they saw the scattered detritus of emigration: old clothes, some stained with blood, and pots too heavy to carry. There had been a serious drought and they met Indians seeking new homes because the lack of water and grass had driven away the buffalo and deer. The threatened attacks did not occur.

In the spring and summer, South Pass is a benign, wide expanse of sagebrush. To the north, the southern end of the snow-capped Wind River Mountains come to a mildly declining end, and to the south, low mesas rise to break the skyline. In between these two landmarks, the gentle rise of the pass, almost twenty miles broad, fills the eye.

The first trappers to traverse the slopes of South Pass were members of the Astorians heading back from the mouth of the Columbia in 1812. While they were delighted to be shown this easy route, its full significance for future expansion did not dawn on them.

In 1824, Jedediah Smith had some inkling of its importance but could never have imagined the flood of pilgrims who would use it two decades later to reach their hoped-for heaven. Bonneville, who hauled the first wagons over the hump, showed that this was a feasible route to the enticing west.

The Sweetwater River runs to the east, and Pacific Creek, at times barely discernible, flows to the west. When Jedediah Smith crossed the Divide, he did not realize he was heading down to the Pacific until he saw that the creek was running westward. To the Indians, this was a well-known route through the mountains, but they did not understand the importance of a pass accessible to wagons and crossing the Continental Divide. They had no idea that by showing the pass to Smith, they were ensuring their own displacement, if not their destruction.

South Pass, a few thousand acres of scrub grass, sand, and sagebrush, was more important to the opening of the West than any other piece of real estate of similar size and conformation. The dramatic route of Meriwether Lewis and William Clark over the Lemhi and Lolo passes is of interest only to tourists and aficionados of the Lewis and Clark heritage; it was never used to expand the West. But more than 400,000 emigrants crossed over South Pass.

Abert's orders were to explore the route to the pass, then turn for home. By the time his party crossed into the valley of the Green River, his official work was finished. Looking north, he could see the snow-covered peaks of the Wind River Mountains, and, setting aside his orders, he turned toward them.

Frémont's first plan was to circumnavigate the range, going north up the western edge and turning east around the northern edge of the mountains before making his way back to Fort Laramie. But he soon realized that his supplies would not last long enough and the sight of the high peaks gave him the idea to be the first man to climb what he thought was the tallest mountain in America.

A lake (Boulder Lake) lay at the foot of the peaks, bright blue in the summer sun, surrounded by trees that afforded shelter, firewood, and grazing for the mules. Some of the men were left here, and Frémont with fourteen others, each mounted on a mule, and with Carson as the guide, made their way through the forest, northeast, to what seemed to be the tallest peak. It looked so close that everyone thought that the summit could be reached within a day, or perhaps two. Like Pike before him, Frémont was deceived by the crystalline clarity of the air into thinking that the climb would be an easy ramble. It did not take them long to realize how wrong they were.

Carson was not used to the intricacies and unexpected obstructions of a mountain range. And although the peak could still be seen tantalizingly close, another difficulty always got in the way: a narrow couloir too steep to climb or an unscalable cliff. And to add to their troubles, several of the party began to suffer from acute mountain sickness. Frémont had a splitting headache and vomited so badly that he could not continue.

Preuss became separated from the main party, lost his footing, and slid precipitously down a snow slope into a pile of rocks. Fortunately, he was not badly hurt. The precious barometer, with which Frémont was going to measure the altitude at the summit, fell and broke. But with great ingenuity, it was repaired with glue made from buffalo bones and deer hide.

It was obvious at the end of the first day that they had underestimated the distance to the mountain they called Snow Peak, now called Frémont Peak (13,745 feet), and they camped on hard granite slabs by the side of a small lake with an island. Thinking that the trip would only take a day, they had not brought enough blankets and food and they spent an uncomfortable, unexpected night out.

Another day was spent searching for a route. Preuss climbed higher than anyone else and was surprised to see Frémont and the others below him. He was carrying the barometer and took a pressure measurement, although he was not at the summit. Frémont was still sick and sent men back for more food and blankets. The next day, refreshed and after a warmer night, he was ready to climb to the summit. Frémont arranged to be the first to reach the summit, which was so small that only one man could stand on it at a time. The view was fantastic and Frémont, clutching an American flag, was thrilled by the feeling of standing on top of the world.

The climb was, in its way, a singular achievement. This was the first time a mountain of this size had been climbed in America (at least by a white man), with no other intent than to get to the top. Climbing for fun or to achieve dramatic "firsts" was only in its infancy in Europe. Mont Blanc had first been climbed in 1786 and the Alps were the playground for adventurous Englishmen and their stalwart Swiss guides. For Frémont, this was a pure ego trip, one that could be described to Jessie in glowing terms and would serve to show his adventurous spirit. His success would bring praise and adulation. If it had turned out to be a disaster, there would have been hell to pay.

The descent to the lake took little more than a day and the group headed for the Sweetwater River and the way home. But the way home was not as easy as was hoped. Somehow, events never were that easy for Frémont. When the party reached the Sweetwater, Frémont inflated the rubber boat. All went well until they hit some rapids and the boat capsized, tipping valuable supplies and instruments into the water, including a book with all the astronomical observations. The boat was abandoned and walking on bare feet through cactus country, they picked a precarious way toward Fort Laramie. Miraculously, one of the men fished a book out of the river: the astronomical observations, the scientific basis for Frémont's later report to the Topographical Engineers. Forty-two days after setting out, they walked back into Fort Laramie.

When Frémont finally reached Saint Louis, he left almost immediately for Washington to rejoin his wife, who was expecting a child, and to report to the authorities and his father-in-law.

The report that Frémont wrote with the help of his wife, Jessie, became a best seller, opening the eyes of the public to the adventure of western travel and providing scientific information about the land between the Missouri and the Rockies. The heroic young explorer with a pretty young wife, an influential father-in-law, and the writer of a best-selling government report was poised for greater adventures.

The Second Expedition

Frémont worked hard after his return from the first expedition. The report for the Corps of Topographical Engineers was long. Writing did not come easily to him and the stress gave him bad headaches and nosebleeds. Jessie became not only his amanuensis, but also his ghost writer, elaborating his account of the journey, sometimes with descriptive license. The report so touched the public's yearning for true tales of

American heroes that Henry Wadsworth Longfellow considered writing a poem about the expedition.

Oregon beckoned the public as a potential agricultural paradise. In February 1843, the Senate passed a bill authorizing the establishment of a series of forts along the emigrant route to Oregon. The House of Representatives failed to pass the bill, but the Oregon momentum swayed Abert sufficiently for him to order Frémont to lead an expedition to find another western route south of those previously found and to proceed to the Columbia River.

Frémont hurried to prepare and obtain supplies that included a substantial armory of weapons, including a mountain howitzer and 500 pounds of ammunition. He claimed they would be traveling through hostile Indian country and would need the weapons. The howitzer was dragged and hauled for thousands of miles before being abandoned without firing a shot in anger.

On May 22, 1843, Abert wrote a stinging letter to Frémont, who was already at Westport Landing preparing for the expedition. Frémont's wife, Jessie, received the letter in Saint Louis and opened it (although it was not addressed to her). The letter, which castigated Frémont for buying the unnecessary howitzer, ended by saying, "If there is reason to believe that the condition of the country will not admit of the safe management of such an expedition, and of course will not admit of the only objectives for accomplishment of which the expedition was planned, *you will immediately desist in its further prosecution and report to this office.*" (Emphasis added)

Jessie immediately sent off a message to her husband, "You must not ask why: start at once, ready or not." The urgency of the letter was unmistakable and Frémont's faith in his wife was unshakable. He left immediately. Abert's letter lingered, unread by its rightful recipient.

Frémont led a corps of thirty-nine well-armed men, with "Broken Hand" Fitzpatrick as guide, Preuss as cartographer, and a German artillery officer. The expedition, slowed by hauling the heavy howitzer, finally reached the site of modern Pueblo, Colorado. Carson, hearing about the expedition, left his wife of five months and hastened to Frémont's camp, where he was welcomed and reemployed as a guide.

Taking a route north of the Wasatch Mountains, Frémont went down the Bear River valley to the Great Salt Lake where he arrived in September. The route then took them north to Fort Hall and along the Snake River until they reached Fort Walla Walla on October 25. Preuss, always a gloomy observer, thought the Hudson's Bay Company treated the local Nez Perce Indians like slaves.

The expedition stopped at a Methodist mission at The Dalles that reminded Frémont of the comforts of home. The main party never traveled farther west, but Frémont went downstream to Fort Vancouver, the

Hudson's Bay Company headquarters. He only spent a couple of days there before returning to The Dalles. He never went to the ocean, claiming lack of time—a strange decision after a journey of thousands of miles to reach a goal only forty miles away.

If Frémont had followed his orders to the letter, he should have turned around and returned to Saint Louis. But he had other plans. When Abert wrote, if the conditions " ... will not admit of the only objectives for accomplishment of which the expedition was planned ... " did he have at the back of his mind that Frémont, who had gone beyond his orders during the first expedition, would do the same this time? If so, his worries were well founded.

Fitzpatrick and his men who had been intentionally left behind rejoined the group. Frémont collected supplies and more than 100 horses and mules in preparation for a journey south. They were about to enter unknown territory. Up to this point, they had been traveling over established routes, able to pull their supplies in carts. Now they would be going over rough, mountainous terrain without carts—but they were still pulling the big brass howitzer.

The expedition left The Dalles on November 25, 1843. The plan was to move south through the Cascades to the east of the Sierra Nevada and then recross the desert toward the Great Salt Lake. But there was always the possibility that the plan might have to be changed and they would have to cross the Sierra Nevada to California. The plan might have been sensible earlier in the year, but crossing the Sierra in the middle of winter was bound to carry unreasonable risks. But as Kit Carson wrote later, "Nothing his explorations required was impossible for him to perform."

There was another objective: to find the Buenaventura River that had been described by early Spanish explorers and drawn on Humboldt's map of the West—the same map that had deceived Pike about the origins of the Arkansas River. Frémont's hope was that it would prove to be a navigable route out of the mountains to the Pacific, but it was a figment of the Spanish explorer's minds.

On the journey to Klamath Lake, they met Indians who were friendly, others who were aggressive, and some who had never seen white men before. The only time the howitzer was fired was to impress some Indians whose smoky fires could be seen but who had done nothing to cause alarm. The noise impressed the Indian guides and caused the fires to disappear. No one was hurt because it was not fired at a real target.

By January 16, 1844, Frémont had to make a decision. He was in a place with plenty of water and grass and could have waited out the winter. The local Indians were bringing them cutthroat trout two to four feet in length. But Frémont was suspicious of their intentions. So he used strange reasoning to reach a dangerous conclusion. He thought that the state of his horses was so bad that the only way to save them would be to cross the mountains; this despite the fact that the Indians told him the snow in the mountains was forty feet deep.

Were Frémont's stated and (later) written reasons the real ones for crossing the mountains in the middle of winter? Did Frémont have some secret reason for getting to California? We shall never know. But we do know that the same single-minded reasoning that took him into the jaws of danger this time would lead him to disaster five years later.

On January 25, the men were slightly northeast of what is now the northern tip of Yosemite National Park. From that point, Frémont and Carson set off to scout a route, passing through Devil's Gate. They rejoined the group and led them along the same way, climbing above 7,000 feet. Here, at last, they abandoned the howitzer. They met several groups of Indians who discouraged them from going on. Nothing would deter Frémont, but by offering enough presents to make a young Indian "richer and better clothed than any of his tribe had been before," he managed to persuade him to guide them.

Snow fell and was soon a blizzard. They rested. Then ten men on the strongest horses bashed their way through the deepening snow. That day, they covered only a few hundred yards. Frémont, who had been ahead of the party, turned back and learned that the group was in chaos, men and horses unable to push their way ahead, abandoning equipment and supplies. They all turned back to a lower altitude where they met another group of Indians who were so discouraging that their young Indian guide deserted.

February 6. Frémont, Carson, and a few men started on snowshoes, climbing to a summit from which Carson, who had passed through the Sierra in summer as a young boy, recognized some landmarks. On February 10, they established a camp with grass for the horses. But by this time, the group was spread out over twenty miles. The snow was so deep that some of the horses almost "drowned." The men tried to stamp out a passable route. Snow was still falling. Food was running low, and a message was sent back ordering horses to be killed for meat. But the meat did not arrive and the advance party killed and ate their only dog. Over the next few days, the remainder of the party straggled into camp.

Frémont had spotted what is now Lake Tahoe and pushed ahead on foot. He turned back to camp to find that the men and fifty-seven horses had reached a grassy haven at the summit of Carson Pass. The date was February 17. On the twenty-first, they descended toward the west, hoping "to escape into the genial country of which we had heard so many glowing descriptions." But the "genial country" was not yet within their reach. The route was steep and rocky in places, covered with thick pine trees in others, and underfoot the frozen ground was dangerously slippery.

The state of the men and horses was disastrous. They killed another horse for food. From a high ridge, they looked down onto the Sacramento

Valley. "No one," wrote Frémont, "who had not accompanied us through the incidents of our life for the last few months, could realize the delight with which we looked down upon it." They knew they were not far from Sutter's Fort, and by March 6 the advance detail came out on to flats that were covered with spring flowers and green grass. Frémont later wrote, "When we arrived at the fort we were naked and in as poor condition as men could possibly be." But they were alive.

Johann August Sutter, a Swiss-born American who had become a Mexican citizen, received them politely. They bought a large number of mules and returned to rescue the other men. Many of their original horses and mules had died by falling off the slippery trail, losing valuable equipment in their loads. Only half their horses survived the hellish traverse of the Sierras.

The Mexicans had learned of the arrival of the Americans and sent soldiers to interrogate and, presumably, evict them. But Sutter asked Frémont to leave before the Mexicans arrived.

The beauty of the California spring must have seemed like heaven to the refreshed and strengthened men. "Our road was now one continuous enjoyment," wrote Frémont, describing their journey down the Central Valley. An Indian told them that the route they proposed to take east across the desert was harsh and without water. The party was by this time dressed in wild clothing and mounted on more than 100 horses and mules. The route was easy. Food was plentiful. Life was sweet—for a time. Frémont decided, having explored the length of the Central Valley, that the elusive Buenaventura River did not exist.

The expedition entered the barren, dry Mojave Desert. The days of plenty were finished. At first, they followed an old Spanish trail that led alongside the Mojave River but soon disappeared into the desert. They collected a Mexican and his son whose herd of horses had been stolen by Indians. Carson and Alexis Godey set off to recapture the horses. Although considerably outnumbered, they attacked the Indian village, killed and scalped two men, and returned triumphantly to Frémont, happy in their belief that they had taught the Indians a righteous lesson. Preuss thought the two victors were worse than the Indians they killed.

The expedition had entered the Great Basin. During the day, heat waves flickered and shimmered off the sand; at night, cool air made travel bearable. They passed the skeletons of horses, gaunt memorials to the hardships that faced them. One of the camps had a now familiar name, Las Vegas, where there was good grass (but no casinos!). One man died from an accident with a gun; Indians killed another.

Near the Great Salt Lake, they met Joseph Walker, the first white man to see Yosemite, who agreed to be their guide. Two months later, they arrived back at Westport. Frémont quickly became a hero, the most famous explorer in the country, a man who could disregard the orders of Washington and still enhance his reputation. The government printed 10,000 copies of his report, once again written with Jessie's devoted help. (Only 1,417 copies were printed of the first edition of Lewis's and Clark's journal.) John Charles Frémont, promoted to brevet captain, was ready to lead another expedition, but he could not read the future. His fame had flown as high as it would go.

The Third Expedition

Frémont, now thirty-two years old, was at the height of his power and influence; therefore, it was not surprising that Abert appointed him to lead another expedition to the West, backed by $50,000 in congressional support.

Abert's orders were clear but not very exciting. Frémont was told to stay east of the Rockies, explore the upper reaches of the Arkansas and Red Rivers, and be back in Saint Louis before the end of the year. It is not clear why the orders were so circumscribed and historians have long believed that Frémont actually had secret orders to go to California. The area Frémont was to explore was already relatively well known, and he would be most unlikely to make any important discoveries. A routine expedition, and not one to suit Frémont.

When Frémont reached Saint Louis, the men for his expedition were already being chosen. Such was his fame that a huge, excited crowd of volunteers had gathered and he had to hide from the public. The expedition was well equipped. Every man received weapons, saddle and bridle, a horse or mule to ride, and a pair of pack animals. Seventy-four men, including five Delaware Indians to act as hunters, set off from Westport on June 26, 1845.

The expedition reached Bent's Fort by the middle of August. There they rested and resupplied. Frémont wanted Carson as a scout and sent a messenger to his ranch, where he was trying to settle down with his wife, Josefa, hoping to start a family and a business. When Carson heard that Frémont was at Bent's Fort and wanted him as a guide, he immediately sold his ranch. Little did he know that he would not see his wife for two years.

The long train of men and animals left Bent's Fort on August 16 and, in the next weeks, made its way up to the present site of Denver, then through the mountains to the Great Salt Lake. Beyond the Great Salt Lake lay a long, dry stretch of hot desert, a potential death trap for both men and horses.

Frémont had a good plan. Carson went ahead to scout out the land and find water. If he found water, he was to send a smoke signal and Frémont would bring on the party. Carson, in his memoirs, wrote, "We traveled about sixty miles and found neither water, nor grass, nor a patch of vegetation, with the ground as level and bare as a barn floor. ... He (Frémont) camped one night, and then the next evening at dark he completed the crossing, having lost only a few of his animals." This was a typically laconic comment by Carson on a difficult crossing during which the loss of animals was expected. Carson leapfrogged ahead a couple more times and finally they came out into grassy country at the base of the Sierra. Weeks had passed and Frémont was beginning to worry about the onset of winter. His memories of crossing the Sierra in the middle of winter must have been painful and instructive.

On December 4, a pass—later called Donner Pass, of ill fame—opened in front of them, and as there had not yet been heavy snow, they were able to cross to the west side in four days. They dropped down 4,000 feet in four hours and entered a land of tall red pines filled with "the dim religious light of religious aisles." Later, Frémont would say, optimistically, that their success showed that it was possible to go from the Great Salt Lake to California in only thirty-five days. Sutter's Fort was the first stop after crossing the mountains. Sutter was away from his home and his deputy, at first, could not supply all Frémont's demands for mules and supplies. Frémont became angry and mules and supplies soon appeared.

California was in a state of geopolitical upheaval. The governor in Monterey, Governor José Castro, was having a major dispute with the governor in Los Angeles, Pio Pico. The capital had been moved from Monterey to Los Angeles; the two governors were fighting for power and Pico was planning to march north to attack Castro. Back in Washington, President John Tyler had signed an order for the annexation of Texas and war with Mexico was imminent. Many of the settlers in California welcomed Frémont's arrival and assumed that he was under orders from Washington to help them gain independence from Mexico.

When Sutter returned home, he told Frémont that on his previous visit the Mexicans had tried to evict him. Frémont had not been aware of this and decided that it would be both politic and interesting to go to Monterey, where there was an American consul, Thomas Larkin.

Sutter issued Frémont with a passport to ensure his safe passage. When he reached Monterey, Frémont presented himself to Larkin and to General Castro, who wondered what an American officer was doing in Mexican territory with a company of men. Frémont claimed that he was merely a surveyor and scientist and had come to Monterey to get supplies. Castro doubted the story and told Frémont to leave the area. Frémont retreated into the hills, where he built a rudimentary fort and cut down a slim tree for a flagstaff from which he defiantly flew the American flag. Castro sent a force to the foot of the hill but did not attack. Carson wrote sarcastically, "We remained on the mountain for three days and had become tired of waiting for the attack of the valiant Mexican General."

The truth was that neither side wanted to fight. On the third day, the American flagstaff fell to the ground and Frémont, taking this as an excuse (or an omen?), withdrew. Walker, who had recently rejoined the group, thought that Frémont was a coward and departed on his own.

Frémont and his men traveled north, back to Sutter's fort and then farther north to Lassen's Ranch. The settlers in the area complained that the Indians were planning a major attack. They asked Frémont for help. Always one to find a way out of a tricky situation that would leave him without blame, Frémont said that his men could not officially attack the Indians. If, however, some of his men wanted to participate, he would release them temporarily and they could go as individuals.

The massacre that followed was a blot on Frémont's record, although he did not see it that way. About fifty men found the Indian village, where, according to some grossly exaggerated accounts, 4,000 to 5,000 Indians were having a war dance. The small group of settlers swept in, firing and slashing. During the next three hours, they killed between 150 and 170 Indians, mostly women and children. Carson thought this was good "chastisement" for the Indians, but also described the massacre (it would be impossible to call it a battle) as "perfect butchery."

The men returned to Lassen's Ranch, self-righteously triumphant, firm in their belief that they had taught the Indians a necessary lesson.

On April 24, Frémont and his reorganized men rode north to Klamath Lake, intending to find a route to the Oregon Territory that might be easier than the one through South Pass. On May 8, two Americans rode into camp on exhausted horses, saying that they were the advance party for Lieutenant Archibald Gillespie of the U.S. Navy, who was coming with special information for Frémont. Gillespie, who would play a less than heroic part in later events, had come from Washington via Hawaii, Vera Cruz, and Monterey to meet with Consul Larkin. His secret orders were to inform Larkin that war was imminent between Mexico and the United States and that he was now a confidential agent of the government. Having delivered these instructions to Larkin, he decided to find Frémont, 500 miles away, and give him the news about the impending war.

When Gillespie did not appear for a couple of days, they worried that he had been killed by Indians. On May 9, he rode into camp and delivered the news to a delighted Frémont. From this moment on, Frémont considered himself an active officer of the U.S. Army. That night, reassured by Gillespie that the Indians had not followed him, Frémont, for the first time, did not post any sentries.

Most of the men were fast asleep near the campfire, but Frémont was awake, perhaps contemplating his new status. The mules, tethered nearby, stirred in the dark but quietened when Frémont walked down to see what was happening. Suddenly, there was a loud "crack" and then Carson was heard shouting, "Indians, Indians!" In an instant, the camp was in an uproar, the men grabbing the rifles by their sides. The cause of the "crack" was immediately obvious: Basil LaJeunesse lay dead, his skull split wide open by an axe.

A brief, wild battle ensued and only finished when the Indian chief was felled by five bullets. The final score: LaJeunesse and two Delaware Indians on one side and fifteen to twenty attacking Indians on the other. As soon as dawn lightened the sky, Frémont and his sad procession left, the bodies of their friends slung over mules to be buried a few miles away.

On May 13, far away and unbeknownst to Frémont, the United States declared war on Mexico. In his mind, Frémont was now commanding a U.S. force against the Mexicans. His father-in-law, Senator Benton, had long dreamed of the Pacific Coast as the western boundary of U.S. territory, a necessary stop on the Road to India. Frémont must have had thoughts of a glorious future in this endeavor.

Events were quickly moving out of his control. On June 4, settlers, eager to form an independent California, captured the sleepy town of Sonoma, now famous for its wines. The Mexican commander, not unsympathetic to being taken over by the United States, regaled his captors liberally with brandy and was then delivered to Frémont, who in turn sent him to Sutter's Fort. Sutter, a Mexican citizen, was now an "enemy." Frémont put Edward Kern in charge of the fort and told him to lock up anyone who disobeyed him.

The men who captured Sonoma hoisted a makeshift flag with a bear on the background and inscribed "Republic of California." They became known as the "Bear Flaggers."

Early in July, U.S. naval ships under the command of Commodore John Drake Sloat appeared off Monterey, took control of the town, and raised the U.S. flag. Within a few days, the U.S. flag flew over Yerba Buena (the future San Francisco) and Sonoma. Frémont, going south to meet with Sloat and becoming increasingly enchanted with California, named the narrows north of Yerba Buena the Golden Gate.

California fell like a ripe plum into the hands of the Americans. Commodore Robert F. Stockton took over from the ailing Commodore Sloat and shipped Frémont, Carson, and their men south to San Diego. A two-pronged advance, Frémont from the south and Stockton from the north, captured Los Angeles. The future state was divided into three administrative zones—south, central, and north—with Gillespie in charge of Los Angeles. Frémont was the military commander and, a little later, governor of California. The Mexican population was offered full U.S. citizenship and everyone seemed to be happy. But trouble was brewing in Los Angeles. A popular uprising evicted Gillespie, an authoritarian and unpopular governor who escaped to Monterey.

Meanwhile, Carson had been sent east, carrying letters for the president telling of the bloodless acquisition of California. In New Mexico, Carson met General Stephen Watts Kearney, who was on his way west with a small force guided by Broken Hand Fitzpatrick. Kearney, hearing the good news, immediately sent half of his troops back to the east, guided by Fitzpatrick, and continued west, guided by Carson (who was angry because he had hoped to visit his wife).

At San Pasqual, Kearney's force was surrounded and severely trounced by General Don Andrés Pico from Los Angeles. Carson and a junior officer escaped at night by crawling on their hands and knees for several miles to call for help from Commodore Stockton. Kearney was rescued and Los Angeles recaptured. When Frémont finally reached Los Angeles, the city was already under Kearney's control. The golden ring had slipped from his fingers.

During the next few months, Kearney, who was senior in both age and rank to Frémont, argued back and forth about who was governor and who was military commander. The argument was finally settled when a letter arrived from Washington confirming that Kearney was in command. After a final confrontation, Frémont accepted the reality of the situation.

Kearney was recalled east and took Frémont with him, a prisoner in fact, if not in name. Arriving at Fort Leavenworth, Frémont was arrested and charged with mutiny, disobeying orders, and conduct prejudicial to military discipline. Despite the most energetic efforts of Senator Benton and other supporters, Frémont was court-martialed on November 2, 1848. The court found him guilty on all counts and ordered his discharge from the army. President James Knox Polk remitted the sentence, but Frémont, saying that he wanted "justice not clemency," voluntarily resigned from the army.

The Fourth Expedition

Frémont's court-martial left him in disgrace. He was only thirty-six and had fallen from the heights of fame to the depths of disgrace in less than a year. But despite that, he was not dispirited. Characteristically, he blamed his downfall on politicians and officers in the army out to destroy him. In his mind, he was not at fault.

Within a few months, under the influence and power of his father-in-law, another expedition was planned. Senator Benton had for a long time dreamed of developing a railroad from coast to coast. But first, a route had to be surveyed. The line of the thirty-eighth parallel was chosen as a possible route, a choice based on few facts.

This was a chance for Frémont to get his name honorably back in the headlines. His father-in-law tried unsuccessfully to raise money in the Congress but managed to collect sufficient private funds.

Frémont began to collect a group of men, including some who had traveled with him before: Alexis Godey, Edward Kern, and Charles Preuss.

The weather was already deteriorating when they reached Bent's Fort. The local mountain men said the snow was too deep. Frémont's route would take him through several mountain ranges in the middle of winter in an area that, year by year, has the heaviest snowfall of the region. The veterans of the mountains knew the mountains were tough in the summer and impassable in the winter. But Frémont was not about to be put off. He had traversed the Sierra Nevada in winter when others had said that it was impossible. The mountains ahead of him could be no worse than those he had conquered before. And the added incentive of mapping out the first route for a railroad was irresistible.

Frémont, however, did not have a guide. Carson was settling down and would not join the expedition. Instead, Frémont hired "Uncle Dick" Wootton, who soon quit because he thought the journey too hazardous at that time of year. In his place, Frémont hired William Sherley Williams, "Old Bill Williams," as he was known. Williams was an experienced mountain man and guide who, like many, had been born in the east and moved west with his family as a young man. When Frémont found him, he was down on his luck, fond of the bottle, and probably very glad to have a chance to earn some money, although what he was promised was not great. He was tall, gaunt, and weather-beaten, with a face scarred by smallpox. He had been with Frémont for a short time on the third expedition but had left long before they reached California. This time, after traveling with the group for some days, he signed up when the expedition was near present-day Pueblo.

Frémont could have followed several safer routes than going straight across the mountains. But his stubborn nature would allow only one way to achieve his purpose: follow the parallel and see if a railroad route opened up.

In November, the party moved to Hardscrabble, a tiny collection of adobe houses east of the Sangre de Cristos, where they were able to collect feed for the more than 100 mules that they were going to take to carry supplies for thirty-three men.

By December 3, the party had struggled through the Sangre de Cristos to the Great Sand Dunes along almost the same route as Zebulon Pike. But instead of turning south, as Pike had been forced to do by the Spanish, Frémont turned northwest across the barrens of the San Luis Valley, heading into the menacing peaks of the San Juans.

At this point, Frémont had a major difference of opinion with Old Bill. Frémont wanted to head straight west into the mountains, although it was quite apparent by this time that the Sangre de Cristos alone made building a railroad impossible along the thirty-eighth parallel. Old Bill wanted to turn south and bypass the San Juans. Even if he was not as familiar with the mountains as he claimed, he knew them well enough to know that continuing into them would lead them into a morass of high, snow-filled passes, deep valleys, and impossible peaks. Frémont prevailed.

Within a few days, they were pushing their way through deep snow, and the diaries of the men soon began to give clues about difficulties ahead. Frémont himself wrote little about this expedition and what is known comes almost entirely from journals kept by his men and from letters he later wrote to Jessie. The lack of a formal report diminishes our knowledge of how he felt, what he was thinking, and how he made his decisions. His letters to Jessie are self-serving and he blames others for the disasters and for his decisions as though both were out of his control.

The snow fell with increasing ferocity, accompanied by biting cold winds and temperatures well below zero. Even a modern expedition equipped with cold-weather gear and riding snowmobiles would have had an extremely difficult task fighting its way across the mountains and dealing with blizzards and drifting snow that was sometimes fifteen to thirty feet deep.

Micajah McGhee wrote that their lips were so stiff from the ice that they could not speak and their long beards and eyelids were frozen. The animals were soon starving. The corn they had brought from Hardscrabble was finished and the deep snow made it impossible for the mules to find grass. Whenever they could, the men camped in small groves to shelter from the storms. They climbed to nearly 12,000 feet, sometimes advancing only a few hundred yards in a day. As the mules died, they were butchered and eaten, but as they too were starving, they provided barely enough meat to make soup for the men.

The depth of the snow can be calculated from the remains of the campsites that have been found in modern times. David Roberts (acknowledging the pioneering investigations of Patricia Joy Richmond), in his gripping account of the journey, A Newer World, described visiting some of the old campsites in the late 1990s and finding rotting tree stumps, some of them cut more than fifteen feet from the ground—stark evidence of the depth of the snow when the trees were felled for firewood.

The conditions became worse, the snow deeper, the blizzards more intense. There was no game and the men ate tallow candles. The mules, starving and freezing, cried out in their misery. They all showed the signs of starvation, eating their bridles and saddles and gnawing the tails and manes of other mules. Even when the expedition was at its highest point (11,800 feet), more than 100 mules were still alive. But every day, the surviving mules became fewer. They dropped beside of the trail, and died.

At Camp Dismal—an appropriate name—one of the men later described how they spread a large rubber sheet on the open ground, covered it with blankets, and then pulled more blankets over themselves as they hunkered together, trying to keep warm. In the morning, they were often covered by deep snow.

Despite the horrendous conditions and the hopelessness of finding a route for a railroad, the morale of the men stayed remarkably strong. But cold and starvation began to take their toll and some of the men began to despair of ever surviving to reach civilization.

On December 22, Frémont finally decided that they would have to turn around and seek lower ground if any of them were to live. He hoped they could reach a New Mexican town, resupply, and take up the search again. His decision to turn back was long overdue. Christmas Day, as on so many expeditions, was spent in miserable conditions but lightened by an attempt to celebrate with extra rations. They ate elk stew, coffee, and biscuits, even drank some alcohol, and tried to pretend that turning around and heading south would bring relief. But the unexpectedly rich food exacted its price: their bellies reacted with cramps and vomiting. When Frémont wrote to his wife describing Christmas, he said that though his heart was filled with "gloomy and anxious thoughts," he was wondering what she was doing and imagined the comforts of home—thoughts expressed by millions of men at Christmas far from home, at war, on expeditions, or stranded in remote and desperate situations.

Frémont sent ahead a small group of the fittest men to find help and return with mules and food. He chose Henry King to be the leader; Old Bill was a member of the group, but not the leader. There was much discussion about how long it would take to reach the New Mexican town of Abiqui, about 150 miles away. Even the longest guess, sixteen days, proved to be far from the truth. They had been able to travel only two to three miles a day, so it is surprising that they did not come to a more realistic calculation. The men who were going to make the "dash" for help were already weak and half starved, they did not know the route, and could only carry a small amount of food. They set off on December 26, full of hope, carrying guns, ammunition for hunting and protection, blankets, sugar, and a few pounds of mule meat.

Splitting the group may, at the time, have seemed to be a good idea, but it left the weaker members to their own devices. And they were made to carry telescopes, sextants, surveying equipment, and heavy volumes of legal books that Frémont was determined to preserve. Did Frémont hope to retrieve them and continue his survey? Starvation and cold may have impaired Frémont's thinking. He was so fixed on an unachievable aim that he lost sight of the most important objective: saving the lives of his men. By the time he decided to turn around, many of the men were too weak to survive.

Frémont's later letters to his wife showed that he believed that many of his men were weaklings and responsible for the disaster that overwhelmed the group. "The courage of the men failed fast; in fact, I have never seen men so soon discouraged by misfortune as we were on this occasion;

but, as you know, the party was not constituted like the former ones." He was failing as a leader and would fail even more before the survivors staggered and crawled to safety.

The rescue group soon needed to be rescued itself. They had hoped to reach the Rio Grande valley in one day, but it took them three. By the time they arrived in the valley, they were out of food and "hungry as wolves." Their feet were frostbitten and swollen and they were unable to get their boots back on again after they had taken them off. But the boots had other uses—as food. They wrapped their feet in rags and crept along on the bloody soles at a rate of two or three miles a day. Their visionary hope of being back at the camp with help in sixteen days was an impossible dream. Now they were struggling for their own lives, living off any scrap of leather they could boil or roast over the fire.

Walking became easier on the flat of the valley, but the weather was bitterly cold, and there was no shelter against the wind screaming over the plain. Their snow-blind eyes felt as though they were filled with red-hot sand. Snow goggles would have been a gift from heaven. Stumbling and starving, they groped their way south, half blind. Almost within sight of the Rio Grande, King, the leader, announced that he could go no farther and lay down by the trail. No amount of urging could persuade him to move. The next day, another member of the group went back and found him dead. That night, the man who had found King dreamed of a well-filled kitchen and endless food but woke to a belly cramping for lack of food.

At this point, the story takes a gruesome turn. It is almost certain that a decision was made by the group to eat King's body. Who made the decision and how it was carried out is not known, but Preuss, a meticulous keeper of the facts, later confirmed that the surviving members of the rescue group lived off the body, perhaps for several days. Naturally, some have said that this did not happen and that scavenging animals ate King's body. But the accounts by others would tip the balance of evidence the other way.

Meanwhile, back in the mountains, Frémont was pushing his men to their limits. Eventually, he went ahead with a small group of the fitter men, while the others, too weak to continue, set up camps on their own. The group was falling apart; it was every man for himself. The crowning insult came when Frémont told the men staying behind that they would have to speed up, because as soon as he reached a town, he was leaving for California.

The rescue group was near death when Frémont overtook them six days later. They were, he said, "the most miserable objects I have ever seen." Their lives were saved by the food he was able to give them. He told his wife that he arranged for them to be carried on horses, but Thomas Breckenridge, one of the survivors, later wrote that they had to crawl on bloody feet for the last forty miles.

Frémont reached Taos and sought out Carson, whose wife nursed him back to health. While he was recovering, there were men still creeping out of the mountains, and Godey, without waiting, turned around to save them. He picked up survivors one by one. Ten of the original thirty-three men and all the animals perished. Despite Frémont's obvious failings as a leader and his rapid departure for California as soon as the men reached Taos, Godey remained completely loyal to him, praising the leadership and endurance of a man that others regarded as an egotistical scoundrel.

Needless to say, the railroad was never built along the line of the fateful thirty-eighth parallel.

The Fifth Expedition

The fifth, and last, of Frémont's expeditions was, perhaps, the least necessary and least productive of all his voyages.

After his fourth expedition, Frémont spent time in California at his newly acquired estate, then spent twenty-one days as a senator in Washington. Because gold was found on his property, he became very rich. He thought that his exploring days were over, but somewhere hidden in his psyche the urge to explore still lay dormant. His father-in-law still thought that the thirty-eighth parallel offered a route for a future railway or road (although he recognized that a railway engine could not get over the San Juan Mountains). The government was searching for routes for the railways and under the Pacific Railroad Survey Act of 1853 had sent out several surveying expeditions. Captain John Gunnison followed the thirty-eighth parallel. The thirty-fifth parallel was surveyed by Lieutenant Amiel Whipple, and the thirty-second by Lieutenant John Parke and Captain John Pope. Gunnison had already gone ahead of Frémont and crossed the San Juan Mountains in the summer but was killed by Indians in Utah.

We would know little about Frémont's last expedition if it were not for the delightful journal of Solomon Nunes Carvalho, a photographer and artist signed on by Frémont at the last minute. An interesting man, Jewish, artistic, and a city slicker who had never saddled a horse, he signed on because of his faith in Frémont. Although he did not go all the way to California, he recorded the journey through the San Juan Mountains, a journey that tried the perseverance and determination of the group.

Frémont wanted to show that the San Juans could be crossed in winter. He started from Westport on September 22, 1853, heading for Bent's Fort, but soon became ill with a severe leg infection and had to turn back, assuring his men that he would soon return. The day he rejoined the group was almost apocalyptic. The prairie was on fire, the smoke darkening the sky, the flames an orange menace along the horizon. The Delaware Indians gave a loud "Whoop!" when they saw Frémont accompanied by other members of the group, including "an immense man on an immense mule ... galloping through the blazing element in the direction of our camp. ... No father who had been absent from his children could have been received with more enthusiasm and more real joy."

After resupplying at Bent's Fort, the troop moved west to the Sangre de Cristo Mountains. At the summit of Robidoux (Mosca) Pass, Frémont pointed forty miles across the San Luis Valley to the San Juan Mountains and, with a voice breaking with emotion, related to Carvalho some of the terrible events of his previous visit to the area.

This time, crossing the mountains, while still a trial that wore down both men and animals, did not end with one-third of the men dying. Carvalho wrote about the difficulty of taking daguerreotypes at thirty degrees below zero while standing in waist-deep snow. He recalled a scene when one mule slipped, pulling fifty others down a snow-covered slope, tumbling with legs flailing and loads flying in every direction. Then as the cold, altitude, lack of food, diet of horse meat, and struggles with the snow-drifts sapped his strength, Carvalho fell farther and farther behind, determined to take the pictures that Frémont had hired him to take or die in the attempt.

Once they reached the west side of the mountains, Carvalho and another man, Oliver Fuller, became weaker and weaker. Fuller's horse died and he had to walk in tattered moccasins, his feet swollen with frostbite. Two Indians helped him into camp, but he died the next day. "A journey like the one we had passed through," wrote Carvalho, "was calculated to expose the thorough character of individuals; if there were any imperfections, they were sure to be developed. My friend, Oliver Fuller, passed through the trials of that ordeal victoriously."

Fuller's death caused Frémont, remembering the horrors of his previous expedition, to make everyone take an oath that they would never indulge in cannibalism.

Shortly after Fuller died, they reached the Mormon settlement of Parowan, where Carvalho left the expedition. They had lived on horse meat for fifty days and he could go no farther. "My hair was long and had not known a comb for a month, my face was unwashed ... my fingers were frostbitten, and split at every joint; and suffering at the same time from diarrhea and the symptoms of scurvy ... I was in a situation truly to be pitied."

Carvalho left the expedition and took a long time to recover his health. He eventually reached Salt Lake City, where he was invited to stay with Brigham Young, his nineteen wives, and thirty-three children. He refused the kind invitation but continued to stay in the city and study the Mormons, appreciating their kindness but being highly critical of polygamy.

Frémont continued across the desert and reached California to live on his estate, La Mariposa.

8

Sir John Franklin
(1786–1847)

The Man Who Attracted Disaster

*A sad tale was never told
in fewer words.*

—*Francis Leopold McClintock*

John Franklin was born only ten miles from the sea but never heard the waves crashing on the beach until he was in grammar school. The sight and sounds of the sea must have made a deep impression on him, because although his father intended that he enter the ministry, John had another idea: he wanted to be a sailor. His father tried to discourage this dangerous idea by sending John on a sea voyage, but the journey on a merchant ship to Lisbon only reinforced his determination. So he joined the Royal Navy, as many young men and boys did, as a midshipman at age fourteen, reporting to HMS *Polyphemus* under the command of Captain John Lawford. One year later, he took part in the bloody Battle of Copenhagen.

His next assignment was even more adventurous. He sailed on the *Investigator*, commanded by his cousin Captain Matthew Flinders, on a great circumnavigation of the coast of Australia. They left England in June 1801, but after the *Investigator*'s timbers rotted and the ship was laid up in Sydney, Franklin was sent back to England on the *Porpoise*. Two ships, the *Cato* and *Bridgewater*, lying in Sydney harbor waiting to go to Batavia, asked to sail along with the *Porpoise*. The three ships sailed along the Barrier Reef, but during the night, the *Porpoise* ran aground on a reef. The *Cato*, coming to investigate, ran aground on the same reef, losing her masts. During the next night, the *Cato* broke up and three boys drowned as they tried to swim to a rescuing gig. At low water, the stores on board the *Porpoise* were off-loaded onto an island and a signal sent to the *Bridgewater*. The captain of the *Bridgewater* sailed off to India, where he reported that all hands had been lost from both the other ships.

Captain Flinders decided to go for help and, in the largest cutter available, sailed 750 miles to Sydney. Flinders arrived back at the reef some weeks later to find his men in good shape and already trying to build a ship on which they could sail home if no rescue came. The rescue ships took them to Canton, from which they sailed back to England.

Franklin was immediately ordered to the *Bellerophon* and in October 1805, as the midshipman in charge of signals, took part in the battle of Trafalgar, a battle that changed the history of the world. The *Bellerophon* suffered many casualties, including her captain, who was shot through the chest by a sniper in the rigging of one of the French ships. There were forty men around Franklin on the poop during the engagement; thirty-two were killed or wounded. Franklin was unscathed.

Over the next few years, Franklin's naval career was filled with war and bloodshed. He was promoted to lieutenant in 1807, took part in the blockade of Flushing, and sailed to America, where he was wounded during a battle capturing five American gunboats. He took part in a land engagement in Louisiana and was commended for heroism. He returned to England in 1815 as the Napoleonic War was coming to an end.

The First Expedition

After the war was over, Britain no longer needed a huge fleet and was mistress of the seas. Many officers were laid off or put on unpaid reserve, but Lieutenant Franklin, probably because of his varied and distinguished service, was retained.

The Royal Navy turned its attention from defeating Napoleon to exploring the unknown corners of the world. John Barrow, second secretary of the Admiralty for the next forty years (some people believed he behaved like the first secretary), became the mastermind of British explorations, sending ships and men around the world. His greatest hope was to find the fabled Northwest Passage along the northern shore of the North American continent. If there was not a passage around America, perhaps one could be found north of Russia. So on January 14, 1818, Franklin was appointed to command the *Trent*, a hired brig, which, together with the *Dorothea* under the command of Captain David Buchan, was to explore the possibility of a northeast passage. Both ships had been refurbished before setting out, but the shipwrights who worked on the *Trent* were careless and it did not take long at sea to discover that she had some serious leaks that badly needed repair in Spitsbergen.

This was not the first attempt to find a northeast passage. In 1590, Willem Barents, a Dutch sailor, had tried to explore this route and had discovered the island of Spitsbergen but had not succeeded in sailing farther. A whaling industry started as early as 1611 and several nationalities, including the French, British, Russians, and Dutch, all laid claim to the whaling rights. Between 1669 and 1778, more than 14,000 Dutch vessels visited the island, catching nearly 60,000 whales. By the time Buchan and Franklin visited, the Russians were the only remaining inhabitants of the island. The voyage was a continual battle against ice and wind and they had to retreat to Spitsbergen again to make repairs before they could return home without having found any way to enter the Northeast Passage. (Roald Amundsen finally sailed through the passage from 1918 to 1920, having already successfully sailed through the Northwest Passage from 1903 to 1906.)

The Second Expedition

The Lords Commissioners of the Admiralty were still obsessed with trying to find the Northwest Sea Passage and planned a combined mission. Captain William Parry would lead a naval expedition into Lancaster Sound and sail westward, while Franklin, who had just been promoted to captain, was commissioned to lead a land expedition. He was thirty-three years old, experienced in battle and exploration by sea, and somewhat familiar with Arctic conditions, although he knew nothing about Arctic travel by land. He had never been on, let alone led, a land-based expedition (except for a short time in Louisiana), and some doubted his physical fitness. George Simpson, governor of the Hudson's Bay Company, said "With the utmost exertion he cannot walk above eight miles in one day."

Franklin and his men would go west from the Hudson Bay, paddle down the Coppermine River, and then explore eastward. In retrospect, the belief that a small, inexperienced party and a number of Canadian voyageurs could explore the entire coast of the continent east of the Coppermine River and meet with Captain Parry was naïve, at best. The planners did not understand the geography of the area nor the extreme difficulty of travel along a complex coastline in birch-bark canoes, constantly battered by storms, and fighting the shifting pack ice that could crush even the strongest ships. Even nowadays, only massive icebreakers and nuclear submarines are capable of forcing a way through this maze of danger.

Many expeditions had already tried to penetrate the passage from the east and all had failed. Some had been imprisoned in the ice for as long as four winters; others had met what they thought were impenetrable barriers of ice and had turned back. Captain James Cook tried to enter the passage from the west and was rebuffed by the ice of the Bering Sea. Franklin was to try a new approach, starting in the middle of the continent and slowly easing his way to the east. If he met Captain Parry coming from Lancaster Sound, he would sail home with him. If he did not succeed in meeting Parry, he would make his way back overland. It all sounded very simple.

The expedition left Gravesend on May 23, 1819. The other members of Franklin's party were Dr. John Richardson, who acted as both doctor and naturalist; two midshipmen, George Back (who would later rise to fame as an Arctic explorer in his own right), and Robert Hood, both of whom were good artists and were to make maps and drawings; and a seaman who acted as Franklin's servant, John Hepburn. After reaching Canada, the group planned to recruit voyageurs to paddle the birch-bark canoes and Indians to act as hunters. The navy still did not think it proper that officers should hunt or carry loads.

The crossing of the Atlantic was made in convoy with three other ships, the *Eddystone*, the *Wear*, and the *Harmony*, all filled with Scottish emigrants for the Earl of Selkirk's settlement on the Red River. What should have been a routine voyage to York Factory turned into a nightmare. As soon as the ships entered the Hudson Bay, they encountered the worst of Arctic weather: impenetrable fog, strong winds, wild currents, icebergs, and an unfriendly shoreline of rocks and steep cliffs. Franklin's account was full of remarks such as "an alarming view of a barren rugged shore within a few yards ... prospect most alarming ... seemed to be no probability of escaping shipwreck ... violently forced by the current against a large iceberg lying aground." The *Prince of Wales* struck a rock and her hold filled with four feet of water. The elderly and the children were transferred to the *Eddystone* for fear that the ship would sink. But heroic efforts by the crew, energetically assisted by the younger women who pumped as strongly as the men, combined with the efforts of the ship's carpenters, staunched the flow of water. The ships pulled into the harbor at York Factory on August 30, relieved to have arrived without loss of life or cargo.

The governor of the factory greeted Franklin and his men but soon told them that there would be no cooperation between the Hudson's Bay Company and the North West Company. The two companies were at each other's throats, both commercially and literally: fighting had broken out between the traders in vicious competition for the furs. Despite these gloomy prognostications, Franklin went ahead with his preparations. Governor William Williams provided him with the largest boat on the station, and on September 9 they prepared to leave, planning to go to Cumberland House, where they would spend the early winter. It was soon obvious that their boat was overloaded and a lot of bacon, flour, rice, tobacco, and ammunition had to be returned to the company store. Franklin was assured that supplies could be obtained inland, so they left to a salute of guns and three rousing cheers.

After a long and laborious day of dragging the boats against strong currents, they made camp and Franklin was able to record, "We retired with our buffalo robes on, and enjoyed a night of sound repose." Later, he would remember nights of "sound repose" with fond nostalgia.

Apart from heavy rain and the labor of hauling the boats upstream, the journey to Lake Winnipeg was relatively uneventful. By early October, the weather was turning very cold. The scenery varied from swampy flats to rocky canyons through which the river rushed. "I shall long remember the rude and characteristic wildness of the scenery which surrounded these falls," wrote Franklin. They noted the "lop-sticks," trees stripped of their lower branches that the Indians used to mark their routes. One day, Franklin fell into the river and damaged a valuable chronometer necessary for the measurement of longitude. Fortunately, it could be repaired.

By October 22, they reached Cumberland House—and just in time. Within days, the rivers froze, making further travel by boat impossible. They had gone 700 miles since leaving York Factory but had many miles to go before reaching their intended winter base at Fort Chipewyan on Lake Athabasca. They set out again on January 18, 1820. But now they traveled with dogsleds and on snowshoes. The British naval men were totally inexperienced in snow travel and the bindings of the snowshoes galled their feet and made them swell painfully. The restful nights at the start of the voyage changed into shivering hours lying on pine branches. The mercury in the thermometer froze, but not before it registered forty degress below zero. Hot tea froze in the tin cups before the men had time to raise it to their lips. They reached Carlton House, rested for a couple of days, warmed up and changed their clothes, and pushed on. Fresh food was in short supply and they relied on pemmican.

On March 25, the weather was so bad—Franklin called it "boisterous"—that they had to stop and shelter for a day before reaching Fort Chipewyan, where they were greeted hospitably by the traders of the North West Company. They had gone 857 miles by boat and snowshoe, a remarkable achievement for men who had never traveled in the Barrens before.

Their weeks at Fort Chipewyan were not wasted. They spoke with Dogrib and Copper Indians about the route ahead. Franklin ordered the building of a thirty-two-foot birch-bark canoe for the next stage of the journey, big enough to carry 3,000 pounds of supplies and six men. Richardson and Hood had stayed behind to bring up more supplies, but their news was not good. They had been unable to get the supplies they needed and one of their men had drowned in a rapid. Franklin accepted the news with characteristic sangfroid. "The prospect of having to commence our journey from hence, almost destitute of provisions and scantily supplied with stores was distressing to us." To say that the news was "distressing" was a major understatement. When they finally headed north, on July 18, twenty-three strong, they only had provisions sufficient for one day, including two barrels of flour, chocolate, arrowroot, portable soup, and some preserved meat. They hoped to be able to catch fish and shoot caribou enough to meet their needs, but their hopes were not met. On the first day, they caught only four small fish and they were lucky to shoot a buffalo as it crossed the river.

On July 27, they reached Fort Providence on the Great Slave Lake and met Mr. William Wentzel of the North West Company who would accompany them and assist with their dealings with the Indians. They also met Chief Akaitcho, a Chipewyan who undertook to send hunters with them and guide them. He would play a very important part in their subsequent trials.

Franklin had thought that perhaps he could descend the Mackenzie River, but he was advised by Akaitcho to use the Coppermine to reach the coast, as there were more caribou along its valley and the food supply of the expedition would be more assured. On August 2, in high spirits, the small flotilla of canoes pushed off across the lake, heading for the Coppermine River. They soon found that the Indians who were with them, who traveled much more lightly, managed the portages easily and quickly. The heavily equipped Canadians had to make four times as many trips around each portage as the Indians.

The labor of the portages and the roughness of the trails took their toll. The men were exhausted and several of them developed swollen legs. Food was in very short supply and the Canadian voyageurs, used to generous rations of fat-filled pemmican, nearly mutinied. Franklin had to threaten punishment, although they did not come under naval command and there was no real punishment he could administer. Fortunately, the hunters shot two caribou and full bellies restored morale.

By August 19, the expedition had reached a critical point. They had reached a lake where Akaitcho said they should stay for the winter. There were fish in the lake and caribou would pass nearby. If they went farther, they would march for eleven days without wood for fires, the weather was about to deteriorate, and they might starve because the caribou were leaving the river valley. Franklin, as happened more than once when the British navy met the wisdom of the locals, wanted to push ahead against advice. But Akaitcho said that he could not be responsible for their safety, and although he would send men with them, those men would be regarded as dead as soon as they set off. Common sense prevailed and Franklin agreed to stay at the lake and build a fort for the winter.

Fort Enterprise rose quickly from the tundra. Houses were built on three sides of a square: one for the officers, one for the men, and a storehouse. Early in October, thousands of caribou passed nearby and they were able to stock up with meat. But their ammunition was running low and they would have been in a bad situation had not Back and Wentzel volunteered to return to Fort Providence to get more tobacco and ammunition. The main party was well supplied with food and the storehouse contained the carcasses of 100 caribou and 1,000 pounds of dried meat and fat.

Back and Wentzel started for Fort Providence on October 18. By the middle of November, no news had arrived that the two men had reached

Fort Providence safely and the Indians thought they had probably fallen through the ice on a lake. But a Canadian, Solomon Bélanger, arrived to tell them that all was well. He had marched without stopping for thirty-six hours and arrived with his clothes stiff with ice and his hair and beard a matted, frozen mass. He was an alarming sight coming in out of the storm, but he brought letters from England that cheered everyone. He was not, however, able to bring the ammunition that was so badly needed for hunting because he had been robbed by Dogrib Indians. They received only 100 ammunition balls and had to distribute some of them to the Indians, their hunters. By the time Back returned, on March 17, he had traveled more than 1,000 miles on snowshoes and sleds.

The temperature dropped to fifty-seven degrees below zero. Trees froze and the axes splintered as they were used. However, the days passed quickly. The officers wrote in their journals, read and reread the newspapers from England, took short walks in the woods, and played games with the men in the evenings. Every Sunday, Franklin conducted a religious service attended by the Catholic voyageurs, even though they could not understand the prayers. Their diet was mostly caribou and fish, brightened in January when some men arrived with two kegs of rum. They also brought powder, ammunition, and tobacco. But the temperature inside the houses was so cold that the rum turned to syrup and the fingers of the men froze to the dram glasses. About this time, two Eskimos, Augustus and Junius, joined them and would be invaluable interpreters when they reached the coast.

On April 4, the last supplies arrived from Fort Providence, and in return, a message was sent out asking that a ship be made available on the Hudson Bay in the event that they reached there. Franklin was ever the optimist!

As spring approached, food was running short. Indians encamped near the Fort were starving and could be seen picking through the snow near their houses, searching for edible remains of bones, hides, and deer's feet. Franklin tried to keep morale high by arranging snow slides down a nearby slope. This was a good idea and kept the men cheerful until a fat Indian lady on a sled crashed into Franklin and sprained his knee.

The migrating caribou returned and famine was relieved. By the end of May, the signs were propitious: the weather was warmer, the caribou had returned, and geese and ducks had reappeared. They were ready to leave for the Coppermine.

Dr. Richardson was first to leave, on June 4, with fifteen voyageurs, two Indian hunters, and a mixed party of Métis women and children—twenty-three in all. Each man carried eighty pounds, either on his back or on a sled. The canoes, to be used later, were dragged on sleds pulled by four men and two dogs each. At Marten Lake, they found that wolverines had eaten their cache of food. Point Lake, through which the Coppermine River ran, was reached on June 20, and they met Akaitcho, who told them that his hunters had used up all the ammunition they had been given. Now the only food they had was 200 pounds of dried meat and a little salt to be shared among twenty-three hungry mouths. They had not yet reached the ocean.

Dragging the canoes on sleds was difficult so Franklin decided to abandon one, leaving more men free to pull the remaining loads to the end of the lake to embark on the river. But the river was still frozen and they could not launch the canoes until July 1. As Franklin wrote, "There was no retreating after we had once launched into the stream, and our safety depended on the skill and dexterity of the bowmen and steersmen." The river was swift and dangerous and Franklin decided that no rapid would be run until the bowman had decided it was safe. The precious surveying instruments were removed from the canoes and carried around the rapids.

Lack of food was an increasing problem. One day, they might shoot several musk ox, then they would go without meat for several days. When they had killed more than enough for their immediate needs, they waited a day to dry out the rest of the meat. They encountered grizzly bears, whose meat became a major part of their diet, for they were common and easy to approach.

Planning the food supply for later in the summer was extremely important. Franklin always knew they might be stranded by bad weather or severe early winter blizzards. He was wildly optimistic in his expectation of the distances they could cover. He hoped they might reach the Hudson Bay or Repulse Bay, a mere 700 miles east of the mouth of the Coppermine River. He still expressed these hopes while they were traveling only a dozen miles a day. He even thought about wintering with Eskimos.

In mid-July, they entered Eskimo country and became much more wary. The constant warfare between the Indians and Eskimos demanded that they post sentries at night. When they reached the Bloody Falls, made famous by Samuel Hearne's account of the massacre of the Eskimos, they finally saw a few scared individuals who escaped to the other side of the river. In looking around, they came across grim reminders of the massacre three decades before: whitened skulls and bones lying among the rocks. Their Eskimo interpreter, Augustus, was able to understand the local dialect but was unable to convince the Eskimos that the white men meant no harm and wanted to give them gifts. The Eskimos fled their camps, leaving howling dogs and all their possessions behind. As a sign of friendship, the expedition left behind some copper vessels and small pieces of iron, knowing that iron was more valuable to the Eskimos than gold.

Both Augustus and Junius, "who had rendered themselves dear to the whole party," went ahead, seeking Eskimo families. They found one old man who was unable to run away because of age and decrepitude. At first, he was terrified and, thinking that he was going to be killed, lunged at Augustus with a spear. The poor old man was easily restrained and, with reassurance, he became friendly and promised to give them some dried meat he had stored in a secret place. When they told him that they had Indians with them who were anxious to make peace, he was very pleased and hoped that the rivalry between the peoples could end.

On July 20, 1821, they set sail on the Hyperborean Sea, the Arctic Ocean, in birch-bark canoes. The Canadian voyageurs were frightened of the sea as they had never seen such water before. The naval hands in the party were glad to get off the rushing river and onto an environment that Franklin called "an element more congenial with our habits." The element may have been more congenial, but it was dangerous. Impenetrable fog, pack ice that gripped the fragile canoes, and gales combined to terrify the voyageurs. The waves broke over the canoes, soaking the men who were already unhappy because they were hungry.

The supply of food reached dangerously low levels. "Our stock of provisions being now reduced to eight days' consumption, it became a matter of first importance to obtain a supply." Once again, caribou or bears were found and the critical moment was postponed. But Franklin suspected that some of the hunters, wanting to turn for home and afraid of a catastrophic lack of food, were letting up in their hunts so that they could say that there was no food to be found. The expedition made its way eastward along the coast to Bathurst Inlet. When they found that the inlet ended in a river, they sailed north and east again before finally deciding that winter was imminent and they had to turn back. On August 25, east of Bathurst Inlet, at Turnagain Point, Franklin decided that they could go no farther and would have to return to Fort Enterprise to spend the winter.

The expedition sailed south into Bathurst Inlet and up the Hood River. Soon they came face-to-face with an insuperable barrier, the Wilberforce Falls, 250 feet high. Farther progress on the river was impossible, but they still needed canoes for crossing rivers. Each man, except the officers, carried a hundred-pound load and two men portaged canoes. Their march into hell started on August 31.

Summer turned into winter in a single day. Snow fell, the ponds froze, and they were soon without food, except for a little pemmican and portable soup. The portents for survival were bad. There was no firewood and the moss for fires was too wet to burn. They faced forty days of travel with little hope of food and warm shelter in an area with few caribou and where the terrain made a hunter's task almost impossible. The bleak, treeless land afforded no cover for shelter or for a hunter to sneak up on a herd of animals. Chief Akaitcho had warned them of the dangers of the Barrens in the middle of winter. They would soon learn how right he had been.

They ate only two small meals a day. In early September, Franklin fainted and had to be revived with soup. A plan to split the party and send the strongest travelers ahead to find the Indians was abandoned when one of the canoes was smashed. They had to stay together because they needed at least one canoe to cross the rivers that lay between them and their destination. They ate the last of the pemmican and were reduced to eating *tripe de roches*, a bitter lichen that provided minimal nourishment and caused many of the men to have severe belly cramps. They shot a musk ox, but its meat did not last long and they were soon reduced to eating scraps of skin and bone from a deer killed by a wolf. Soon they were eating burned caribou skin and old moccasins.

The situation deteriorated rapidly. One of the men nearly drowned while crossing a river. He was pulled insensate from the freezing water and was revived by being wrapped in blankets between two naked men. Several hours passed before the freezing man was rewarmed to normality.

As they struggled through deep snow, staggering and falling from exhaustion and starvation, some men were left to die. Franklin knew that they would all die unless they found Indians to rescue them. He sent Back to Fort Enterprise to find Indians and food. But when he arrived, the huts were empty, there was no food, and there was only a note to explain why it had not been possible to stock the fort. Akaitcho had failed to keep his promise to leave Fort Enterprise well supplied with meat, a failure unexplained in Franklin's journal.

The party divided again. Franklin and seven men pushed ahead, following Back and his companions to Fort Enterprise, but when they arrived, they also found the fort abandoned, with broken windows and filth deep on the floor. Back had moved on, intending to go for help to Fort Providence, 140 miles away. He and the others with him were too weak to snowshoe all the way to Fort Providence, but after three weeks of severe privation, living on scraps of dead caribou, they found Akaitcho's camp. They were saved, but could they get help to Franklin?

Most of Franklin's men were too weak to help those who had been left behind, but two went looking for Indians who might help. Meanwhile, back at the camp where the men too weak to go on had been left, a terrible drama was playing out. Michel, an Iroquois guide, asked Dr. Richardson for an axe to cut up the carcass of a deer. He returned to camp later, behaving in a strange way and saying that the two men he had gone back to help had both died. He brought some meat with him he said had come from a wolf killed by a caribou. The meat had a strange taste and Dr. Richardson became suspicious that the Indian had murdered the others and then resorted to cannibalism. The meat was human. Richardson and his friend Hepburn feared that Michel, whom they regarded as a homicidal maniac, would kill them. They watched his every move and made sure they were never alone. Eventually, Richardson made a fateful decision: he took his revolver and executed Michel.

The men waiting in hope at Fort Enterprise were so weak they could not even raise a rifle to shoot at passing caribou. When Richardson joined them, he was horrified at their appearance. He wrote in his journal, "No words can convey an idea of the filth and wretchedness that met our eyes on looking around. Our own misery had stolen upon us by degrees, and we were accustomed to the contemplation of each other's emaciated figures, but the ghastly countenances, dilated eyeballs and sepulchral voices of Captain Franklin and those with him were more than we at first could bear."

The surviving men's legs were swollen with edema. They were so thin that lying on the cold ground was agony. They had pleasant dreams about food, but they were just fantasies. "Dear me," wrote Hepburn, "if we are spared to return to England, I wonder if we shall ever recover our understanding." Their minds were beginning to wander.

Richardson, writing after the events to the father of one of those who had died, softened the story by saying, "Our sufferings were never acute during the march, the sensation of hunger eased after the third day of privation, and with the decay of strength the love of life decayed. We could calmly contemplate the approach of death."

On November 7, the men at Fort Enterprise heard a musket shot. A party of Indians, sent by Back, had arrived with food and appeared to the starving men as veritable giants of strength. The men gorged themselves on the meat the Indians brought but paid the price of satiety with severe indigestion. Within ten days, their strength returned and they were able to proceed slowly back to civilization. They had been sixty days without adequate food, many days with no food, and showed the classic symptoms of severe starvation: extreme weakness, apathy, mental disturbances, swelling of the ankles, and obsessive dreams of food. They became irritable, argumentative, and even violent. Then when help came, they overate, despite a warning from the doctor. But with good food, physical recovery was quick. Psychological recovery was probably much slower.

As they made their way precariously back to safety, they praised the Indians for the tender care they provided, supporting them on the trail, feeding them like children, "evincing humanity that would have done honour to the most civilized nation."

The survivors were greeted in London as heroes. They were fêted, wined, and dined, and asked to give speeches, and the hardships they had endured only made them more admirable heroes. The "man who ate his boots" became the talk of the town. Nothing was said about the execution of Michel or the possibility of cannibalism.

Franklin had more pleasant and urgent thoughts in his mind. He was courting a charming young lady, Eleanor Porden, well placed in society, beautiful, a poet, and erudite. When they married in 1823, Franklin did not realize that her frail beauty was due to tuberculosis. It was a strange union. He was a phlegmatic naval officer, devoted to the service. She was interested in the affairs of an intellectual society into which he did not fit. Nevertheless, she bore him a daughter and, as a dutiful naval wife, made no complaint when her husband was ordered to return to Canada. Before he left, she made a silk Union Jack to be carried to the Arctic Ocean. Many months later, Franklin would unfurl it on the Arctic coast.

As the time approached for the expedition to leave, it became obvious that Eleanor was dying and that after he had left they would never see each other again. Being an extraordinarily realistic woman, she made her will and settled all her affairs before he left. To the modern reader, Franklin sounds cold and heartless and his actions hard to condone. But as a naval officer, duty came before affection and family.

Despite unexplained misgivings by Franklin, Back, who had been promoted to lieutenant, was offered a place on the team, which he readily accepted.

The Third Expedition

Franklin's memories of the horrors of the Barrens must still have been vividly clear in his mind in 1823 when he was asked to lead another expedition to cover much of the same ground he had struggled over in 1821. Why would a man who had nearly died and had resorted to eating his boots want to go back for a second course? But a request from the Lords Commissioners of the Admiralty was an order and the public adulation with which he had been received only confirmed his view that he was the only man for the job.

Franklin's previous expedition had been planned to explore the coastline east of the Coppermine. This expedition was to explore both east and west of the Mackenzie, with Franklin going west and Dr. Richardson going east. In this way, the coast between the Mackenzie and Coppermine rivers would be explored, filling in a gap on the map, and at the same time extending the knowledge of the coast even farther west. Once again, there was a hope that the coastal expedition could join with a seaborne expedition from the west. Captain Frederick Beechey would sail around the Americas, up the West Coast, and through the Bering Strait. As with the previous expedition, the plan was impossibly optimistic, but, fortunately, the outcome would be less disastrous.

The Admirality supported the expedition fully. The supply of food was greater and three small strong boats had been built for the coastal exploration, more seaworthy than the birch-bark canoes used on the first expedition. The boats were to be manned by naval seamen, not by Canadian voyageurs. But, as before, they would rely on Indian hunters to supply them with food.

The expedition sailed from Liverpool on February 15, 1825. Franklin left with a heavy heart, knowing that he would never again see his wife of only eighteen months. She died while they were at sea, and Franklin did not learn of her death until he arrived in New York. From New York, they traveled to Montreal, and from there to Georgian Bay, Fort William, Lake Winnipeg, and Fort Chipewyan. Franklin and Richardson had pushed ahead, but Back caught up with them at Fort Chipewyan, a place very familiar to him from his classic winter journey in 1821.

The first task was to descend the Mackenzie River from the Great Slave Lake to the Great Bear Lake, where they intended to spend the winter and where Peter Dease of the Hudson's Bay Company had winter quarters.

The Mackenzie River is broad, muddy, and, for the most part, easy to navigate. So they lashed the canoes together and drifted down the river, using sails. At Fort Norman, they met Augustus, their Eskimo interpreter whose services had been so valuable four years before.

Back was sent up the Bear River with supplies to the fort that was being built, while Franklin continued on down the Mackenzie to make an initial reconnaissance of their route. Richardson was dispatched to the eastern end of the Great Bear Lake to explore its shores.

Both Franklin and Richardson returned from their preliminary trips and the group settled into the new buildings of Fort Franklin. The voyageurs who had helped paddle the canoes thus far were sent back to Fort Chipewyan for the winter.

The main building of Fort Franklin measured forty-four by twenty-two feet, had a plank floor, a fireplace, windows closed with caribou membrane, and well-chinked walls. The officers had their own bedrooms and the men slept in two adjoining bunkhouses. They were snug for the winter, which passed with its typical routines: catching fish, cutting firewood, reading, playing card games, listening to educational lectures from the officers, sketching, and smoking their pipes. On Sundays, Franklin expected a full turnout for divine service.

Despite planning and constant fishing, by February their diet was reduced to pemmican. Fortunately, the caribou returned and starvation was forestalled.

The voyage down the Mackenzie began at the end of June 1826. The specially built boats, *Lion*, *Reliance*, *Dolphin*, and *Union*, and a freight barge made a gallant sight as they set off, the sailors dressed in special waterproof uniforms of bright blue and red, made from rubberized cloth by an inventive Scotsman, John Mackintosh.

The delta of the Mackenzie River breaks into east and west branches. Franklin and Richardson parted at Separation Point, probably wondering if and when they would see each other again. Franklin and Back, with fourteen sailors and marines and accompanied by Augustus, took the western branch, sailing in *Lion* and *Reliance*. Richardson and Lieutenant E. N. Kendall, in *Dolphin* and *Union*, sailed down the eastern branch.

Of the two groups, Franklin had the greater problems. After reaching the ocean, they encountered an avaricious group of Eskimos. *Lion* and *Reliance* were some distance offshore and ran aground when the tide receded. As soon as the Eskimos realized that Franklin was giving out presents, dozens of kayaks came out from the shore. Inquisitive and greedy hands explored the contents of the boats and removable items were quickly passed from person to person. Back's pistol was stolen and, at one point, Franklin was a virtual prisoner in his boat with two strong men pinning his arms to his sides. Had it not been for the forbearance of the sailors and marines, the interpretive skills of Augustus, and the intervention of a senior Eskimo leader, the incident could easily have turned into a disaster. Had one man fired a single shot and killed an Eskimo, there would have been heavy casualties on both sides. When threatened with guns, the Eskimos kept their distance. Common sense prevailed and the two boats were able to escape to the west. Later, through Augustus, they learned that the Eskimos had been planning to kill them.

Coastal sailing was demanding. Shifting ice pack, shallow water, and strong winds and currents made progress slow. But mile by mile, they crept past Herschel Island, Manning and Foggy Points to a spot west of Prudhoe Bay, where Franklin decided they had to turn around. There were no signs of Captain Beechey and the *Blossom* and Franklin did not want to be caught by another winter. They had charted 375 miles of coast and found it unsuitable for large ships and without possible harbors. The findings were negative, but they filled an important gap in the map of the northern coastline. Reluctantly, on August 16 they turned around and sailed back to the Mackenzie River and Fort Franklin after traveling more than 1,000 miles.

Dr. Richardson and his party had already arrived at Fort Franklin when the western party returned. They, too, had dealt with thieving Eskimos but had the advantage of sailing before the prevailing winds. Reaching the mouth of the Coppermine, they turned south, as far as Bloody Falls, where they abandoned their boats. They packed their belongings and instruments into seventy-pound packs and trekked across country to the east end of the Great Bear Lake, where they met a large canoe from the fort. They had been away for seventy-one days and the two explorers together had covered 2,048 miles. Their surveying had been so accurate that the longitude and latitude of the mouth of the Coppermine was only off by twenty seconds (two and a half miles). And Franklin found that Hearne had been off by only seven miles.

The party arrived back in London in September 1827, having filled in the details of more than 1,100 miles of coast. Franklin, who was knighted on his return, could justifiably be pleased with himself. He returned with his boots uneaten and without the loss of a single man.

The Fourth Expedition

Franklin's return to London was tinged with sadness. He had never seen his young daughter because he had been absent when she was born. He did not remain unmarried for long. Fanny Griffin—later to be known as Lady Jane Franklin—had already set her heart on marrying the famous captain and was soon in hot pursuit of him. They married and he was soon appointed to be governor of Van Dieman's Land—present-day Tasmania—a penal colony at the far end of the world. He spent six unhappy years before being recalled home, thinking that his career had come to an end. One of the few pleasant occasions was the visit of two ships, *Terror* and *Erebus*, that had just explored Antarctica. As Franklin was entertained on board, he cannot have dreamed that the *Erebus* would later be his tomb.

Sir John Barrow, by now eighty years old but still the dominant force in making plans for naval exploration, decided that one final attempt should be made to find the Northwest Passage. This was to be the navy's largest, most extravagant expedition. There was much discussion among the Arctic experts about who should lead this great endeavor. The first choice was Sir James Ross, who had recently returned from a successful exploration of the Antarctic, but he did not think himself suitable (he recognized he had a problem with alcohol). The next possibility, Commander James Fitzjames, was deemed too young. Another experienced Arctic leader, Francis Crozier, who had been second in command to Ross, was also proposed but did not think himself physically fit enough. Despite this, he was eventually chosen as Franklin's second in command. While this discussion was going on between their lordships, Lady Jane had been pushing the candidacy of her husband. At last, Franklin was asked to come to the Admiralty for an interview.

Captain Sir John Franklin, showing the portliness of one who had indulged too much and exercised too little, was questioned at length and it was pointed out to him that he was sixty years old. "No sir," he replied, "I am only fifty-nine." He was appointed. Two ships, the *Erebus* and *Terror*, the same ships on which Franklin had been entertained in Tasmania, were selected, reequipped, and elaborately stocked. Both ships were fitted with twenty-horsepower coal-driven railway engines to supply both power and central heating.

Every conceivable comfort and luxury was planned. Libraries of more than 1,000 books and musical organs were provided for both ships and the food supplies for at least three years were liberal beyond the dreams of the most imaginative seaman: 9,500 pounds of chocolate, 7,000 pounds of tobacco, 137,000 pounds of flour, 9,200 pounds of lemon juice for the prevention of scurvy, 35,000 pints of liquor, and 1,900 pints of wine. In addition, there were large supplies of soap, candles, warm-weather clothing, and wolf-skin blankets. No details were spared, including the 8,000 tins of canned meat, soup, and vegetables. The ships' chandlers at Gravesend made handsome profits. As Scott Cookman has written in his well-researched book *Ice Blink*, the canned food, supplied by a criminally greedy contractor, Stephan Goldner, was probably responsible for many of the subsequent deaths. Goldner cut every possible corner to sell poorly prepared, contaminated food to the Admiralty. The canned food, thought to prevent scurvy and be a reliable source of food that would last several years, turned out to be poison.

The general opinion was that with Franklin in charge, success was assured. But not everyone was happy. Crozier, the second in command, had a premonition that he would not return from the voyage. Perhaps he was depressed because Sophie Cracroft, Lady Jane's niece, had just rejected him in love. Franklin himself was not too happy with the omens. His wife had made a silk Union Jack and, thinking it to be a pleasant surprise, had laid it across his feet while he was taking a nap. He awoke to find himself draped

Canned Food

In 1795, Napoleon offered a prize of 12,000 francs to anyone who could invent a method for preserving food. A former candy maker, baker, brewer, and vintner from Paris, Nicholas Appert, worked for fourteen years and devised a method for preserving food by packing it in glass containers and then placing the container in boiling water and sealing out all air. He did not realize that he was sterilizing the contents. That explanation would have to wait for the work of Louis Pasteur in the 1850s.

Three Englishmen, Peter Durand and Bryan and John Hall, developed a method for putting the food in metal cans rather than in breakable glass jars. By 1818, the British navy was using 24,000 cans of preserved foods every year. So by 1845, when Franklin's expedition started out, canned meat had been used in the navy for many years.

in the flag and had a tantrum because a flag was only draped across the body of an officer after he had died.

Franklin received specific orders about the route to attempt. He was to enter Lancaster Sound through Baffin Bay and proceed as far west as practicable. If halted by ice, he was to turn south and find a route along the coast. Less than 200 miles of coast remained to be surveyed and Barrow thought that this must be accomplished by a British Naval expedition for fear that some other nation might solve the puzzle first. The vagueness of the orders and the impossibility of communication with the ships after they had entered the Arctic made confusion certain and greatly reduced the chances of rescue if anything should go wrong. Perhaps that was why no official contingency plans were made for rescue.

The constantly shifting conditions of the pack ice demanded that Franklin be given a free hand to choose whatever route opened before him. Authorities sitting in London could not dictate what that route might be. Ross cautioned Franklin to leave many traces of his progress, such as cairns, notes, and easily visible landmarks. He even volunteered to mount a search if nothing had been heard from him by 1847. Franklin thought such plans were unnecessary.

On May 19, 1845, with flags flying, the *Terror* and *Erebus*, carrying a crew totalling 134 officers and men, sailed off into oblivion. (Five men were sent back from Greenland: the luckiest men in the crew. One hundred and twenty-nine officers and men were on board as they left for the Arctic.) The clumsy ships were towed by steam-powered ships up the coast to Stromness in the Orkneys. They then proceeded to Greenland, where they received supplies of fresh meat. Franklin sent a letter to his wife in which he wrote, "I am entering on my voyage comforted with every hope of God's merciful guidance and protection." Captain Fitzjames wrote home, saying how pleased he was to have Franklin as his commander "who improves very much as we come to know him." In Baffin Bay, the expedition met two whaling ships, the *Prince of Wales* and the *Enterprise*. One of the captains recorded that all was well and that Franklin expected to complete the expedition in good time. No one ever saw them alive again.

Three years passed before Ross took two ships to search for Franklin. In the next decade, the Admiralty and Lady Jane mounted the largest and most prolonged searches ever, by sea and land. The toll of men who died, went mad, mutinied, were court-martialed, frostbitten, developed scurvy, starved, and drowned is a story too long and detailed to relate here. Ships were sent from the east and west, became caught in the ice pack for several winters, were abandoned, and then found again. One ship, the *Resolute*, that was abandoned by its crew was found by an American whaler, sailed to New York, refurbished, and presented to Queen Victoria as a goodwill gesture. It was finally broken up and from its wood a fine desk was made that was then presented to the American president and placed in the Oval Office of the White House. Lady Jane raised thousands of pounds to finance and equip three expeditions and the Admiralty spent many more thousands to send ship after ship into the cold grip of the ice, only to return with shattered crews and no information. One ship, under the command of Captain Richard Collinson, came as close as any to finding the endpoint of the expedition but turned around before a discovery was made. Even had he found signs, it is doubtful that anyone would have been found alive.

The first evidence of what had happened came nine years after the expedition had set out with such high expectations. Eskimos told John Rae of white men dragging a boat across the tundra and later being found dead. They found human bones in the cooking kettles. When this story reached England, there was an immediate uproar that anyone might suggest that men of the Royal Navy could be forced to the final extreme of cannibalism. Rae was accused of trying to hide the fact that the Eskimos had murdered the men. Even Charles Dickens, with the evidence given to him by Lady Franklin, wrote a stinging article criticizing Rae's evidence (but not Rae) and defending Sir John's men. It was a strong racist and class-conscious Victorian statement of the superiority of the white man over the "Esquimaux." Dickens wrote: "We believe every savage to be in his heart covetous, treacherous and cruel: and we have yet to learn what knowledge the white man—lost, houseless, shipless, apparently forgotten by his race,

Rescue Expeditions

More than 1,000 books, articles, and historical papers have been written about the Franklin Expedition. The number of search-and-rescue missions has been quoted as between twenty and seventy. W. Gillies Ross has concluded that there were seven overland or coastal expeditions, thirty-two by sea, involving forty-one ships, of which forty wintered over in the Arctic for at least one season. According to Ross, only twenty true search expeditions reached the Arctic. Others were mounted to supply the search ships, to search for the searchers, or were aborted before they got near the Arctic. Some expeditions had a double purpose: to catch whales and search, or to explore the coast and keep and eye open for any signs. The first definitive information about Franklin's fate came from such an expedition: Rae's exploratory land voyage from 1853 to 1854.

plainly famine stricken, weak, frozen, helpless, and dying—has of the gentleness of Esquimaux nature." He believed the Esquimaux were responsible, but, above all, he did not believe that English officers and gentlemen were capable of cannibalism.

Rae had arrived in London after the start of the Crimean War, and the Admiralty, which had spent more than £600,000 financing many expeditions, was probably relieved to stop sending more expeditions. But Lady Jane wanted still more expeditions to obtain remains and try to visit possible sites. The Admiralty agreed to two more attempts, but the most important expedition—and, as it turned out, the most productive—was one financed by Lady Jane.

In 1857, Captain Francis Leopold McClintock was commissioned by Lady Jane to sail a tiny yacht, the *Fox*, on a last attempt to gain more information about the final days of the expedition. He had been on three previous Arctic expeditions, including one in which he had made a sled trip of 1,238 miles in 106 days searching for Franklin. Lady Franklin already knew in her heart that her husband was dead. He would have been seventy years old and his survival would have been a miracle.

On April 18, 1857, the *Fox*, a former luxury yacht that weighed only 177 tons, set sail from England to Greenland. The first winter was spent in the ice of Melville Bay and a second winter was passed in Bellot Strait, farther to the east. (Lieutenant Joseph-René Bellot had been a favorite of Lady Jane and had drowned on a previous rescue expedition.) In the spring of 1859, McClintock and his second in command, William Hobson, started out separately with dogsleds to explore King William Island. They knew from Rae that this is where they would find evidence of the expedition's end. McClintock went down the east side of the island and sent Hobson to explore the west coast. Toward the southern end of the island, McClintock came across the skeleton of a young man lying flat on his face. From the way he had knotted the kerchief around his neck, he concluded that he had been a steward. The Eskimos had told Rae that the men fell down dead as they walked and the position of this body suggested that the man had dropped in his tracks. Proceeding west along the southern shore and then turning north up the west coast, McClintock found a message from Hobson that a cairn had been found with a written message telling the exact date of Franklin's death and indicating that the survivors were heading south to try and reach the Great Fish River.

The paper on which the message had been written was a standard navy form asking any finder to send the information back to the Admiralty. The first part of the message was dated May 28, 1847, and ended, "All well." The second part of the message, scribbled around the edges of the form and dated April 25, 1848, told a different story. Sir John had died on

June 11, 1847, less than a month after the first cheerful message. The ships had been abandoned on April 22, 1848, "having been beset since 12th September 1846." Nine officers and fifteen men had died and the remaining "105 souls under the command of F.R.M. Crozier landed here ... and start tomorrow, 26th, for Back's Fish River." Hobson and McClintock could only guess at the causes of this catastrophe. As McClintock wrote in his memoir, "In the short space of twelve months how mournful had become the history of Franklin's expedition."

Farther north, a pile of clothing, four feet high, lay on the tundra. As none of the garments were marked with names and no note explained the reason for the clothes, the finding remained a mystery.

The most revealing and gruesome finding was an upturned boat containing two skeletons and surrounded by an astonishing collection of items: clothes, loaded guns, silk handkerchiefs, toothbrushes, tea, and chocolate. The boat was built from special lightweight wood and was mounted on a massive sled. But it must have weighed at least 1,400 pounds, a nearly impossible load for weakened men to drag across the tundra. Surprisingly, the boat's bow was pointing north, as though the party was trying to return to their ship.

Previous searchers had discovered the expedition's first winter camp on Beechey Island (1845 to 1846), so McClintock knew from the note in the cairn that the ships had spent two brutal winters off the coast of King William's Island. Such a trial would guarantee that when the men finally escaped the ships, they would be suffering from scurvy, semistarvation, and other diseases and barely able to haul a sled-borne boat across the ice and tundra. That they had managed to bring the boat across land to where it was found was a miracle of endurance and courage.

McClintock met several groups of Eskimos from whom he was able to purchase silver spoons and plates marked with the initials and crests of individual officers. He also learned from them of a ship that had run aground on the eastern shore of the island containing the body of one large man with big teeth. The message in the cairn had told of 105 souls, but they had found only three skeletons. Where were the others? How did these findings fit with the stories of many bodies and cannibalism?

McClintock returned to England, carrying with him the written message and the definitive date of Sir John's death. But many unanswered questions remained for later explorers to unravel.

The final story may never be told, but putting together the information found on the ground and the verbal accounts from Eskimos, some of whom had met the unfortunate, weakened survivors, it seems as though a few men returned to the ship, but many made their way across to the mainland where they died at the mouth of Chantrey Inlet. There, at Starvation

Cove, another boat and many skeletons were found with signs of cannibalism. Some men may have survived even longer, as the Eskimos told of hearing shots later on, as though from men hunting.

The Canadian author Farley Mowat, when a young man working in the far north, came across a cairn that contained a wooden box, obviously old, that could have been placed there by a Franklin survivor or by Samuel Hearne. And in recent times, the forensic anthropologist Dr. Owen Beattie exhumed the bodies on Beechey Island, the first wintering camp of the expedition. Evidence from them and from other remains found on King William Island indicated that the men had possibly been suffering from lead poisoning. He and his associates also found bones that had obviously been cut with saws and a skull with similar evidence of intentional entry.

Cookman has made an excellent case that the canned food was infected with botulism, a deadly poison, well known to grow in badly preserved canned food. Botulism would explain the deaths of so many officers—who ate more of the canned food than the rest of the crew—and the sudden deaths of the men struggling to leave the ship. They might have been eating food directly from the cans, food in which the botulism organism had not been killed by cooking. As botulism attacks the nervous system, it would not be surprising for "men to die as they walked," as described by the Eskimos.

Apart from the note in the cairn, no other documents were found. The Eskimo told Rae that there were many papers and books in the ship that ran aground, but they were all thrown away or destroyed by winter storms.

Few disasters have been the object of so many investigations and searches. Some of the facts are clear. All the men died. Some possibly died as late as 1850 and probably indulged in cannibalism to avoid starvation. But by the time the men resorted to cannibalism, there was no hope that they could reach safety. They were too weak, their food had run out, there was no game to hunt, there were no hunters, and the nearest help was 1,000 miles away. They must have died knowing that help was impossible.

McClintock, in his wonderful account of the search for remains, wrote of the document found in the cairn, "A sad tale was never told in fewer words." How true.

9

John Rae
(1813–1893)

The Man Who Walked on Snowshoes

For he'd found the Northwest Passage and
the fate of Franklin's crew.

—From "John Rae" by Jim Smith

If you study a map of the northern coastline of Canada and the United States, you could on the innocence of paper trace half a dozen obvious routes through the Northwest Passage. It looks so easy that you wonder why it took four centuries of exploration, hundreds of painful, cold, scorbutic deaths, cannibalism, fights, crushed ships, broken hearts, claims and counterclaims, political intrigue, and scarred reputations to find the final link between the Atlantic and Pacific Oceans.

Lady Jane Franklin made the most mendacious claim on behalf of her dead husband, Sir John Franklin. She was determined that some shred of fame—rather than infamy—be salvaged from the disasters of his life and persuaded the Admiralty to say that he had discovered the passage when he had not been within miles of it. Robert McClure, searching for Franklin's lost expedition, also claimed to have found the passage. True, he saw one end of a possible route, but he never sailed through it. Only one man could claim to have found the true passage: John Rae. And only one man could claim to have been the first to sail through the passage that Rae had discovered: Roald Amundsen, who took three years to sail its course in a wisp of a boat, far different from the hulking icebreakers that now carry rich tourists along the famous route.

Rae was born within the solid stone walls of Clestrain House in the parish of Orphir, near the town of Stromness, in the Orkney Islands on September 30, 1813. His father, John Rae Sr., was the manager of Sir William Honeyman's estate and also the agent for the local office of the Hudson's Bay Company. His job was to arrange all the supplies and fresh water for the ships of the company when they stopped at Stromness before sailing west to the Hudson Bay. He recruited crew for their ships and employees for the company. At that time, three-quarters of the men who worked for the company were Orcadians. The men were tough and used to a cold, wet, stormy environment. The company offered an escape from poverty. Being Calvinistic Presbyterians, they were honest in trade, hardworking, and used to a disciplined life. Yet they were independent, self-reliant, surprisingly well educated, and capable of working on their own in isolated places. They were the ideal men for the Hudson's Bay Company.

The Orkney Islands, almost seventy in number, lie between the north coast of Scotland and the Shetland Islands. They sit in the windblown ocean on the same latitude as Oslo and Stockholm to the east and Churchill in the Hudson Bay to the west. And Stromness lies only one degree south of the tip of Greenland. Few trees cover the rolling hills and steep cliffs drop precipitously to the sea. The winters are dark with wet, stormy days; but in the summer, when the days are long and sunlit and the hills are covered with waving grass and thousands of bright flowers and a million keening seabirds nest on the cliffs, the islands are a magical place.

In such a place, Rae grew to manhood. He was the fourth son in a family of nine children. Physically strong, long-limbed, and adventurous, he was happiest when he was hunting, fishing, climbing the cliffs for birds' eggs, or sailing the family boat, the *Brenda*, with his brothers. He became oblivious to cold and rain and was equally at home striding across the moors with his musket or sailing the wild sea. Two older brothers had joined the Hudson's Bay Company, but John wanted to become a doctor. So at age sixteen, in 1829, he went south to the University of Edinburgh, the preeminent medical school of his day.

John had little time—and perhaps equally little money—for anything but study. But 1829 was an interesting period. The famous body snatchers William Burke and William Hare who supplied cadavers for anatomy dissections had been executed for murder only one year before. The Royal Infirmary, the main hospital, was building a new surgical wing with an operating room large enough for an audience of 400 students. Each operation was announced by the ringing of an outside bell, and if the bell rang on a Sunday, the minister of nearby Greyfriars Church stopped preaching because all the students in the congregation would get up and leave. The city was agog with activity. Men were seeking the vote and trade unions were gaining power. But this was of little interest to John. He transferred from the university to the Royal College of Surgeons and received his diploma as a licentiate of the college in 1833. As soon as he arrived home, he joined a Hudson's Bay Company ship, the *Prince of Wales*, as surgeon.

John signed up for only one voyage, but Mother Nature and the thrill of the Arctic changed his future, and fourteen years passed before he saw the shores of Orkney again. As the ship's surgeon, he enjoyed the comfort of a cabin and good meals with the captain. Below decks, typhoid broke out among the poor passengers, testing the skills of the newly qualified doctor. Fortunately, no one died. As they sailed into the Hudson Strait, the pack ice entrapped the ships, delaying their arrival. Two ships had been sailing in tandem and the *Prince of Wales*, heading for Churchill, turned for Charlton Island, 800 miles farther south. Unlike many of the passengers, Rae enjoyed the challenge. The island had been abandoned and they had to rebuild the houses and send a boat south to Moose Factory for supplies. Many of the people died from scurvy, but in the spring Rae found cranberries and cured the survivors. He hunted ptarmigan, seals, and duck and canoed around the ninety-six-mile coast of the island. In July, the stranded passengers loaded the *Prince of Wales* and sailed south to Moose Factory where the chief factor, John MacTavish, promptly offered Rae a five-year contract as surgeon and clerk. Rae agreed and the acceptance of the contract changed his life and a nation's knowledge of the Arctic.

Rae stayed at Moose Factory for ten years. In his autobiography, written many years later, Rae described the factory as "a very happy home to me." The factory was, in many ways, better than his home in the Orkneys. The married men and the factor lived in comfortable houses and the annual visit of the supply ship brought liberal quantities of food, wine, and luxuries. The unmarried men lived in Bachelor's Hall, where the parties could turn wild, especially at Christmas and New Year's. Workshops and warehouses completed the small community. The surrounding country was wooded and filled with wildlife, a wonderful hunting ground for an eager young man who was already a crack shot.

At first, Rae agreed to stay if his only duties were medical. But he soon found that he did not have enough medical work and began to take charge of the warehouses, the packing of furs to be sent to England, and the trading post, where the local Indians brought the furs they had trapped in the winter. This brought him into close contact with the Indians and it was not long before he was learning the Cree language and studying the native culture and way of life. To him, everyone could teach him useful skills.

The general philosophy among the company men was that the Indians could live life their way, but it was neither right nor useful to "go native." Most of the company men stayed within the relative comfort and safety of the factory and seldom ventured far afield. But Rae had other aspirations and a different attitude. He wanted, one day, to explore that immeasurable land to the west, where it was possible to travel for thousands of miles without encountering another settlement, and he had an insatiable curiosity to learn more about the native people for whom this land had been home for thousands of years.

A hunchback, Cree became Rae's constant hunting companion and taught him how to stalk and kill, how to dress and clean animals, and how to cook them with delicacy. He observed the women making beautiful clothes, preparing moose leather, and threading the beads that decorated the jackets and skirts. Like Samuel Hearne, Rae soon learned that the women, Cree, and Eskimo, were essential partners in survival, and to the men of the factory, the women gave sweet companionship. Officially, the company frowned on marriage with native women. But unofficially, the companionship of country wives was encouraged. Not only did the relationships lead to happier men, but they also sealed the bonds between the traders and the native population. While Rae did not describe specific friendships, he was certainly attracted to, admired, and presumably consorted with the "tawny damsels," as Meriwether Lewis described them. Sir George Simpson, governor of the Hudson's Bay Company, had several wives and fathered a number of children, all of whom he abandoned when he finally retired to England.

Rae was careful in choosing his traveling companions. He wanted excellent hunters, strong snowshoe walkers, and, among the Eskimos, experts at making snow houses. Some of the company men scorned men who were "half-breeds"—half Cree and half English or Scottish. Rae thought they made the best hunting companions.

Rae proved to be a snow walker of astonishing speed and endurance. On one occasion, he walked 100 miles in forty-eight hours. He wrote, "A long day's march on snowshoes is about the finest exercise a man can take." His explorations, mostly on snowshoes, covered thousands of miles and were mostly done with pleasure, not with complaint.

Sir George Simpson, the legendary governor of the Hudson's Bay Company who traveled wearing a top hat in a special canoe paddled by the best voyageurs, became aware of this young doctor who had learned to master the wilderness. In 1843, he asked Rae to come to Montreal to discuss the exploration of the north coast of Canada. In September of that year, Rae left Moose Factory and made his way to Montreal by canoe. Rae reached Montreal in December and spent Christmas in fine style in Simpson's mansion. He explored Montreal while discussing the more serious business of how best to survey the coast. He returned to Moose Factory early in 1844, traveling by himself on snowshoes, a distance of 700 miles. He described the journey home as "my first comparatively long journey." Not long after returning to the factory, he received instructions from Simpson to meet him in July to make final decisions. This was an official letter appointing him as the leader, because "you are one of the fittest men in the country to make the exploration."

The task was daunting. An earlier expedition by Thomas Simpson (not related to the governor) and Peter Dease had charted about 150 miles of coastline. Rae's plan was to sail north up the Hudson Bay and then cross Boothia Felix, an area that was thought to be an island. He could then travel west along the coast and, with luck, discover the Northwest Passage. Success in finding the passage would be an enormous feather in Rae's cap and a triumph for the company and Sir George. Although Sir George took all the credit for devising this plan, it seems certain that Rae, the more experienced traveler by land, made most of the plans. Rae's experience over the years at Moose Factory had readied him for an adventure of this sort. He was familiar with the Eskimos' way of life and could understand their language. The skills he lacked were in measuring longitude and latitude and in mapping. To acquire these skills, he traveled to Red River—now the city of Winnipeg—where there was someone to teach him. Unfortunately, the teacher died. Determined to get the instruction he needed, Rae waited for the winter, then, with his two companions who had come from Moose Factory, he snowshoed 1,200 miles to Sault Sainte Marie with a dog team. The rugged journey lasted two months, during which Rae actually gained weight! Rae finally went to Toronto to learn how to use a sextant.

Rae received his orders to sail north from Churchill and explore west from Fury and Hecla Strait to the mouth of the Castor and Pollux River. Robert Ballantyne, a company employee and later a well-known author, described Rae as a man of a "pushing, energetic character" with a much better understanding of the problems involved in exploration than George Back and Franklin.

Rae's plans were met with skepticism and few volunteers for such a dangerous trip that would require spending a winter in the far north, something never done before by white men. However, he was able to recruit a friend, John Corrigal, and Richard Turner, a Métis boatbuilder. He arrived at York Factory in October and decided to wait until spring before continuing on to Churchill. He found that two York boats, keeled wooden boats that could carry large loads in shallow water, had already been built for him. He was challenged by others to sailing races and must have felt like a boy back in Orkney, racing and beating whoever wanted to test their skills against his.

Rae was thirty-two, in the prime of his health and strength. As Ken McGoogan wrote in his biography of Rae, *Fatal Passage*, "He must have known that he could not only out-sail, but also out-hike, out-shoot, out-hunt, out-track, out-snowshoe, out-canoe, out-survey, out-smart, and out-survive any man in North America—certainly any European."

Spring of 1846. Rae was waiting at York Factory for the ice to break so that he could start north. But spring was slow to come to the Hudson Bay and it was not until June 12 that Rae and his ten men were ready to leave. Six of the men were Scottish, four from his home in Orkney; and two were French-Canadian, the Métis carpenter Turner, and a Cree hunter. They were about to start on the adventure of a lifetime. They were well supplied with food, guns and ammunition, stoves and cooking pots, fishing equipment, and a collapsible rubber boat. The two boats, the *North Pole* and the *Magnet*, were packed, the men aboard, and to the sound of a seven-gun salute, they pushed off.

The plan called for them to be away for fifteen months, but they only carried food for three. Rae's hunting skills would be put to the ultimate test, or they would certainly starve.

By the end of June, they had reached Fort Churchill, the former Prince of Wales Fort. Two new men were added to the group, one of whom, Ouligbuck, had traveled with Franklin, Dease, and Thomas Simpson. They left on July 5, 1846, and wandered slowly up the coast, stopping to collect botanical specimens and shoot game. At Repulse Bay, they found a small group of Eskimo, from whom Rae learned that an expanse of sea lay to the northwest, about forty miles away. Rae changed his plans and decided to haul the boats across the Melville Peninsula to the mouth of the Castor and Pollux River. They began to pull the *North Pole* across what would later be called the Rae Isthmus. It was a tough job. The boats were heavy and the men had to alternate between hauling the boats and sailing across small lakes. They arrived at the western shore, facing the Gulf of Boothia, and found two old Eskimo who explained the geography to them. From this information, they concluded that Boothia was a peninsula and not an island. But Rae still had to prove it.

The coastline is so complicated that it is hard to visualize the geography without continually looking at a map. But imagine Rae's route in this way: three peninsulas project northward, like the index, middle, and ring fingers of the left hand. The outer two peninsulas are long and the center one is like a middle finger bent against the palm. The index finger is Melville Peninsula, the doubled up middle finger is Simpson Peninsula, and the ring finger is Boothia Felix.

Repulse Bay lies at the outer (eastern) base of the index finger. Committee Bay separates the index and middle fingers, and Fury and Hecla Strait lies across the tip of the index finger. Pelly Bay is located at the eastern base of Boothia (the ring finger), and Lord Mayor Bay is halfway up the eastern shore of the same finger.

During the remainder of summer 1846, Rae and four Eskimo hauled the *North Pole* across the base of the Melville peninsula to Committee Bay. He soon realized that he would not have enough time to explore farther up the coast and returned to Repulse Bay, where the party spent the winter of 1846–1847. On April 5, 1847, they set out again on foot and followed a torturous route from Pelly Bay to Lord Mayor's Bay, up the Melville Peninsula, and ending at Repulse Bay. The sea was still frozen and they had to wait until August 12 before the ice broke and they could sail back to Churchill and York Factory, arriving on September 6, 1847. They had been away for fourteen months, had charted more than 650 miles of hitherto unexplored coast, had spent a winter living off the land, and had not lost a single man. When they arrived back, they still had eight bags of pemmican and four bags of flour. Before they left, one old Scotsman had advised them to take as few men as possible, for none of them would return alive. Not only had they returned alive, but they had returned in fine fettle and with food to spare.

The bare facts of the story do not tell the lessons learned. Along the way, Rae had listened to Eskimos describe the land, the rivers, and the sea and realized that he could rely on their knowledge of the geography. During the long, dark winter, they had lived in a stone house with a roof of deer skin and Rae had observed that the igloos of the Eskimo were much warmer than the house in which they had shivered. He also learned that an igloo could be built in about an hour. Rae discovered that the runners of the Eskimo sleds, made from rolled caribou skins covered with frozen moss and ice, were much lighter and faster than his heavy metal runners. These were lessons that he was quick to learn and apply to his own methods of travel.

The winter in stone houses was long and dreary. The men often stayed most of the day in their sleeping bags in order to stay warm (the coldest temperature was forty-seven degrees below zero), but Rae had brought copies of Shakespeare's plays to read and, reading by the light of dim oil lamps, was able to while away the hours. Before winter set in, he shot more than 60 caribou and 170 ptarmigan and caught 116 salmon and trout. Even with this good supply, they began to run short of food and had to go on reduced rations as the winter ended. Christmas and New Year's Day, however, were both lightened with good food, brandy, and a game of soccer, using a ball made from inflated caribou skin.

Travel was extremely hard, especially up the west coast of Melville Peninsula. The walking alternated between slushy, cold sea water, waist-deep snow, and ice. Rae later wrote it was one of the hardest trips he had ever taken, but it increased his experience and his reputation as a remarkable wilderness leader.

While Rae and his men were isolated on Boothia Felix, the final stages of Sir John Franklin's last expedition began to play out less than 200 miles to the west. Franklin died on June 11, 1847, while Rae was waiting at Repulse Bay for the ice to break so that he could return to Churchill. When he returned to York Factory, he found a group of British soldiers and sailors waiting to find the Franklin expedition; Sir John Richardson, who had accompanied Franklin on both his land expeditions, had been commissioned to lead an overland search up the Back River. Rae had never been impressed with Franklin's wilderness skills and feared that he and his men had probably perished. But within three weeks of hearing the news about the rescue expedition, Rae was on a company ship returning to England.

No official plans had been made to rescue Franklin if he did not reappear within a previously agreed time. Sir James Ross had already started out to look for his friend and the British government asked Richardson, who was fifty-nine years old, to lead another expedition. Ross was to search by sea and Richardson by land. Richardson read of Rae's exploits in the *Times* and knew, instinctively, that he wanted Rae to accompany him on his Arctic search. Rae knew Richardson's name in connection with his previous trips but had never met him. They arranged to meet and Rae readily accepted Richardson's invitation.

Richardson's plan was to descend the Mackenzie River and explore eastward along the coast, repeating the voyage he had made with Franklin. Richardson and Rae sailed from England on March 25, 1848. After arriving in New York, they made their way to Montreal, and then traveled west to Sault Sainte Marie, where Rae collected a group of voyageurs and Indians. They followed the standard fur trading route to Norway House, where they met the British servicemen Rae had already encountered at York Factory. Rae immediately became concerned at the lack of experience and training the soldiers and sailors had, and their poor clothing and equipment. The journey north was no cakewalk for the servicemen. The Methy Portage, the longest, hardest portage in Canada, was almost their undoing. They could only carry half the loads of the voyageurs and grumbled and complained about the food, the mosquitoes, and the weather. Their clothes were already in tatters and, as they were issued only one suit a year, they had no hope of immediate improvement. The portage that could be covered in four days by experienced trappers took the soldiers eight days of sweating and cursing. But it was done and they arrived at Fort Resolution on the Slave River on July 15.

The party then split. A small group was sent to Fort Confidence on the Great Bear Lake to build winter quarters. Richardson, Rae, and eighteen men sailed across the Great Slave Lake and started down the Mackenzie River. They reached the Arctic coast on August 3, after a relatively easy voyage. Rae was constantly pushing the group to go faster and travel farther. He was worried about starting such a long voyage so late in the season. But by the time they reached the coast, they had traveled 3,616 miles from Sault Sainte Marie in ninety days: an average of forty miles per day.

As soon as they took to the sea, they were assaulted by a large group of thieving Eskimos, and Richardson must have recalled their behavior in 1825. Rae ordered his men to fire their muskets in the air and the Eskimos pulled back. Rae wrote later: "The Eskimos are the most daring and impudent scoundrels I ever saw." But, wisely, he did not want to get involved in a battle that would cause loss of life.

At first, all went well. They made good progress, but after Cape Bathurst, ice slowed their progress, giving Rae an opportunity to go ashore and hunt to supply the group with ample meat. The soldiers, because of their unwillingness, or inability, to carry heavy loads, slowed down their progress, irritating Rae, who was used to voyageurs who carried dauntingly heavy loads. Rae tried to shame the men into carrying heavier loads by carrying one himself, but to no avail.

As they traveled along the coast, they left cairns and caches of food for possible survivors of the Franklin expedition. Ice damaged the boats and on September 1 Rae decided that they could go no farther. This decision confounded the plans for the next summer to search Wollaston Land. Richardson decided that the next summer's search would have to be done by Rae alone. They prepared for the march to Fort Confidence and Richardson, who was as religious as his old companion of the trail, Franklin, led the men in prayer before they moved off. The men carried seventy-pound loads and Rae carried nearly as much, carrying the precious surveying instruments. Even Richardson carried a small load but had to stop because of an attack of chest pain, probably due to blocked arteries to his heart (angina). He also suffered from similar cramping pain in his legs, due to blockage of the arteries to the leg muscles. Rae was worried that he would not be able to continue. He recovered, but if Rae had known more about heart disease, he would have been extremely worried for Richardson's life. They reached the Coppermine and were able to arrive safely at Fort Confidence to spend the winter.

Chief Trader John Bell had done a great job in preparing their winter quarters. The old buildings had been burned to the ground, but this had not stopped Bell from constructing solid new houses for the men. The group was too large to be totally accommodated in the fort and some of the men were sent to a nearby island, where there was wood and game. The camp was soon organized and the men detailed to their various duties.

Rae received the unwelcome news that he had been put in charge of the Mackenzie District of the Hudson's Bay Company. The promotion meant that he could not accompany Richardson home to England. The party divided. Rae chose six men to accompany him, including the Eskimo interpreter Albert One-eye, one of his favorite workers. The remaining men, mostly military, went with Richardson back to Montreal.

Rae and Richardson had developed great respect for each other. Richardson was an excellent naturalist and subsequently published two volumes of observations on the wildlife of the Arctic. During the winter the two spent together at Fort Confidence, they must have had long discussions about what they had seen and done, apart from speculating about the disappearance of the Franklin expedition. Richardson had struggled with Franklin on his first Canadian expedition, which had ended in cannibalism, and he would never have agreed to come on the search, at age fifty-nine, except to find a close friend. He had a phenomenal memory for poetry and regaled the group with long recitations, much to Rae's enjoyment.

As Richardson was getting ready to leave, Rae received new orders from Sir George Simpson to search Wollaston and Victoria Lands for Franklin. This did not please him but gave him an opportunity to explore another part of the coast and perhaps unlock another clue in the puzzle of the Northwest Passage. The one consolation was that he was ordered to return before the end of the summer.

Rae left Fort Confidence on June 9, 1849, to find the Coppermine still frozen. Eventually, the river opened and they were able to proceed north up Coronation Gulf. To reach Wollaston Land, they had to cross the Dolphin and Union Strait. It was frozen solid. Several weeks passed and the sea did not open. On August 19, they tried to make some progress but made no headway, and on August 25, they turned for home.

At Bloody Falls, James Hope proposed to haul the boat up the river with only two men aboard. All went well until the tow rope broke and the two men jumped ashore in panic. Rae and Albert One-eye raced down to grab the boat. Albert managed to grab it with a hook, but before Rae could help him, Albert was swept into the rapid and disappeared from sight. Rae and the other men searched in desperation, but Albert had drowned.

Rae became deeply depressed. Albert was the first—and only—man that Rae lost on any expedition. He never forgave himself for what happened, even though there was nothing he could have done to save Albert. Visiting Bloody Falls a year later, Rae went into the woods and wept.

The expedition was a failure. They had not been able to cross the strait to reach Wollaston, their last boat had been destroyed, and, worst of all, Albert had died. Rae reported the failure to the governor and made his way to Fort Simpson to take up his company duties.

An unexpected visitor arrived at Fort Simpson: Lieutenant W. J. Pullen of the Royal Navy, who had searched along the coast from the west and then turned up the Mackenzie to find winter shelter. Pullen had already made an extraordinary voyage. He had come up the West Coast and joined HMS *Plover*, a supply ship that remained on station in the Bering Strait from 1848 to 1854. He and his men left the *Plover* at Wainright Inlet in Alaska and sailed along the coast in two boats on a vain search for Franklin, who was hundreds of miles to the east. His crew was exhausted and must have been glad to see the comparative comfort of Fort Simpson, although Rae thought the fort uncomfortable and cold. Their plan was to return to civilization, but Pullen stayed all winter with Rae.

Rae made a trip in May 1859 to collect furs that had been trapped. When he returned, he heard a shocking story about an HBC employee, James Stewart, who had made a journey of more than 1,000 miles to find out why he had not received any winter supplies. He had stopped at an HBC station, called Pelly Banks, that was in charge of Pierre Pambrun. The story he learned from Pambrun was horrifying but not beyond imagination.

The station accidentally burned to the ground and the men were left destitute and starving. Pambrun left the station, ostensibly to allow the others to have more food. When he returned, he found only one man alive, William Foubister, and immediately concluded from the bones in the fireplace that Foubister had eaten his dead companions. Later, he found Foubister cooking broth that contained unmistakable human bones. Foubister would not confess to Pambrun's shouted demands for an explanation, and when Pambrun returned two days later, he found Foubister dead, his Bible by his side. Rae was furious that Pambrun had saved his own life at the expense of two others, but there was nothing he could do about it. Life on the Barrens was cruel.

When the ice on the Mackenize River broke, Rae, Pullen, and the chief trader hauled their heavy loads of furs upstream, heading for the Great Slave Lake and the route back to Montreal. But Rae would go no farther. A messenger told him that he had to renew his search for Franklin at once. The political pressure in England had grown to a bursting point. Franklin, or his remains, had to be found at all costs. Along with the orders from Simpson came a sugary letter from Lady Jane herself and another from Sir Francis Beaufort, the chief hydrographer of the Admiralty, saying that he wanted to "add my voice to the moans of the wives and children of the two unfortunate ships" and telling Rae that his mission was holy.

Pullen received word that he had been promoted to captain and was also ordered to resume the search for Franklin. Rae was faced with a dilemma: he did not have enough supplies to equip both expeditions. He gave Pullen what he could and then wrote to Sir George outlining a plan. Before the thaw, he would travel north with dogs, cross the Dolphin and Union Strait, search Wollaston and Victoria, and return to the mainland before the sea ice broke. In the meantime, his men would bring boats to the Kendall River. By that time, the sea would be open and he would be able to turn back down the Coppermine River and search the coast. It was an ingenious, daring two-part plan to satisfy the requirements of the Lords of the Admiralty in London.

Rae traveled the usual route over Methy Portage with the furs, collected more men, and started back. He had to discharge some inexperienced men and was fortunate in hiring a boatbuilder from the Orkneys, George Kirkness. They were back in Fort Confidence by mid-August and made preparations for the winter and the spring expedition.

The winter was tough. Food was scarce and starving Indians had to be fed. But two boats were built and Rae spent his time helping with the chores and doing company business.

Rae departed Fort Confidence on April 25, 1851, on another incredible expedition that would take him thousands of miles by dogsled, snowshoe, and small boat, during which he would find pieces of wood that clearly came from a British government ship—but from which ship?

Rae had sent supplies ahead to be cached and brought men with him to carry extra supplies and then turn back. He had stripped down his own equipment to a minimum, carrying only "a spare woolen shirt or two." (His economies are reminiscent of the famous argument between two British mountaineers, Eric Shipton and Bill Tillman, about whether it was necessary to take a spare shirt on a three-month climbing expedition in the Himalayas.) He took no tents, but would rely on snow houses. He carried enough food for thirty-five days. No detail had been forgotten. His years of experience in the Arctic would pay off and his methods of travel be vindicated.

On May 2, the men who had been hauling the supplies turned back and Rae and two men, Peter Linklater and John Beads, pressed on. The sea ice was smooth, but the sun was so bright they had to travel at night to avoid snowblindness. They crossed the Dolphin and Union Strait and reached Wollaston Land. It was believed that Wollaston and Victoria were separate islands, but Rae's journey along the southern coast and up the east coast proved that they formed a single large island.

They met bad storms; one of the men was frostbitten. They encountered friendly Eskimos who had never seen Europeans and had no news of big ships. As they surveyed the land, they named prominent features after distinguished associates: Richardson Islands, Cape Back. On May 24, Rae decided to turn back. As he overlooked Prince William Sound, he little knew that only ten days before a sledding group from HMS *Investigator* had been on the other side of the sound.

They crossed the Dolphin and Union Strait safely as the sea ice was starting to melt and moved overland to the Kendall River. On the way, Rae shot a musk ox bull, whose skeleton he took back to England. The traveling became more and more unpleasant, with the wet, soggy tundra, small ponds, and constant wading in freezing water. They lost their cooking utensils and had to eat off flat stones. The lemmings were so abundant that the dogs were able to feed themselves. A few days later, Hector Mackenzie and eight men arrived with the boats built during the winter. Now Rae could revert to his boyhood, sailing a small boat along the coast. But first, they had to navigate the raging Coppermine River, full of snowmelt.

Rae waited several days before venturing down the river, but finally ordered the boats into the river. The run was exciting, and the portages went well. At Bloody Falls, Rae went off by himself to meditate on the disaster of Albert's death. When they set out on the sea, Rae found to his dismay that none of the men knew how to handle a sailing boat and the first days were spent in teaching them the elements of tacking and luffing.

The sea ice parted and they sailed north up Coronation Gulf to Cape Barrow, where the ice was thick but not impassable. They met Eskimos who, like others they had questioned, had neither seen nor heard of white men or big ships. If they had been able to sail farther east, they might have found evidence of the Franklin expedition, perhaps even saved some of the documents that later Eskimos threw away because they were of no value to them. Instead, Rae sailed north to Victoria Land.

Victoria Land has a waist, with two inlets pushing in from the eastern and western sides. Cambridge Bay, the inlet on the east, was deep enough to make a good harbor. Sailing east, they continued on around the coast, rowing and sailing against strong winds, but, eventually, they reached Pelly Point, directly opposite Cape Franklin on King William Land, where relics of the lost expedition would later be found. They were within almost visual distance of making discoveries that many explorers had sought so diligently. Rae tried to cross the strait—later named the McClintock Channel—but was stopped by ice. He must have been halted close to the point where *Erebus* and *Terror* sank.

In Pine Bay, one of the men found a piece of wood, six feet long with a squared-off bottom, stamped with a broad government arrow and with a piece of white rope nailed to it with copper tacks. They had certainly found a relic from a British ship, but so many ships had been searching for Franklin that Rae could not say with assurance that the wood had come from either of Franklin's ships. But it would end up on the desk of the First Lord of the Admiralty as evidence. Rae did not really expect to find evidence of the Franklin expedition in this area and had said as much in a letter to Sir John Richardson. He thought remains would be found farther north, but did not think that anyone would still be alive and knew in his heart that he was conducting a useless search.

The small group turned back, sailing around the south coast of Wollaston and then some distance up its west coast. Nothing was found, and by September 10, they were home at Fort Confidence. Rae only stayed one day. He gave orders to shut down the fort, pay off the men, and leave. He was going back to England, come hell or high water. He had just sailed 1,390 miles in a small open boat and charted more than 600 miles of unexplored coastline and had covered more than 8,000 miles, overall, in a vain search.

After reporting to Sir George Simpson, Rae sailed from New York and arrived in England in April 1852. The city was full of rumors about the Franklin expedition. Lady Jane was still prodding the Admiralty and Rae met Robert McCormick, who was about to set out on yet another search, with five ships. They discussed the direction the men might have gone, assuming that they lost their ships. Some thought the men would have gone south—a long and almost hopeless choice; others, including Rae, thought they would have gone east to the supplies left in previous years on Somerset Island.

The Royal Geographical Society awarded Rae its coveted Founder's Gold Medal, but he was in Orkney with his ailing mother. The Hudson's Bay Company was losing enthusiasm for searching for Franklin and wanted Rae to complete his survey of the north coast. Rae suggested taking boats up the west coast of the Hudson Bay, then heading west to explore the western coast of Boothia, filling in some of the few remaining gaps on the map. (If the many searches for Franklin had done nothing else, they had greatly increased the charting and surveying of the complicated shoreline of the north coast. Very few gaps remained uncharted.) Rae did not want to make this trip himself but was persuaded that he was the best leader, and perhaps he had a lingering thought that he might find the last link in the Northwest Passage. In the meantime, he enjoyed the social whirl of London as well as grouse shooting on the moors of Orkney and hunting on the estates of the aristocracy. He watched the ceremonial magnificence of the Duke of Wellington's funeral and received a generous reward from the government for his services in Victoria Land.

In November 1852, Rae wrote to *The Times* explaining that his next expedition gave no hope of finding Sir John. Little did he know how wrong he was. He left London in March 1853, anxious to return to the Arctic, his true home.

Passing through New York, Rae had himself photographed by Matthew Brady. Rae, full-bearded with thinning hair on top, stands erect in a smart, long-tailed suit, his right hand, like Napoleon's, tucked into his waistcoat. Dressed like this instead of in the furs of an Eskimo, he looked more like a successful business tycoon than the finest Arctic explorer of his era.

He quickly made his way to Norway House, where he was joined by John Beads, James Johnston, and Thomas Mistegan, an Ojibwa hunter. They arrived at York Factory in June 1853. He had already made arrangements for two boats to be built strong enough to withstand the buffeting of the sea but light enough to be portaged. The larger boat was twenty-seven feet long; the smaller boat was twenty-four feet long. Rae recruited another Orkney man, James Clouston, an experienced sailor, and made him steersman of the larger boat. The supplies were ready: biscuits, tea, flour, pemmican, blankets, moccasins, warm clothes, and gifts for the Indians. They left on June 24 to the traditional gun salute and huzzahs from the crowd. The journey north was not easy. The sea was shallow, they had to stand off the coast, and they had problems with the pack ice, having to leap out of their boats onto passing floes. They hauled their boats through freezing water, a task that Rae regarded as "no great hardship."

After reaching the Prince of Wales Fort, they were joined by Marko Ouligbuck, an Eskimo with whom Rae had worked before. Rae was not keen to take him on as he thought he was a liar, but he was assured that in the intervening years Marko had grown up and was now a reliable interpreter, speaking English, Cree, and French, as well as his own languages.

Farther north, in Chesterfield Inlet, they began to go up an unknown river but were stopped about seventy miles from the Great Back Fish river, which they were seeking. The rocky shield of northern Canada was far too difficult for portaging a boat and they had to turn back. Rae sent some of the men back to York Factory and decided to sail to Repulse Bay, winter there, and continue in the spring. He continued with the larger boat and seven men, including Mistegan and Ouligbuck. They arrived at Repulse Bay in August and immediately set about getting ready for the winter. The prospects were grim. They did not have enough supplies to last the winter, there were no signs of local Eskimos or game, and, having spent one winter at Repulse Bay, Rae knew well the rigors of withstanding the bitter cold, darkness, and isolation of the camp. He called his men together and asked them what they wanted to do: stay or go back? The answer was unanimous: they would stay for the winter.

Rae and Mistegan, both excellent hunters, shot caribou, ptarmigan, marmots, and one musk ox and soon had enough to get them through most of the winter, although all the men knew that they might have to go on short rations. The men lived in snow houses, and Rae lived by himself—he could not tolerate the smoke in the mens' houses—in a leather tent, with his belongings laid out in precise detail, everything from his socks to his rifle in its appointed place. When the snow was sufficiently deep, he built himself an igloo. Because he was the sole occupant, it was bitterly cold. Christmas, as usual, required an attempt to celebrate with venison and a small allowance of brandy.

Because they had not been able to find any Eskimos, they had no dogs. Hauling the sleds was the only option and they planned a short trip to leave a cache. Up and down the ridges they kept going, covering eighty miles before they cached some food and lightened the loads. They returned to Repulse Bay to make preparations for the longer spring expedition. Rae calculated that their loads would add up to 820 pounds, not including guns and ammunition and trade goods for the Indians—more than 200 pounds per sled. When the time came, they still had not found any dogs. Three men were left behind, including a disappointed Mistegan. He was a skilled hunter and could keep the group supplied with food.

Rae and four men (Beads, Johnston, John McDonald, and Ouligbuck) put their shoulders into the harnesses and left Repulse Bay. The plan was still the same: to cross Boothia Peninsula and survey its west coast. They had supplies for sixty-five days.

Within a few days, McDonald developed chest pains and was sent back to Repulse Bay to be replaced by Mistegan, who was delighted to leave camp. They opened the cache at Cape Lady Pelly and found everything in order. Now pulling heavier loads they pushed ahead, building igloos every night. Rae's daily routine was rigorous: a small breakfast; no lunch, except for some munching on the trail; and a simple but filling dinner at night.

They had started early in the season and had to deal with extremely cold weather. Two of Beads's toes froze badly, a potentially disastrous injury. One day, because of the terrible weather, they only went a mile and a half. Rae was still anxious to obtain dogs, so he sent Mistegan and Ouligbuck ahead, looking for help. They returned within a day with seventeen Eskimos, some of whom were old friends. They gave Rae's group no useful information, and the next day, when they left, Ouligbuck left with them. Rae could not afford the loss of one man and chased after him. Ouligbuck was full of remorse and returned weeping. His reasons for leaving were never explained to Rae's satisfaction, but he was back with the group and worked hard.

Soon they met two other Eskimos who were willing to talk and share their dogs. Rae immediately noticed that one of the men, In-nook-poo-zhe-jook, was wearing a gold cap band. He said that it had come from the place where the white men had died, although he had not been there himself. Rae later wrote: "They did not know the place, could not, or would not explain it on a chart." Rae bought the cap band. Could it have come from Franklin's men? The story grew more detailed. The white men had died ten or twelve days' journey to the west in a place the Eskimos had never visited and which would now be under a blanket of winter snow. All Rae could do was urge them to pass the word around that he was interested in more relics from the dead white men and more information about their deaths.

Rae decided to leave Beads and Johnston behind while he went ahead with Mistegan and Ouligbuck. They took a small supply of food and made for the mouth of the Castor and Pollux River. They reached the sea on April 27, 1854. Among old Eskimo caches, they found the remains of a cairn that had probably been built by Thomas Simpson in 1839. It was empty.

The three men moved north, up the west coast of the Peninsula, hoping to reach Bellot Strait. On May 6, they were looking over a wide sea channel where the maps indicated that there should be land. The maps were wrong. Rae could see that the ice was thin and concluded that in the right season, this channel would be open. Without fully realizing it at the time, Rae had discovered the final link in the Northwest Passage. He was looking at the channel down which Amundsen would sail in 1905. Others who claimed to have found the Northwest Passage had never seen this channel. Their claims were false and only Rae's information would later be confirmed. Despite this finding, many books still falsely claim that Franklin or McClure discovered the Northwest Passage.

The journey back was hell for Beads. His feet were excruciatingly painful, but he refused to be pulled in a sled. But hauling the sleds was easier than during the outward journey. At Pelly Bay, a large group of Eskimo had more clues to the final days of Franklin's expedition, including a silver spoon with the initials "F.R.M.C." scratched on the surface. Rae thought that perhaps the spoon had belonged to McClure. In fact, it had belonged to Francis Crozier, the second in command to Franklin.

Back at Repulse Bay on May 26, they found more Eskimos with relics to trade and, at last, Rae knew their stories were about the Franklin expedition. The white men had been seen four years before, dragging a boat. One of them had a telescope strapped to his back. They were moving south on King William Land. Later, at least thirty bodies were found near the mouth of the Great Fish River, and according to the Eskimo, there was strong evidence that they had indulged in cannibalism: the food kettles contained human bones. In his later report, Rae wrote: "From the mutilated state of the many bodies, and the contents of the kettles, it is evident that our wretched country-men had been driven to the last dread alternative as a means of sustaining life."

The story was all hearsay, but Rae was confident enough in the reliability of the Eskimo to know that it was true. He listened in horror, realizing the enormity of the news he would have to carry back to London. Later, he would be asked why he did not turn back and visit the sites where the white men had been seen, but the sledding season was nearly over and he did not want to spend another winter at Repulse Bay. Also, he did not have a boat to take him across the strait to King William Land. He knew the news was definitive: the many relics he obtained were proof in themselves. His duty was to return to London as fast as he could, report to the Admiralty, and stop the need for useless searches.

Packing up the relics, including a silver plate inscribed "Sir John Franklin, K.C.H.," Rae hurried back to board a ship for England. He arrived in London on October 22, 1854, bearing tragic but historic news. In the days to come, he would wish that fate had not destined him to be the messenger.

Rae was unpleasantly surprised to find that the *Times* had already published details of his report. He had written to the newspaper but did not expect the letter to arrive and be printed before he was able to report to the Admiralty. Like many political "leaks" in modern times, the consequences were immediate and unpleasant.

He was received with civility by the Lords of the Admiralty and showed them the relics, including the silver plates inscribed with the initials and coat of arms of Sir John Franklin. The evidence he gave them of the deaths of the men was so convincing that the names of the men were soon struck from the navy rolls. As far as the Admiralty was concerned, the fate of the expedition had been decided and no further searches were needed. But Rae had to deal with more potent foes than the Admiralty.

The interview with Lady Jane Franklin was icy. She was willing to accept that her husband was dead but would not believe that there had been cannibalism, even though he was not responsible for the dreadful acts. She recruited others to support her disbelief. Sir John Richardson—who had himself executed an Indian he suspected of cannibalism and knew well the terrible psychological trauma of starvation—roundly criticized his former friend for not personally verifying the facts firsthand. Charles Dickens leapt into the fray and published two long articles in his magazine, *Household Words*, in which he displayed his personal racism and Victorian-era prejudices that British officers could do no wrong and that white men were always superior to "savages" in behavior and morals. The public was led to believe that the "Esquimaux" had probably murdered the men and then lied to exculpate themselves. Rae knew from years of experience that the Eskimo would not lie about the deaths of thirty or forty men. He had traveled with and lived with these people. He had relied on them for his own safety. But how could he convince an aristocratic widow, white-faced with fury, who would not even talk to him? The messenger was dead.

Other incidents infuriated Rae. New Admiralty maps ascribed the discovery of sections of the northern coast that he had charted to naval men. Rae's protests produced smooth answers but no promises of changes. Part of the problem may have been a rivalry between the navy and the Hudson's Bay Company. The navy thought they were entitled to all the discoveries and resented the fact that men from the HBC had made significant discoveries more economically and with no loss of life. Rae threatened to publish his complaints in the *Times*. Changes were made.

The government had long said that they would give an award of £10,000 to anyone who was able to determine the fate of the Franklin expedition. Rae knew nothing about this reward. He was isolated in the wilderness of northern Canada when the reward was announced and did not know about it until the Admiralty told him that he was entitled to it. Despite protests from Lady Jane Franklin, he was given the money and was immediately accused of returning with his news solely to receive the reward. Rae divided the award and gave £2,000 to his men, even those who had remained at Repulse Bay. Rae's portion, £8,000 (the equivalent of $600,000 today), added to his accumulated pay was more than enough to support a good living, so he resigned from the Hudson's Bay Company, which he had served for twenty-three amazing years.

Rae was never knighted, but Francis McClintock, Lady Jane's hero who found the written evidence that her husband was dead, was promoted to admiral, knighted, and received numerous awards and public adulation.

After his resignation, Rae returned to Canada and went into business with his brothers in Hamilton. There he met and married Kate Jane Alicia Thomson, a beautiful, talented woman. Rae did not sit back and vegetate. He made long trips across Iceland and in western Canada surveying routes for telegraph lines. But after he married, he and Kate never lived permanently in Canada. They had a home in London and moved between there and the Orkneys. They were married for thirty-three years but had no children. Rae remained very active to the end of his life, hunting in the north, exercising with the volunteer army, and always walking, walking, walking.

John Rae, the greatest Arctic traveler of his day, died on July 22, 1893, in his bed. His last words were, "Oh, my darling wife, all is over, oh my darling wife, oh my darling wife."

Part Two

10
Survival
Who Lives, Who Dies, and Why

The first virtue of a soldier is endurance of fatigue:
courage is only the second virtue.

—*Napoleon Bonaparte*

How did they do it? How did they survive? These are the obvious questions raised by the stories of our heroes: William Bligh and his men crossing the Pacific in a tiny, crowded boat; John Charles Frémont struggling with fifteen-foot snowfalls in the San Juan Mountains; Samuel Hearne in the Barrens, starving and sheltering under a deer hide tossed over his back. "Ye Gods!" we think, "I could not survive that." Yet millions of people across the world have survived wars, concentration camps, attacks by machete-wielding murderers, fires, earthquakes, and tsunamis. Why do some people survive, yet others die?

The American Alpine Club publishes yearly accounts of all mountaineering accidents in North America and analyzes them under three headings: conditions (the conditions before and at the time of the accident), acts (actions taken after the accident), and judgment (judgment before and after the accident). The same scheme can be used to help us understand how Bligh, Zebulon Montgomery Pike, and others might have avoided getting into trouble and how they survived.

The word "conditions" in the context of an accident usually refers to the weather at the time of the accident. The weather conditions that the explorers encountered covered every conceivable variation except tornados, earthquakes, and tsunamis. From summer desert heat to Arctic winter blizzards, the explorers faced them all. Many explorers have described the weather day by day. Susan Solomon, a climatologist at the National Oceanic and Atmsopheric Administration, made a retrospective analysis of the weather during Captain Robert Scott's fatal return from the South Pole in 1913. Solomon found, by comparing modern observations with those made in 1912 to 1913, that Scott experienced the coldest weather for 100 years, a factor that contributed to the fatal end of his expedition. She also compared the weather observations made by Meriwether Lewis and William Clark as they traveled through the Bitterroots with modern measurements made over many years. She found that Lewis and Clark experienced average weather conditions for the summer. They did not, as some authorities have guessed, experience unusually severe snowfall.

Wilderness has been described as a malevolent force. *The Savage Mountain*, for example, is the title given by Charles Houston to his account of attempting to climb K2, the second highest mountain in the world. Colonel Spencer Chapman, a British officer, spent three years behind the Japanese lines in Malaysia after the fall of Singapore. Many of the soldiers who escaped into the jungle gave up and died. They did not die from disease or injury but having been born and raised in cities they regarded the jungle as a malevolent force. Chapman believed that the jungle, like all natural environments, was neutral in the battle for survival. This concept applies to all expeditions. The environment is not hostile: it is neutral.

The experience and training of each individual embarking on an expedition, the choice of which men to take, knowledge of the country to be explored, as well as the supplies taken and the overall trip planning all contributed to the conditions of the expeditions outlined in this book. Lewis and Clark, John Rae, and Alexander Mackenzie had been tried and tested by years spent in the wilderness. They had acquired the needed skills, they knew how to lead, and they made the appropriate plans. Some of the others did not plan as carefully and did not have the same background experience. Their lack of experience, the absence of good plans, or bad judgment all contributed to the troubles that hit them.

Through the prism of two centuries, it is easy to judge that some of the expeditions should have been better prepared. But in those days, what would "better prepared" have meant? Could they have selected better men, better equipment, had better maps, or had more food? The answer to many of these questions is no. Lewis and Clark's expedition was the most successful expedition of its time, largely due to Thomas Jefferson's driving obsession with details: he insisted that Lewis acquire the best knowledge of the land and its peoples; he persuaded Congress to provide money for supplies and sent Lewis to get the best equipment at the arsenal; he instructed Lewis on the objectives of the expedition, how to achieve them, and when to give up, if necessary; and Jefferson knew that a military expedition would be glued by a code of discipline that would not apply to a band of trappers and traders.

Expeditons are affected not only by the backing they receive, but by the care with which they are prepared. The expeditions of Frémont and Pike were backed by the U.S. government, but Pike was hurriedly pushed into his expeditions by General Wilkinson. Frémont received good financial backing but had to make preparations rapidly and chose only a few of his men with care. Mackenzie spent two winters planning his journeys and knew the caliber of the men who would travel with him. The Hudson's Bay Company had employed John Rae for ten years before he embarked on his first major voyage. He prided himself on being able to make extended expeditions at about a tenth of the cost that the British navy spent for the same results. Even though he traveled cheaply, by living in snow houses and living off the land, he planned each trip with precision and foresight.

The correct choice of companions may be the most important component of the conditions. Those embarking on modern-day expeditions prepare to the nth degree. The participants are subjected to physical and psychological tests, in addition to having to be experts in their fields; expedition leaders do not chose sailors for mountaineering trips or scuba divers for explorations of deserts and jungles.

To be successful, the leader of an expedition should choose the other members taking into account their skills, temperaments, and experience. Frémont's choice of men was usually sound. Kit Carson proved to be an excellent guide, time and time again. He was courageous, tough as nails, and had years of travel in the West under his belt. Frémont wrote of him, "A braver man than Kit perhaps never lived, in fact, I doubt if he ever knew what fear was." He was a renowned Indian fighter who had killed his first Apache when he was only fifteen. Frémont anticipated battles with the Indians and Carson was the sort of man he wanted beside him when the shooting started. Frémont compared the courage and coolness of Carson, Alexis Godey, and Dick Owens to Napoleon's marshals. His judgment was beyond reproach. In contrast, Pike chose his men at the last minute and called them "damned rascals." But considering what he put them through, they remained remarkably loyal. One man, Private Henry Kennerman, who had been demoted from sergeant to private on the first expedition up the Mississippi for destroying and stealing the expedition's property, signed up again for the second expedition but promptly deserted. He was not a good choice, but Pike prepared for his second expedition so quickly that he was glad to recruit anyone with experience, even if he could not be trusted.

John Wesley Powell chose men who had been with him before and whom he knew to be skilled hunters and mountain men, but he never imagined that river skills would be more important than being a crack shot with a rifle.

John Franklin, for his overland expeditions, chose a small nucleus of naval men and then surrounded himself with a larger pick-up group of voyageurs and Indian hunters. The majority of the men—and the few accompanying women—were total strangers whose loyalty he had to trust.

On his last expedition, the crews of the ships were said to have been hand-picked. That was true of the officers, but we do not know how the volunteers were chosen to make up the rest of the ship's company. Once they embarked, the glue of naval discipline, loyalty to the service, and genuine loyalty to their commanding officer held them together.

One characteristic common to all the men of these stories is that they were extraordinarily tough and able to ignore cold, wet, heat, pain, and discomfort. Even Franklin, who was scoffingly dismissed as being unable to walk more than eight miles, proved amazingly resilient and optimistic in the face of conditions of the utmost severity. The men of those days led hard lives. They had seen others die violent deaths. Hearne and Franklin had seen friends blown to smithereens by the cannons of the French. Others had watched Indians scalp their friends and, in turn, had lopped the topknot off a few Indians themselves. They did not think that walking thirty miles or riding fifty miles in a day was an achievement of Olympic proportions. Rae snowshoed twenty-four miles between 9:00 A.M. and 3:00 P.M. to visit a sick man, then turned around and returned along the same route that evening, taking time to shoot twenty-eight ptarmigan along the way. Most modern city dwellers think that a twenty-mile walk is remarkable. These men thought it was usual, perhaps even an easy day.

Two forces, ego and pride, drove the leaders and many of the men. The same forces drove them to both achievement and disaster. Mackenzie called on the pride of his men to keep them going when they wanted to quit. Frémont's ego compelled him to leave his dying men behind and head for California, searching for a route for the railroad. Pike's unacceptance of fail-ure would not permit him to give up, even when it seemed that he and his men would die of starvation. Franklin's determination to explore as much of the northern coast as possible made him turn back too late in the season and caused the deaths of eleven men in his group. But four years later, along the same coast, he had learned his lesson and turned around before winter struck. No men died.

Our explorers, with a few exceptions (Charles Preuss on Franklin's first expedition), had lived in the wilderness for years, but their experi-ences did not always fit those of the expedition they were joining. Powell's men knew nothing about running white-water rivers. Pike and Frémont had no experience of high-altitude winter travel. Rae, on the other hand, had been traveling in the Arctic for many years before he ventured across the northern shore, relying on Eskimos as his main companions, men to whom the Arctic was home. Cold and blizzards were their familiar com-panions.

Military-based expeditions had some advantages, of which discipline was perhaps the most obvious. Lewis and Clark picked their men carefully:

unmarried, young, good hunters, used to the discomforts of wilderness travel "to a remarkable degree." The men they chose had slept in rain-soaked clothes, eaten maggot-ridden meat, suffered from malaria, and left their homes and loved ones to seek adventure. A few men who had disciplinary problems during the first summer were sent home after the winter at the Mandan Fort. Despite their diversity in social and ethnic backgrounds, the Corps of Discovery became a tightly knit group, capable of independent action without the presence of their commanding officers. Powell, on the other hand, relied on trappers and mountain men who did not like his military manner and discipline. If he had not been traveling through a canyon from which there was little escape, more of his men would probably have deserted. They had to stick together, there was no alternative. At the end, three of them climbed out of the canyon and were never seen alive again.

The best years to survive hardship are those between twenty-five and thirty-five years of age and almost all the men's ages fell within this range. Though there were exceptions: George Shannon was only eighteen and the youngest man on the Corps of Discovery when he joined, and Sacagawea was only about seventeen and was every bit as tough as the men.

Previous experience and training help in responding to an accident or disaster. Lewis was ordered by President Jefferson to seek technical advice in Philadelphia. Dr. Benjamin Rush gave him medical advice—although they only spent one day together—and also provided a list of medications. The winter spent at Camp Dubois in 1803–1804 was very important to the ultimate outcome. This enabled Clark to sort out the strong from the weak, the troublemakers from the reliable, and to develop an esprit de corps unequalled by Pike, Frémont, and Powell, who picked their men quickly and departed within days. The start of their expeditions was the shakedown.

Equipment and supplies were the next most important prerequisite. Frémont's men were well equipped with saddles, bridles, weapons, and mules. Powell had special boats built in Chicago and brought to the Green River. That he picked the wrong design was hardly his fault, as no one knew the best boat for navigating a river with the strength and fury of the Colorado. Lewis and Clark took nothing but the best. Franklin used birch-bark canoes on his first coastal expedition and learned a lesson. The canoes were never meant to be paddled on the sea. They were fragile and the birch bark and pine resin needed to repair them were unavailable. On the next expedition, he had custom boats built in England, sturdy, yet light, that could be paddled or driven by wind and sails.

The logistical supplies taken by the expeditions varied between Lewis and Clark's seven tons to Rae's one-day supply of food. The amount of food taken depended on the duration of the expedition, the chances of obtaining meat from hunting, and the opportunities to buy or barter food from the Indians. Staple foods, such as flour, rice, beans, and coffee, were usually unobtainable en route.

Powell lost nearly half his staples in the first few days when a boat capsized and he had no hope of resupply until he was able to walk out to an Indian Agency. Lewis and Clark took several tons of supplies, including 193 pounds of "portable soup," a gluelike substance made from calves hooves, or other protein, mixed with vegetables. It was an emergency ration that had been developed for the British navy and used for many years by the American navy and army and would keep without refrigeration for many months; their supply, bought in 1803, was not used until the fall of 1805. Liquor was an important part of a soldier's rations and Lewis took thirty gallons of strong wine and 120 gallons of whiskey. In addition to staples, they took salt pork that they ate when game was in short supply.

Of all the expeditions of that era (except, perhaps, Sir John Franklin's huge naval expedition of 1845, looking for the Northwest Passage), we know more about the preparations for the Lewis and Clark expedition than for any other. We know how much food was bought and every item on his shopping list, including more than fifty medications, surgical and dental instruments, clothing, tools, weapons, and even a collapsible boat (which was later abandoned).

Rae also kept a close record of the food he used, and on one occasion, in preparation for spending the winter in the high Arctic—something no white man had ever done before—he shot 63 deer, 5 hares, 32 ptarmigan, and 172 partridges and caught 116 salmon and trout. He then built four snow houses connected by tunnels so that his men would not need to go outside when the temperature was forty-seven degrees below zero.

Next to food, clothing was most important. Rae used Eskimo clothing with warm gloves and mukluks for his feet. Frémont was well supplied with blankets and a rubber groundsheet to put under the blankets and hides for sleeping. But as Pike confessed, he was totally unprepared for the winter rigors of Colorado. There was a reluctance to "go native," but some of the men must have acquired fur hats to keep warm. Lewis, impressed by the beautifully made conical waterproof hats of the Clatsop Indians, bought a supply for his men. But Lewis's men were well supplied with military uniforms, although these undoubtedly wore out and were replaced with handmade buckskin clothes, including moccasins and leggings. While at Fort Clatsop, the men made more than 300 pairs of moccasins for the return journey—roughly ten pairs apiece for a six-month journey.

Nowadays, everyone going into the wilderness takes—or should take—a medical kit. Big, modern expeditions almost always take a doctor. But that was not always so. Rae was a doctor and could take care of wounds and frostbite, and Franklin recruited Richardson as a doctor and naturalist whose devotion to the sick was an inspiration to everyone. Lewis, probably influenced by Jefferson, did not take a doctor. His mother had taught him about many herbal medicines and his experience in the army had familiarized him with rudimentary principles of sanitation.

Apart from arrow and gunshot wounds, animal bites, and limb fractures that an expedition might anticipate, there were many diseases that could just as easily devastate a group. Yet we know nothing about the medical preparations made by Frémont, Pike, and many others, nor how they treated medical problems when they arose. On his second expedition, Pike was accompanied by Dr. John H. Robinson, who was not recruited as a doctor but because he had business to do in Santa Fe. At one time, nine of Pike's fifteen men were suffering from frostbite but were left to treat themselves while Pike and Robinson moved on across the Sangre de Cristo Mountains. Robinson left the expedition early to go to Santa Fe, knowing that sick men had been left behind. This was hardly the action of a conscientious trip physician.

Not all the problems were due to lack of preparation. Pike and Frémont both exceeded their orders, making their problems a combination of poor conditions, bad judgment, and wrong actions. Pike, going up the Mississippi, knew that the northern winter was desperately cold, yet he decided not to return before the rivers froze as he had been ordered to. He had no winter clothes and both he and his men suffered from a decision that left them freezing. When he tried to climb Snow Mountain (Pikes Peak) on his second expedition in "snow middle-deep," he had to turn back because the distance to the summit was too great, "together with the condition of my soldiers, who had only light overalls, no stockings, and were in every way ill provided to endure the inclemency of the weather."

After his first near disaster in the Sierras, Frémont knew how dangerous the mountains were in winter. He knew enough to make sure their moccasins and leggings were in good shape and he bought what he thought was enough corn to feed the mules, but it ran out long before they reached the most difficult part of the trail. About the food for his men, he wrote to Senator Thomas Hart Benton before venturing into the mountains, "We have a small store of provisions for hard times." He had been warned that the snow depth in the San Juans was greater than the locals had ever seen it before, yet he persisted in going ahead, without an "exit strategy."

A few years later, in 1853, he followed the same route, wanting to prove that a winter traverse of the San Juans was possible, although Senator Benton knew that it was impossible to build a railway through the mountains. As he stood near the summit of the pass through the Sangre de Cristos, he recalled the terrible time he had experienced on the previous expedition. On this expedition, only one man died from starvation, exhaustion, and hypothermia. Once again, Frémont came through unscathed, a testament to his endurance, not to his judgment.

The National Outdoor Leadership School, in Lander, Wyoming, classifies the hazards leading to accidents as objective and subjective. The obvious objective hazards are those such as avalanches, deep, fast water, weather, and animal attacks. The subjective hazards are, as they state in their instructions, "an expression of our humanness brought by us into the mountains." Before almost every accident, there is a critical point, undetected at the time, beyond which tragedy is inevitable. These critical moments are often caused by subjective hazards, such as a climbing knot left untied, a piece of equipment lost or left behind, the wrong route chosen, or unrealistic planning. On Frémont's fourth expedition, the critical point is not hard to find. He should have turned south after crossing the Sangre de Cristos when Old Bill Williams wanted to turn around. Old Bill's route would have taken them away from the holy grail of the thirty-eighth parallel, but Frémont could not accept that.

Bligh, in contrast to Frémont, could not chose the conditions under which he was set adrift, nor his companions. Their supplies were limited and the mutineers never imagined they would last across more than 3,000 miles of open ocean. Bligh's navigational skills told him how far they had to go, the compass bearings to follow, and how long the voyage would take. He distributed the food with relentless discipline and refused to listen to entreaties to increase the rations. They arrived at Timor with eleven days' food supply uneaten. History has condemned him for the way he treated his men, but the strictness with which he rationed the food and water brought them safely to land. Some of the men praised him; some wanted to kill him. He faced objective hazards by keeping the subjective hazards to a minimum.

Rae and Hearne were both experienced Arctic travelers who had adopted native skills and knew that by accepting these lifestyles, they were accepting safety. The environments they dealt with were harsh and unforgiving, but being physically tough and mentally well prepared, they succeeded. Matonabee told Hearne that the reason for his lack of success in the first two attempts to reach the Coppermine was that he did not take women. Women carried loads, prepared food, made shelters, and were a comfort at night. Instead of adopting a white man's view that women should not have to do those jobs—in addition, the Hudson's Bay Company frowned on their employees having country wives—he took Matonabee's advice and succeeded.

There are great differences between avoiding accidents and surviving them. John Leach, an English psychologist and student of disasters, has provided a method for analyzing the success of individual survivors. To him, there are four distinct phases in any disaster: preimpact, impact, recoil, and post trauma. Within these phases, many factors influence the course of events.

- ➤ **Preimpact.** Some catastrophes, such as 9/11, hit with terrifying suddenness. There is no chance to escape. In other instances, there may be some warning. Premonitory rumbles allow earthquake victims to seek safety before the buildings collapse. In war, air-raid sirens allowed the people of London to run for the shelters before the bombs fell. Prolonged drought in a Third World country allows months for relief agencies to stockpile food. Joseph warned Pharaoh that tough times were coming.
- ➤ The duration of the **impact** can be sudden, chronic, or somewhere in between. On 9/11, the impact period was terrifyingly brief. One minute, everything was normal; the next minute changed the victims' worlds. But a famine starts slowly and lasts for a long time, slipping seamlessly into the phase of adaptation. The survivor may fight back and cope or sink into physical and psychological dissolution.
- ➤ During the phase of **recoil**, the victims know they have survived, but perhaps their town has been destroyed and a long road of hunger, fatigue, and searching for the injured and dead stretches ahead.
- ➤ **Posttraumatic stress** follows recoil. Individuals suffer from sleeplessness, apathy, a sense of guilt at surviving, loss of motivation, and the constant reliving of the horror of the event. This phase may last only a few days, a week or two, months, or the person may never recover. On a social and communal level, domestic violence, alcoholism, murder, and suicide rates increase.

Some personal attributes increase the chances of survival: an ability to remain calm, to analyze what is happening, and act rationally (10 to 20 percent); and a strong motivation, a sense of purpose or loyalty to an organization, and attachment to loved ones, even pets (the attachment to dogs is stronger than the attachment to cats).

Panic, apathy, denial (how could this happen to me?), inappropriate and irrational hyperactivity, such as dashing around doing things that do not help the situation, or becoming too intent on a simple task decrease the possibility of survival. After the first wild moments of flight from the scene, 75 percent of people are stunned into inactivity. They stand around waiting for a leader to tell them what to do and where to go. Some people do not even flee but remain frozen to the spot, unable to move even though others may be directing them to safety.

For survivors, the intensity of the situation induces a narrowing of perception. Time slows down and the mind focuses on the immediate, even if the immediate objective may be illogical. During a life-threatening fire, a person may be intent on saving a treasured photograph. Even more commonly, the victim falls back on instinctive behavior. For example, they may run when faced with a mountain lion, inviting it to chase them.

Most of the problems faced by our heroes were long-term, but there were acute incidents. Boats and canoes capsized, screaming Indians attacked in the middle of the night, men fell off cliffs, rattlesnakes struck, horses slid to their deaths off treacherous trails, carrying with them valuable supplies and instruments. But these were isolated events where the men sprang into action to save the situation. These moments of heart-stopping excitement were interspersed between weeks and months when hunger, cold, lack of clothes, frostbite, snow blindness, and raw survival were the problems of the day.

As might be expected, panic was not the usual reaction of these men during crises. In a moment of panic, Lewis could, in an instant, take command. He and six men were coming back to the river from an exploratory hike on the prairie and had to climb along a steep place that dropped ninety feet into the river. Lewis crossed first and almost fell, but Private Richard Windsor slipped, then froze halfway across, shouting for help. He was hanging by his fingertips, with his toes barely dug into the soil. In a calm voice, Lewis told him to reach for the knife that hung at his waist and cut a step in the face of the claylike cliff. Lewis encouraged him quietly and, overcoming a moment of panic, Windsor crabwalked to safety.

Toussaint Charbonneau also panicked when the pirogue he was sailing was hit by a gust of wind, nearly capsizing the boat and spilling much of the valuable cargo into the water. Lewis, standing on the bank, was so alarmed that he began to take off his jacket, intending to swim out and rescue the situation. Two people on the pirogue, Pierre Cruzatte and Sacagawea, saved the day. Cruzatte threatened to shoot Charbonneau if he did not do as he was told and Sacagawea calmly reached overboard and began to retrieve valuable papers that were drifting away. That evening, Lewis wrote in his journal, "The Indian woman to whom I ascribe equal fortitude and resolution with any person on board at the time of the accident, caught and preserved most of the light articles which were washed overboard." Sacagawea was one of the 10 to 20 percent calm responders to crisis.

Periods of long-term stress were standard. When food was short, the trail a torment, and the weather buffeted them into submission, the men reacted in different ways. Frémont, writing later to his wife about the horror of Camp Dismal, described that his men's courage "failed fast." And after December 26, when the rescue party had trudged off down the mountain to seek help, morale and discipline blew away in the blizzard. One man wrote in his journal, "If we ever get out of here, it will be a miracle." Frémont was making them carry heavy, useless survey instruments when they would have been better off carrying extra loads of mule meat. Finally, when Frémont pushed ahead, telling the dispirited and exhausted men that they should hurry up, because, by the time they reached Taos, he would be on his way to California, some of the men curled up by the trail, happy to die. The indomitable Godey managed to rescue some of these men later, but many of them never rose again. How did Godey find the strength when others failed? The will to live is hard to define, but, whatever it is, Godey had it. He probably gave himself tasks to do, one doable task at a time: rescue this man, gather the mules, find the food. He had gone through the same privations as all the others, lacked the same food, lost weight and strength, and was perishingly cold. Yet his response was action, not despair and apathy. Frémont had praised him as a man of great courage, and he was right.

The journals of these adventurers do not display a sense of humor. Lewis could see no humor in a man falling overboard or someone becoming lost. He certainly saw no humor in being shot in the buttocks—although, across the void of 200 years, we can see the humor of a nearly blind man peering through the thick willows while searching for a wounded elk, then firing at the buckskin-clad rear end of his commanding officer.

There must have been humor, black and irreverent, but enough to raise a loud guffaw and a ribald riposte. It is inconceivable that around the campfire with stomachs full of buffalo steaks and a ration of grog to raise morale, lewd jokes and thigh-slapping stories did not rise with the smoke to the star-filled sky. Even in the darkest moments, someone will see the funny side, and the person who sees the funny side is more likely to survive than the man who sinks into a deep depression and apathy. The Old Bill cartoons of World War I and the Willie and Joe drawings of World War II mined a vein of enduring hopefulness. Humor is the spice that keeps men cool, that raises a laugh when everyone should be weeping, and that pricks the bubble of fear or unties the knot in a stomach.

Family bonds are even stronger than humor. Most people who survive being cast away at sea, imprisoned in concentration camps, or in solitary confinement recount that the main source of their strength was a determination to get home to loved ones. That is why interrogators falsely tell prisoners that their families are dead or do not care about them. They are demolishing the prisoner's strongest support.

Clark wanted to marry Julia Hancock before he left on the expedition to the Pacific. When they arrived safely in Saint Louis, he did not go to Washington, like Lewis, but went home to court his sweetheart. (His journal did not reflect his intense longing, because it was an official report to be read by the president, not a personal account of his feelings and emotions.) Imprisoned by snows in the San Juan Mountains on Christmas Day, Frémont—as he later recounted to his wife—had tender thoughts of her in the warmth and comfort of their home.

Lewis, on the other hand, did not have a lady friend to dream about but was strongly attached to his mother. He wrote to her from the Mandan Fort, allaying her concerns and assuring her that all would be well. However, he had another prop: his Newfoundland dog, Seaman. On many occasions he described the sterling qualities of his dog and how useful it was as a guard dog or for catching beaver in the river. When some Indians along the Columbia stole it, he sent men to find it, telling them to shoot the Indians if they did not return it immediately. Frémont had a dog with him in the Sierras, a compagnon de voyage, as he described it, but his sense of attachment was quite different. The dog had grown fat from good attention, and when they ran out of food, they ate it. Even though Lewis was often hungry and dog became a favorite dish in his diet, there were never any thoughts of turning Seaman into a casserole.

It has often been said that there are no atheists in a foxhole. In the face of disaster, people turn naturally to prayer. They may not have worshipped for years and neither know any prayers nor how to pray, but faced with imminent death, appeals to God come to mind easily: "Oh, God, get me out of this." Or the prayer may be an attempt to make a deal, as though God bargains like an oriental carpet seller: "God, if you get me out of this, I will never drink whiskey again." Deep religious convictions were the mainstay of African missionary explorers, such as Dr. David Livingstone. Among secular explorers, religion played a varied part. David Thompson, Canada's great explorer and cartographer, was a profoundly religious man and read the Psalms to the voyageurs sitting around the campfire at night. He saw God's work in the magnificent landscape and sought to redeem his companions, without much success. Sir John Franklin held divine service every Sunday, as was the habit in the Royal Navy. Bligh, too, was religious and gave prayers of thanks when they reached land. Lewis and Clark, however, made no mention of God in their journals and did not feel that they were doing God's work, that the beauty of the land was God's handiwork, or that God was protecting or guiding them; their higher power was Thomas Jefferson.

Loyalty to a leader, a regiment, or a family focuses a person's will to survive. The men of these expeditions were loyal to their leaders. The men who were soldiers were loyal to their service or regiment. The more independent trappers and mountain men would do anything to save a friend but sometimes scorned the government. Their loyalty was earned, not bought. Powell was miserly in the way he rewarded his men. In contrast, the penny-pinching masters of the Hudson's Bay Company accused Rae of overpaying his helpers.

During the past twenty-five years, the strengths needed to survive have been studied and analyzed in great detail and a greater understanding has grown of the aftereffects of severe stress. The explorers discussed here knew nothing of post traumatic stress syndrome (PTSD). We know nothing of the nightmares that some of the survivors of these voyages must have suffered, but we know that Hearne never escaped the sight of the dying Eskimo girl clinging to his legs. It is inconceivable that the horrors they saw and experienced were not played and replayed in their minds for many years. But we cannot say, categorically, that any of them suffered from PTSD. Lewis may have come closest, but he had more than enough other psychological problems to account for his tragic end.

11
Marching on Their Stomachs
Food, Famine, and Cannibalism

They that die by famine die by inches.

—Mathew Henry

Napoleon is said to have proclaimed that an army "marches on its stomach" and the adage applies equally to every expedition, whether in the eighteenth century in North America or in a modern attempt to climb Everest or reach the South Pole. Without enough food, strength fades, morale disappears, determination falters, and depression takes over. The success of the expedition is in jeopardy.

Samuel Hearne joined the Royal Navy as a midshipman when he was only twelve years old and was classed as a "young gentleman." This entitled him to walk on the quarterdeck, a privilege granted only to officers and potential officers, but it did not protect him from the rigors of life below deck in the bowels of the ship: the smells, the cramped quarters, the bantering and hazing by the other midshipmen, and the terrible food.

Food in the Royal Navy in the eighteenth and nineteenth centuries would nowadays be regarded as inedible. Good captains, such as James Cook and Samuel Hood, tried hard to maintain clean ships and put into port often to resupply with fresh food. Even the notorious William Bligh, who had served under Cook and followed his philosophies, tried to obtain fresh food whenever possible. His aim on the journey to the South Pacific was to return without losing a single man to scurvy.

The conditions for the officers in most navies were tolerable, but the sailors and midshipmen lived in dank, dark, stinky conditions. Day after day, a seaman's meal might consist of salt pork, stale and maggot-ridden cheese, washed down with ill-tasting beer. Sir Joseph Banks described the ship biscuit, a rock-hard slab that often had to be soaked in beer to make it soft enough to chew, as "a surprisingly lively insect menagerie."

After a ship had been at sea for some weeks, the bread and meat were full of maggots. Men caught rats and sold them to their mates for five pence each and the beer or rum, on which they depended for a daily shot of relief, began to taste of sewage. The pork was so bad that even boiling it in alcohol could not improve its taste. Fresh food and vegetables lasted for a short time after leaving port, but on a long voyage soon ran out. Sauerkraut was a poor substitute for fresh fruit.

The variety of food eaten by explorers was wide and exotic, more often based on what was available than what was planned. On a long expedition by land, it was obviously impossible to carry enough food for the whole trip. The cooks relied on hunters, either members of the expedition or Indians hired to do the job. Or they bought or bartered for food from the local population. John Rae, an expert shot, preferred to hunt for his group. Meriwether Lewis and William Clark relied on their hunters, especially George Drouillard. Without his hunting skills, the men would have existed on a much skimpier diet than they did. Indian hunters did not prepare for the starvation that would inevitably succeed a period of plenty. Hearne, on his second attempt to reach the Coppermine River, described how the Indians killed several deer and beaver and spent several days in "feasting and gluttony," then, because they hadn't saved any of the meat, were within a short time "in as great distress for provisions as ever."

Naval expeditions were able to take large supplies of food, but also relied on being able to land in ports and buy food. If the landing place was as fruitful and exotic as Tahiti, large quantities of food were readily available. And as vegetables were usually available, scurvy could be cured or forestalled. After 1818, canned foods became available for the Royal Navy and tinned vegetables were a welcome addition to the diet.

The first Portuguese explorers rounding the Cape of Good Hope to India found that by the time they reached the Cape, many of the sailors had scurvy. But fresh fruit obtained from the local population cured them rapidly. Those explorers were the first to discover that a voyage of more than 100 days without touching land and obtaining fresh fruit would always result in an outbreak of scurvy. We now know that their diets were totally deficient in Vitamin C.

When Bligh and his eighteen men were cast adrift in the small boat in which they successfully reached Timor, more than 3,000 miles away, they were allowed to take with them 150 pounds of bread, 32 pounds of pork divided into 16 pieces, 6 quarts of rum, 6 bottles of wine, 28 gallons of water, and 4 small casks for collecting water. Bligh rationed the men to one-twenty-fifth of a pound of bread and a quarter pint of water every day. Fortunately, they encountered heavy rainstorms and collected enough water so that they did not die from dehydration. Toward the end of their voyage, they caught birds, divided up the meat, and gave the blood to the sickest men to strengthen them. When the conditions were really bad and morale was low, Bligh would allow the men a small sip of rum or wine. They often implored Bligh to give them more food, but he insisted on sticking to the minuscule rations he had calculated would last until they reached their destination. When they arrived in Timor, they still had an eleven-day supply of food left.

There were times on that terrible trip when they had plenty of food. On the islands of the Great Barrier Reef, they harvested oysters from the rocks and caught birds. One man slipped away from the group and, in a fit of gross greed, caught and ate nine boobies, ripping their flesh apart and stuffing it into his mouth without sharing any with his mates. He paid for his greed with a violent bellyache.

Bligh's men did not get scurvy because the voyage lasted only forty-eight days and they had just come from Tahiti where their diet was full of Vitamin C. The general condition of the men, however, was beyond belief. Bligh described their appearance: "Our bodies were nothing but skin and bones, our limbs were full of sores, and we were clothed in rags. ... The people of Timor beheld us with a mixture of horror, surprise and pity."

John Wesley Powell, who made a water voyage of a different nature, down the Grand Canyon, traveled with a small group of men skilled enough to supply them with meat, had it been available. But the bottom of the canyon was barren of animals and the few sheep they saw high on the walls quickly scampered out of range of their rifles. They lost food when their boats sank and only had three days' supply remaining when the river burst out of the canyon and they found a settlement of Mormons who fed them generously. They, too, had traveled less than 100 days and thus were not in danger of getting scurvy.

The diet of ordinary people in eighteenth-century America was simple, monotonous, but generally nutritious. People who lived in the country on farms grew much of their food. Gourmet meals were for the rich and aristocratic. The huge multicourse feasts that we imagine, with the diners throwing roasted joints of meat over their shoulders to long-legged, shaggy hunting dogs lurking in the background, were not the regular diet of the men who went on these expeditions. So it is not surprising that they tolerated and survived on diets that modern adventurers would scorn.

Hearne was inured to terrible food long before he joined the Hudson's Bay Company. On the journeys through the Barrens, he experienced the same life as the Indians, one of food aplenty alternating with starvation. The Indians thought that white men could not withstand what was to them a normal life, but the explorers of the fur companies proved that they could not only survive, but were capable of withstanding prolonged hardships. Hearne once lived for several days on chewing tobacco and water while crouched under a leather tent slung over his back, because there were no trees for tent poles. Later, he survived for seven days on cranberries, scraps of leather, and burned bones. The worms and warbles extracted from beneath the skin of dead caribou were the one type of food Indians ate that revolted Hearne. "They are always eaten raw and alive, out of the skin; and are said, by those who like them, to be as fine as gooseberries. But the very idea of eating such things ... was quite sufficient to give me an unalterable disgust to such a repast."

Eating food that was not a normal part of their diet was common for most of the explorers. The men of the Lewis and Clark expedition were strictly meat lovers. After they had crossed through the Rockies, they were in a culture that existed on fish, particularly salmon. Nowadays, we would think "so what was wrong with that?" But the way the salmon was dried and pounded into cakes did not appeal to the men. They had to find additional food and began to eat dogs. The Indian camps were full of dogs, and during their time west of the mountains, the men on the expedition ate more than 190. Clark could not bring himself to eat them, but Lewis and most of the men thought them a tasty addition to their diet. The one dog they would never have eaten was Lewis's Newfoundland, Seaman. On another occasion, they ate whale meat and blubber from a whale that washed up on a beach near Fort Clatsop. Lewis described the taste as somewhere between that of beaver and dog—not a description that resonates with our modern tastes.

Survival sometimes depended more on Mother Nature than on planning. When an expedition passed through an area with ample game, the men could eat like kings. As the Lewis and Clark expedition passed through the Great Plains in the summers of 1804 and 1805, they were surrounded by swarming herds of game. Joseph Fields killed the first buffalo on August 23, 1804, and within a few days, they were encountering thousands more. Hunting became a matter of picking out the choice animals. Lewis recorded in his journal that they were particular to kill only what they needed—but what they needed was considerable. The hunters brought in thirty-two deer, twelve elk, and one buffalo after one hunt—barely enough for three weeks.

Lewis calculated that they needed one buffalo and four deer or a deer and an elk to supply the group for twenty-four hours. At times, the men were eating up to nine pounds of meat a day. If the hunters were very successful, the meat that they could not eat at once was sun-dried and preserved for later use as jerky. Even though there seemed to be an endless supply of meat, they could not tell when the buffalo might migrate and leave them searching the Plains in vain. If they had made their journey in 1800 instead of from 1804 to 1805, they would have traveled during a year of intense drought. The Plains would have been dry, the huge herds of bison might have moved on, and there might have been no game to shoot.

Buffalo, deer, and antelope were not the only sources of meat. At times, they ate horse, badger, dog, bighorn sheep, whale, salmon—fresh, dried, and pounded into cakes—and a wide variety of other fish, including trout and bass. (See table for numbers of animals killed.)

Soldiers in the American army were entitled to a daily ration of one pound of beef or the equivalent amount of pork or fish. When the Corps of Discovery was going up the Missouri in the summer of 1804, the men were eating a ration far greater than that ordained by Congress. They were not receiving the milk and bread, peas, beans, and beer they were supposed to receive, but the substitute diet, which included a gill of whiskey from time to time, was better than anything they would have received on a regular assignment back in Saint Louis.

During the crossing of the Rockies, their rations were barely enough to keep them going. The horses they killed and ate in emergencies were their salvation. The portable soup, of which they took 193 pounds, was a standard emergency food invented in the British navy during the eighteenth century and was also used in the American army and navy. Its preparation varied, but its base was always protein, such as beef or pigs' trotters, to which was added vegetables, spices, and salt. After the ingredients had been boiled, the liquid was poured into a mold. The resulting greasy blocks could be kept in airtight containers for months and years. The blocks were turned into soup by adding water and boiling the mixture. It was barely edible, but it probably tasted better, and was certainly more nutritious, than eating fire-singed moccasins and trousers.

Number of animals killed

Number of animals killed for food on the Lewis and Clark expedition. Bear meat was eaten and bear fat was used as oil.

Animals	Number killed	Animals	Number killed
Deer	1,000	Beavers	113
Elk	375	Otters	16
Bison	227	Geese	104
Pronghorn	62	Ducks	45
Bighorn sheep	35	Turkeys	9
Black bears	23	Grouse	45
Grizzly bears	43	Dogs	193
Horses	19		

Perhaps Lewis and Clark did not take pemmican, the standard fare of the voyageurs, because it was made far from their route by the Indians who lived along the Assiniboine River. It was a high-calorie, nutritious food made from pounded buffalo meat, tallow, and berries. The recipe for a ninety-pound bag included the meat from one buffalo and sixteen pounds of berries. Although it sounds better to eat than portable soup, H. M. Robinson, writing in his reminiscences, *The Great Fur Land*, described it in less than inviting terms: "Take the scrapings from the driest outside corner of a very stale piece of cold roast beef, add to it lumps of rancid fat, then garnish all with long human hairs and short hairs of dogs and oxen and you have a fair imitation of common pemmican."

The diet that Zebulon Montgomery Pike's men ate on the trip up the Mississippi is a good example of the wide variety of animals eaten by these explorers. Among the many foods recorded in Pike's journal were small fish, catfish, perch, deer, bison, bears, pigeons, ducks, geese, swans, prairie hens, pheasants, turkeys, raccoons, porcupines, and wild oats and rice obtained from the Indians. Wolves and mink were also killed, but there is nothing to suggest they were eaten. Wolves were killed because they were thought to

Tripe de Roches

When travelers in the Arctic ran out of food, they sometimes had to resort to eating *tripe de roches*, the tripe of the rocks. This is a lichen (*Umbilicaria dilleni*) that, in wet weather, is a jade green, flat plant attached to trees and rocks. In dry weather as in the winter, when it mostly had to be eaten, it becomes a dry, shriveled-up excrescence that can be found on trees above the snow level, scraped off, and boiled in water. The result is a bitter, gelatinous soup with limited nutritional value that can assuage the pangs of hunger. Some people cannot tolerate it because it causes abdominal cramps and diarrhea.

On John Franklin's disastrous expedition up the Coppermine in 1821, *tripe de roches* became an essential part of their diet when all their food was finished and there were no caribou to hunt.

Labrador tea, brewed from a shrub that grows widely across the Canadian north, was a favorite drink of explorers and a tasty substitute for tripe. It was easily made and, although it was not nutritious, it satisfied the need for a hot drink.

be dangerous, and mink were killed for their fur. Frequently during the winter months, the men went for two or three days without food and then were fortunate to shoot several deer. They were never far from a trading post or an Indian encampment and they would only have starved if they had become incapable of traveling because of injury or extreme weather.

For all of Pike's renowned skill as a marksman, his accounts of trying to shoot buffalo and deer are full of records of wounded animals that got away. He ascribed his failures to the small size of the balls they shot, which may well have been true. The range and power of the muskets available to them was not great and the successful hunter had to be close to his quarry to be assured of a lethal shot.

During Pike's journey up the Arkansas River, they encountered worse conditions and were farther from help than on the first expedition. Often they were without food, but somehow, at the last minute, Pike and Dr. John H. Robinson managed to shoot deer or a buffalo.

There were, of course, also some foods that tasted good. Perhaps the most famous was Toussaint Charbonneau's *boudin blanc*, or white pudding. The Scots eat "mealie puddin'" and haggis, and Charbonneau's white pudding was not dissimilar. A section of the large bowel of a buffalo, used as a sausage skin, was filled with chopped meat, flour, suet, and pepper and salt to taste. The finished delicacy, tied at both ends, was "then baptized in the Missouri with two dips and a flirt, and bobbed into the kettle." It was then fried in bear fat and could assuage the appetite of the hungriest traveler.

Dr. Elaine Nelson McIntosh, a nutritionist, analyzed the caloric, mineral, and vitamin values of the Corp of Discovery's diet. She found that, for the most part, their diet was adequate, except for the period during October 1805 when they were struggling through the Rockies. The intake of protein, carbohydrate, and fat, the basic building blocks of nutrition, were sufficient. Their intake of minerals was marginally adequate, and their diet lacked several vitamins. Although her research indicated a poor intake of Vitamin C, there was no evidence that the men were clinically scorbutic. No particular precautions were taken to ensure that they did not develop scurvy. It was well known that fresh food prevented scurvy and much of the meat they ate barely had time to cool before it was prepared for the pot. Although boiling and roasting destroy Vitamin C, their meat was probably eaten rare rather than well done. The amounts of Vitamin C obviously varied between the fruits and animal meats. Vitamin C content of bison meat is negligible, so they cannot have gained protection against scurvy from that source. But even horse meat contains some Vitamin C, and taken together the fruits and meats they ate contained enough vitamin C to prevent scurvy.

When the men embarked from the Wood River camp early in 1804, they may have been suffering from diets barely adequate in some mineral and vitamin elements because they ate almost no milk, eggs, or vegetables. But whatever deficiencies occurred did not seem to have reduced their capacity for intense physical stress.

Foods that could be kept for prolonged periods of time, such as flour, salt pork, beans, and coffee, were the staples that expeditions bought before they set out. But some explorers were so confident in their hunting skills that they did not want to be burdened with heavy supplies. John Rae set out on a 1,000-mile journey that he knew would take many weeks with only enough food for a day and a half. Few men were that self-sufficient and that self-assured. He did not starve, because he had learned to live off the land. In contrast, John Franklin embarked up the Coppermine on his second expedition with equally reduced supplies, but that was because of poor planning; it was not intentional.

If there is one lesson to be learned from the adventures of these men, it is that determination to live and overcome difficulties was more important than diet. This is a lesson as modern as it is ancient. The concentration camp victims of World War II often survived because they would not let the conditions destroy them. They would search for scraps of food, barter for tiny fragments, and do anything to stay alive. The explorers were driven by the same motives and power.

Lack of water kills much faster than lack of food. There is a saying that you can survive three minutes without oxygen, three days without water, and three weeks without food. In the great southwestern desert, the lack of water quickly became a deadly problem. When Jedediah Smith made his amazing trips between the Great Salt Lake and California, he and his companions came close to dying from lack of water. In 1827, returning from California, accompanied by two men, seven horses, and two mules, the severity of the journey killed five of the horses and one of the mules. Near what is now the Utah-Nevada border, they could not find water. Smith climbed a hill to scope out the landscape. "When I came down I durst not tell my men of the desperate prospect ahead but framed my story so as to discourage them as little as possible." They were "worn down with hunger and fatigue and burning thirst increased by the blazing sands: it was almost insupportable." They dug holes in the sand to find a cooler resting place, and when they saw some mourning doves, they knew that water would be only two or three miles away. But one man, Robert Evans, could go no farther. "We left him with the hope that we might get relief and return in time to save his life." Three miles farther on, they found water. Smith took four or five quarts back to Evans who drank it all and asked Smith why he had not brought more! Later, Smith wrote, "I have at different times suffered the extremes of hunger and thirst. Hard as it is to bear the gnawings of hunger yet it is light compared to the agony of burning thirst."

The explorers of the eighteenth and nineteenth centuries faced many threats, but there was one constant danger that that even the most careful planning could not totally eliminate: starvation hung like a specter over all the expeditions, whether they were by land or by sea. The Native Americans lived one drought, one crop failure, one hard winter away from starvation. Expeditions passing across the land moved under the same threat. Being white and sometimes unwilling to understand or accept Indian culture added to their risks.

Since earliest recorded history, starvation has left a trail of death and misery on every continent and in every era. Major famines occurred 1,800 times in 2,000 years of Chinese history. And in 2004, 5 million children were said to have died from starvation worldwide. The statistics are mind-numbing. In 1943, in the middle of World War II, the province of Bengal in India was hit by a famine that killed more than 2 million people. The rice harvest had failed and the Japanese were knocking on their backdoor. In the government report of the famine, Lieutenant Colonel K. S. Fitch of the Indian Medical Service wrote a description of a starving man that cannot be bettered. "Oblivious of his surroundings and more animal than human, emaciated, dry lips drawn back over decayed and septic teeth, coated tongue, uttering unhuman cries, filthy and scabrous, he represented the nadir of human misery and the epitome of famine."

The stages and symptoms of starvation have been clearly described hundreds of times and all bear a striking resemblance to each other. Whether the victims are prisoners of war, civilians caught in a natural disaster, or explorers stranded far from help, they all go through the same stages and experience the same misery.

In the mid-1940s, Dr. Ancel Keys and his associates at the University of Minnesota, anticipating that many Europeans and prisoners would be starving when World War II ended, embarked on a controlled study of the effects of a severely reduced diet. They wanted to find out scientifically what happens when the body is deprived of food and also what would be the best method to treat victims of starvation. The thirty-six hardy men who volunteered for the study were conscientious objectors who regarded participation as their national service. They received a "semistarvation" diet of 1,570 calories per day for six months. Although the diet was considered semistarvation, the volunteers lost 25 percent of their body weight over the experimental period of six months. There were subtle changes in their behavior. They became preoccupied with food and thoughts of food. Some of them collected cooking pots and pans and were later surprised at the reasons for doing this. There was an increase in the demand for spices and salt and they drank coffee and tea in quantities far beyond their normal habits. Some of the men had to be limited to nine cups of coffee a day. They found other ways to assuage their hunger, such as chewing up to forty packets of gum per day.

Blood samples were taken frequently and they were given psychological tests during and after the period of starvation. This period was followed by three months of rehabilitation and increased diet, during which some of the men ate 5,000 to 6,000 calories per day in splurges of binge eating—almost as much as the men ate during some stages of the Lewis and Clark expedition.

They exercised during the experiment, but their energy expenditure could not compare with that of any of the explorers who kept going while they were starving, accelerating their weight loss. The volunteers' fat and muscles wasted away, their skin became dry and scaly, and their hair fell out. Their defenses against infection were reduced and they became particularly sensitive to respiratory infections.

During the period of starvation, there was a slowing down of physiological functions. The basal metabolic rate (the metabolic rate required to maintain essential bodily functions) decreased, as though the body was shutting down to decrease the drain on its resources. During rehabilitation, the basal metabolic rate increased. The physical changes, apart

Starvation

"First there was loss of natural feeling of well-being. A growing feeling of hunger followed and gradually increased in intensity until, after about three weeks, the whole thought of the POW was concentrated on his food. His chief concern was how long it was to the next meal, and by what means he could supplement his meager rations. This insistent feeling of hunger remained after years of a low diet. It appeared even to increase with time, with the result that the half starved man would go to the greatest ingenuity and dishonesty to obtain small amounts of extra nourishment. Only when death was imminent did the desire for food slowly vanish and the grossly emaciated prisoner become resigned to his fate, of which he seemed to be aware some weeks before it happened. ... None of the other hardships suffered by fighting men observed by me brought about such rapid or complete degeneration of character as starvation."

—Description of the stages of starvation in prisoners
of war in World War II by Dr G. B. Leyton,
who was himself a prisoner.

from the obvious weight loss, included a reduction in the ability of the heart to pump blood, lowered blood pressure, sensitivity to cold, increased urination, and, in some, edema and puffiness of the skin due to the retention of water.

The psychological changes in the volunteers were remarkably the same as those observed in natural starvation: apathy, increased irritability, loss of interest and difficulty in concentrating on tasks, and constant thoughts about food. Their intellect did not suffer, but they became irritable, bad-tempered, and lost their libido. Some of the men became seriously depressed and one volunteer cut off three fingers during a fit of reactive depression. They became more demanding, complaining about the heat of the food they were served, and they were torn between gulping down their food as quickly as possible or dawdling over the meal, stretching out the pleasure as long as possible. They obtained pleasure vicariously from watching others eat and even the smell of food brought intense pleasure. Forty percent of the men said that after the experiment was finished, they would consider a profession that involved food. Some of the men, although they were constrained by their commitment to the program, lost control. One man, while visiting a supermarket, suddenly could not control his hunger and ate sacks of cookies, popcorn, and bananas.

The observations made in these and other controlled studies only put numbers and scientific measurements to what was already known by reading the pages of history. The results, however, do enable us to understand better the behavior of victims in what has been called natural starvation.

In addition to the physiologic changes, nutritional deficits, especially vitamin deficiencies, have a devastating effect on the victim's health. During World War II, American prisoners of the Japanese, languishing for years on a minimal diet, developed profound and unusual vitamin deficiencies. Swelling of the limbs, rashes, and the loss of eyesight and hearing were problems that the doctors in the camps had never seen before. Some men became permanently blind. Beriberi, from the lack of vitamin B, was the most frequent problem, causing burning, swollen feet so painful that the victim could not walk on them.

The world has not lacked for examples of starvation. We have all become used to seeing the pictures of pathetic, huge-eyed, little children from Africa with potbellies and reddish hair suffering from kwashiorkor, a disease caused by prolonged starvation and protein deficiency. During World War II, the Germans decided that some populations were not worthy of life and intentionally starved them to death, giving them a diet of thin potato soup and water with a daily value of 800 to 1,000 calories. The recipients of this vicious regimen died within three months. The experience of others—sailors stranded in lifeboats, explorers lost and out of food, native populations faced with failed crops and drought—have all come to the same conclusion: extreme starvation kills humans in eight to twelve weeks.

Looking back at the experiences of explorers such as Hearne, Franklin, and Pike (and the Indians they met), it is possible to recognize the same patterns of behavior and desire as those found more than 100 years later in the Minnesota volunteers.

Lewis and Clark nearly starved while going west through the Bitterroot Mountains in the fall of 1805. While the weather conditions were not unusual in that area and for that time of year, the struggle through the mountains tested the Corps of Discovery—not forgetting Sacagawea and her eight-month-old infant, Baptiste—to the limits of their strength. The exertion required to push and climb their way through the forests and over the mountains greatly increased demands for energy and food. On the Plains, the men had been eating up to nine pounds of meat a day. While they were waiting with the Shoshones, their intake was reduced, but so were the demands on their energy, because they were not hauling canoes upstream or carrying heavy loads.

When they started through the mountains, their whole metabolic situation changed. There were no large animals to shoot, just a few blue grouse. But they had one resource to use when the situation became bad: horses. They killed three colts as each need arose, and after one meal, Lewis wrote, "We all suped (sic) heartily ... and thought it a fine meal." Technically, they were almost certainly in negative metabolic balance, expending more energy than they took in, but the situation did not continue long enough for them starve.

Thirty-five years earlier, Hearne learned how to survive in the another bleak environment, the Barrens of northern Canada. The Cree and Chipewyan Indians who roamed the millions of square miles to the west of the Hudson Bay lived on the knife-edge of survival, depending on the fickle migratory habits of the caribou for food, clothes, and shelter. Most of them viewed the white men with contempt: they were considered soft creatures, dependant on supplies brought in on ships and unable, or unwilling, to venture far beyond their forts.

Hearne, through determination, self-reliance, and acquired wilderness skills, was one of a handful of white men to prove them wrong. As Hearne traveled with his Indian companions, he suffered the same privations and enjoyed the same occasional feasts. They lived an all-or-nothing existence. The Indians occasionally cached food, if they knew they would be returning along the same route, but it was more common to endure days of starvation alternating with days of plenty. Sometimes Hearne subsisted only on tobacco juice and snowmelt. Then when caribou were killed, they all gorged themselves to the point of incapacity and illness. Hearne regarded this behavior as evidence of a lack of self-control and planning for the future, but overeating is a natural reaction to starvation and was not a weakness peculiar to the Indians. The sailor on Bligh's boat who secretly killed and ate nine booby birds by himself was only following an uncontrollable behavior pattern.

During the winter of 1806–1807, Pike and his men, on their journey through Colorado, were frequently without food for several days. The cumulative effect of those days of want—although they were interspersed with occasional days of plenty—was a progressive weakening of the whole party. Not only did the men become weak, but the horses did as well. A time was reached when neither horses nor men could go any farther.

On January 9, 1807, while staying at their campsite near modern-day Pueblo, Colorado, Pike wrote, "I felt at a considerable loss how to proceed, as any idea of service at that time from my horses was entirely preposterous." He decided to cross the Sangre de Cristo Mountains on foot, and he was fortunate to kill several deer before they left, leaving behind two men to guard the small fort. The remaining thirteen men set out on January 14, each carrying seventy pounds. Within three days, there were no more deer to be found, and nine of the men had frostbitten feet. January 19: "By this time I was become extremely weak and faint, being the fourth day since we received sustenance, the whole of which time we were marching hard, and the last night had scarcely closed our eyes to sleep. ... We were then inclining our course to a point of wood, determined to remain absent and die by ourselves rather than return to our camp and behold the misery of our poor companions."

They were lucky enough to shoot three buffalo, changed their minds about giving up, and returned to camp, where they were happily received by some very hungry men. Three days later, they left again, taking only enough food for one meal, leaving the rest for those who could not travel because of frostbite. The next day: "Again without victuals ... we lay down and strove to dissipate the ideas of hunger and our misery by the thoughts of our far distant homes and relatives."

One man, John Brown, expressed his opinion loudly: "It was more than human nature could bear." Pike ignored the mutinous remark, realizing that "he could not endure fasting. We dragged our emaciated limbs along." Fortune smiled again. The doctor shot a buffalo and they "feasted sumptuously." Pike thanked the men for their fortitude but roundly upbraided the man who had complained. He threatened him with instant death if he should make a similar complaint again.

Pike's outburst was perhaps a justifiable response to maintain discipline in a situation that could easily have fallen apart, but it is also the typically irritable reaction of a starving man. They were all exhausted, ill-clad, cold, and hungry. In addition, Pike had the responsibilities of leadership. And to cap it all, he did not know where he was! On January 25, he wrote, "I determined never again to march with so little provision on hand; for had the storm continued one day longer ... we should have become so weak as not to be able to hunt, and of course, have perished." They continued on, amazingly, for fourteen miles through snow three feet deep until they crossed the Continental Divide, found westward-flowing streams, and came to the edge of the Great Sand Dunes. Within a couple of weeks, Pike was a prisoner of the Spanish and his days of privation were at an end. The men who had been left behind were rescued later.

Cannibalism is the final and most ghastly conclusion to starvation, but it has occurred with surprising constancy from ancient to modern times. Sitting quietly in nice warm homes, the thought of cannibalism is inconceivable. But an American relief worker in Russia after the World War I reported, "To the peasant crazed with hunger, who had come to eating the flesh of animals dug up from the ground, the practice of eating human flesh was not such a long step." Cannibalism may save the survivors, but the psychological and social effects are deep and long lasting: guilt, remorse, horror, and social condemnation.

In the animal world, cannibalism is common. Male bears eat cubs they can catch. Male lions eat the young of other prides. Even among primates, chimpanzees have been known to eat their own species. The big difference between this type of cannibalism and that in humans is that, for the most part, humans resort to cannibalism as a last resort, whereas animals are usually catching readily available food or sometimes trying to gain dominance over a group. (This argument does not take into account those human tribes that have, until very recent times, practiced cannibalism of their vanquished enemies in ritual ceremonies.)

During famines, and among castaways at sea, survivors have often resorted to cannibalism. Murder leading to cannibalism is more rare, although not unknown. For centuries, shipwrecked sailors, floating for weeks in the middle of an ocean, resorted to this ghastly hope for survival. In 1820, the whaling ship *Essex* was hit and sunk in the Pacific by a huge, angry sperm whale. The graphic and tragic aftermath has been brilliantly described in Nathaniel Philbrick's book *In the Heart of the Sea*. The survivors, in two boats, sailed for more than sixty days, emaciated from starvation, hypothermic, with dwindling supplies of food, and so weak they could barely steer the boats. As starving men do, they dreamed of lavish meals. During one night, the boats separated. Each boat was alone, a speck, adrift on the sea. When the first man in one of the boats died from dehydration and starvation, the ten survivors reluctantly decided to turn to cannibalism. Another man died and his body also became sustenance. Then they began to speak of sacrificial death. Lots were picked and men were chosen to die. Eventually, both boats were rescued by passing ships off the coast of Chile. One man who had picked a fatal lot was saved by the appearance of the ship that rescued them but was so traumatized he was insane to the end of his days. But in the other boat, a young man, eighteen years old, was chosen by lot to die. He accepted his fate with resignation, was shot to death and eaten.

Cannibalism was, apparently, not unknown among the mountain men. They were frequently caught in the middle of winter far from civilization with no hope of resupply, other than through the barrel of a rifle or in the wire loop of a snare. During Frémont's fourth expedition through the mountains of southern Colorado, the last survivors of a group trying to find help almost certainly ate the remains of a comrade who had died from starvation. In similar situations, men sometimes volunteered to be killed so that their friends could live. There are no records that these generous, self-sacrificial offers were ever accepted. But on Frémont's fifth expedition, after they had passed through the San Juan Mountains and one man had died of starvation and hypothermia, Frémont called the men together and made them promise that they would never indulge in cannibalism. He must have had painful memories that he was not willing to admit to in writing, for he never mentioned the suspicion of cannibalism in the letters to his wife.

Sometimes there was no game to shoot, no dogs to eat. During the return from Franklin's expedition down the Coppermine River and along the coast, everyone starved; eleven men died. They had been reduced to eating caribou bones, moccasins, and trousers. Men became so weak they could walk no farther. One member of the expedition, an Iroquois hunter, fell behind, saying he wanted to help a dying man, and then reappeared with meat that he claimed was from a caribou killed by a wolf. The other men thought that the meat tasted strange and did not believe him. Dr. John Richardson suspected the Indian of cannibalism, and after waiting in fear for an attack, pulled out his pistol, and executed him summarily. In the final report of the expedition, there was little reference to this terrible event, but Richardson referred to "things which must not be known."

Franklin—by then Sir John Franklin—was later appointed commanding officer of the most expensive and best-equipped expedition mounted by the Royal Navy to find the Northwest Passage. The expedition, which left England in 1845, was supplied with enough food for three years for 129 men. (Franklin thought that on reduced rations the food could have lasted for five years.) Every comfort had been thought of: thousands of pounds of flour, wine and liquor, canned meat soup and vegetables, and large quantities of lemon juice to stave off scurvy. Despite these generous supplies, this expedition was even more disastrous than Franklin's first venture up the Mackenzie River: not a single man survived. Sir John died a natural death while the ships were fast bound in the ice. Others lived as long as two years and died from a combination of diseases and starvation during a doomed attempt to escape south. The Eskimo reported to Rae that white men, hauling a boat, had been seen on a distant island dropping down dead while they marched. They had relics that clearly came from members of Franklin's expedition. But worst of all, they told Rae that there were clear signs of cannibalism. When Rae returned to England, recounted these tales, and showed the relics, there was no doubt that the men had died, but the public refused to believe the story about cannibalism. British sailors did not eat each other, especially officers of the upper social classes. Definitive proof of cannibalism had to await Beattie's investigative expedition in 1981.

Cannibalism is the worst choice facing starving people, a choice that haunts the survivors for the rest of their days, but a choice that has been made for centuries. One man dies and becomes sustenance for the others. The survivors gain strength and there is one less mouth to feed. Philbrick coined the phrase that perfectly describes this terrible dilemma as the "cruel mathematics of survival."

12

Pox and Poisons

Disease, Injuries, Medicines, and Morale

Life is the set of functions which ward off death.

—*Marie-Françoise-Xavier Bichat*
(1771–1820), French surgeon

Medicine in the early years of the nineteenth century was going through dramatic changes. For centuries, the teachings of Hippocrates and Galen had governed the practice of medicine in Europe. But gradually, over the years, with the discovery of the circulation, the invention of the microscope, and slowly changing ideas on the nature and causes of diseases, medical knowledge was being built, like a house, piece by piece, theory by theory. By 1800, there was still an enormous gap between medical knowledge and theory and the ability to treat and heal. Doctors were like hunters going into the field and shooting blanks. A few medications could be used specifically—cinchona for malaria, mercury for syphilis, colchicum for gout—but most therapeutic agents were useless. Most of them did no harm, but some, such as mercury, could be fatal.

The Pilgrims brought no doctors, so they improvised treatments and turned to the Indians for ideas. The Indians used many herbs, but the logic behind the herbs they used had as little scientific basis as that behind the colonists' medications. The Indians used yellow plants to treat jaundice, red plants to treat diseases of the blood, and curly, twisted plants to treat snakebite. There was a theory among the colonists that diseases were best cured by the plants that occurred where the disease occurred. American diseases, therefore, required American cures. The vast array of new plants that the colonists saw provided them with infinite possibilities for new medications. Sassafras, which was unknown in Europe, became one of the most widely prescribed herbs as a diuretic, a diaphoretic (sweat-inducing agent), and cure for scurvy and venereal diseases. It was also a major export from Virginia, second only to tobacco.

Most doctors acquired their knowledge by training as apprentices to other doctors. At first, the aspiring physician would live with his mentor and be given simple tasks. Slowly, by visiting the patient's homes, making up the "simples" in the doctor's kitchen, helping with bleeding, setting bones, and lancing boils, the young man—for there no women physicians—gained enough skill to set up his own shingle and embark on his own practice. A few doctors who could afford the expense went to Europe and the prime place to visit was the University of Edinburgh in Scotland. Dr. Benjamin Rush, who at the request of President Thomas Jefferson advised Meriwether Lewis, studied in Edinburgh, where he gained his doctorate, and later helped found the Pennsylvania College (now the University of Pennsylvania). Of the three doctors who attended George Washington during his final illness, two had studied in Edinburgh, and Edinburgh graduates contributed to the first medical schools in the United States. In Edinburgh, they learned the principles of "animal economy" propounded by William Cullen: nervous power controlled health and disease; diseases were either "sthenic" or "asthenic"—sthenic diseases resulted from overexcitation of the nervous system, and asthenic diseases from understimulation.

During the end of the eighteenth century and into the first half of the nineteenth, autopsy examination of diseased bodies and microscopic examination of tissues enabled physicians such as Rudolf Virchow in Vienna to distinguish between different diseases and identify causes of death. "Noxious humors" and other vague concepts as causes of disease disappeared. The foundations of modern medicine were being born.

Physicians

President Thomas Jefferson had a poor opinion of physicians. In 1807, one year after the return of the Lewis and Clark expedition, he wrote, "One of the most successful physicians I have ever known, has assured me, that he used more bread pills, drops of colored water, & powders of hickory ashes, than all other medicines put together. ... I have lived myself to see the disciples of Hoffman, Boerhaave, Stahl, Cullen, Brown, succeed one another like the shifting figures of a magic lantern, & their fancies, like the dresses of the annual doll babies from Paris, becoming, from their novelty, the vogue of the day, and yielding to the next novelty with ephemeral favor. The patient, treated on the fashionable theory, sometimes gets well in spite of the medicine."

Fevers were common, but their causes could only be classified in general categories. Some diseases, such as syphilis, were known to be "contagious": passed from person to person. Others were "infectious": they were passed from person to person but did not require contact between the victims. The epidemic of yellow fever in Philadelphia in 1793 and the yearly outbreaks of malaria in the spring made it clear that there were different forms of agues, but most of them were ascribed to bad air (malaria) or effluvia from the marshes and swamps (miasmas). Malarial ague, cured by Peruvian bark (quinine), was the only fever with a specific cure and recognized as a specific disease. But all intermittent fevers were called "ague"—some were malaria, some were not. When Lewis had an attack of the ague, he did not treat himself with Peruvian bark, but with a Rush's Thunderbolt (an explosive laxative prescribed by Dr. Rush and liberally dispensed on the expedition). He was better the next day. He obviously did not have malaria. William Clark had a feverish disease while passing through modern-day Montana. It may well have been Colorado tick fever, as ticks were common then and the disease is well known nowadays in that area.

Three-quarters of a century would have to pass before Louis Pasteur, Robert Koch, and others showed that bacteria caused diseases and then associated individual bacteria with specific infections. Anesthesia was not discovered until the 1840s and antiseptic surgery until the mid-1860s. Sir Humphrey Davy discovered the pleasures of laughing gas (1799), but only *suggested* its use for surgery—he did not try it for that purpose. The first anesthetics were used for dental extractions. But on October 16, 1846, William Morton in Boston demonstrated that nitrous oxide could put a patient to sleep for a painful operation. At the end of the operation, surgeon John Collins Warren turned to the gallery of onlookers and spoke the famous words "Gentlemen, this is no humbug."

By the mid-1800s, the center of medical excellence had passed from Edinburgh to Paris, largely through the skill and teachings of Pierre Charles Alexandre Louis. Dr. Louis was the first physician to take medical histories as we know them today. He kept meticulous notes and asked detailed questions about the onset of the disease, the patient's age, and their occupation and family history. He also used simple statistical methods to analyze the progress of diseases and develop a concept of the natural history of diseases, the course a disease takes with and without treatment. One of his first studies was to examine the effects of therapeutic bleeding. He found that bleeding provided no benefits and could make a patient sicker.

In 1826, Théophile Laennec of Paris invented the stethoscope. The first instruments were not what we now see hanging around the neck of every nurse and doctor, but a simple tube, similar to an old-fashioned ear trumpet. It is likely that the surgeons on Sir John Franklin's ships carried such a stethoscope, because tuberculosis was common (and was found in one of the bodies exhumed years later on Beechey Island) and listening for the crackles and wheezes of tuberculous lungs would have been part of a ship surgeon's experience.

Body temperature was not measured routinely in patients until the end of the nineteenth century, although a thermometer for clinical use had been invented at the end of the 1700s. Lewis had a thermometer in his supplies, but it was used for measuring the temperature of the air and water. When Sergeant Charles Floyd fell mortally ill, no mention was made of his temperature, nor was his painful belly examined. Neither Lewis nor Clark were doctors and could be forgiven for not making a diagnosis, but even if Floyd had been living in Dr. Rush's parlor in Philadelphia, his temperature would not have been taken and it is unlikely that his clothes would have been disturbed so that Dr. Rush could feel his belly. Rush might have felt his pulse, looked at his eyes, examined the color of his urine, felt his fevered brow, bled him, purged him, and declared that he had a miasmatic fever. He still would have died.

In 1800, surgery had not advanced in centuries. Amputations, the lancing of abscesses, cutting for bladder stones, bleeding, setting broken bones, and the treatment (if that is the correct word) of the wounds of war were the limits of the profession. Surgeons were regarded as inferior to physicians who dealt out pills and potions and made wise pronouncements about tensions and imbalances in the body. The limits of surgery changed with the discovery of anesthetics, but the ability to open the body painlessly introduced another problem: infection. Surgeons tried to cure hitherto inaccessible problems, but the patients died from infections. That began to change in August 1865 when Joseph Lister, a professor of surgery in Glasgow, Scotland, treated a small boy whose leg had been run over by a cart in the manure-filled streets of the city. The fracture was compound, with the broken bone protruding through the skin. The injury was an almost certain death sentence. But Lister, relying on principles he had developed from the work of Pasteur, treated the wound with carbolic dressings. The bacteria were killed and the wound healed perfectly. A new era had opened, although it was many years before the medical profession universally accepted the principles of asepsis. Of the adventurers studied here, only John Wesley Powell might, theoretically, have been in a position to know something about the need to keep wounds clean, but there is no indication that they knew anything about sterility.

Most wounds were dressed with a topical ointment or a poultice, designed more to give comfort than to kill germs, and roughly bandaged. Some topical agents, such as balsam of Peru (benzoin), were antiseptic, but were not knowingly used for that purpose. When Pierre Cruzatte shot Lewis through the buttocks, Clark treated the wound correctly. The entrance and exit wounds were packed to keep them open and allow any pus to drain out and the wound healed perfectly in a few weeks. Fortunately, the bullet was lodged in Lewis's leather pants, so Clark did not have to go digging for it, which was the standard surgical teaching of the day. Lewis was also lucky that a piece of his pants did not lodge deep in the wound and cause an abscess.

Wounds were not commonly closed with stitches, and in the Lewis and Clark journals, there is only one suggestion that stitches were used. Abscesses were lanced and the pus drained, a procedure that is still an essential part of the treatment of a large abscess. Broken bones were splinted and the setting of bones was a skill in which the Indians were particularly adept. If the skin had not been broken, the limb would heal without complications, except perhaps some unevenness of the bone. If, however, the skin was broken, with a bone end protruding, infection and death were highly likely. It was the remarkable difference in healing simple and compound fractures that led Lister to wonder why some wounds healed without difficulty and others ended so disastrously.

John Charles Frémont, Zebulon Montgomery Pike, and Powell, who all anticipated fighting against Indians, had to be prepared to deal with arrow wounds, but, luckily, none of their men were wounded. Removal of the arrow was always attempted, but, quite often, the head of the arrow remained buried, while the shaft broke away. Methods for extracting arrows and penetrating darts were described in the days of Hippocrates, who was a military surgeon in numerous campaigns. Special instruments, including one called the *belulcum*, were devised as early as 500 B.C. One method was to dilate the point of entrance, insert a split reed along the arrow, thus widening the channel. Special pliers were then passed down the channel to grab the head of the arrow and remove it.

The Indians shot their arrows with remarkable speed, so that multiple wounds were normal. If a cavalry soldier had several wounds, it was not because several Indians had been shooting at him, but because his assailant had been able to fire several arrows so rapidly. The arrows were also shot with amazing force. If a bone did not stop the arrow, it could easily pass through a horse or a bison. It is not surprising, therefore, that the mortality from arrow wounds was high. In 1871, George A. Otis, an assistant surgeon in the U.S. Army, wrote a report on eighty-three arrow wounds. Twenty-six (31 percent) proved fatal, nearly all of them involving the chest or abdominal cavities. There were, however, some amazing recoveries. One soldier was shot from behind; the arrow entered above the shoulder blade on the right side and traveled upward, through the top of the lung, and lodged behind the breastbone. The shaft was removed, but the arrowhead remained in his body for three years. When he reported to a medical officer, seeking a pension, he was in such a state of pain and depression that he was contemplating suicide. The arrowhead was removed (without anesthetic) from behind the top of the breastbone. "The patient, appearing highly gratified at the result, rode to his home. His health underwent a remarkable improvement and, three years later, the operator reported him perfectly well."

Cuts, bruises, boils, and blisters were the order of the day and so common as to be unworthy of reporting. Nathaniel Sergeant Pryor, of the Corps of Discovery, dislocated his shoulder several times, the first time while trying to dismantle the mast of a pirogue. When a shoulder dislocates, the capsule around the joint is torn and subsequent dislocation is common and usually easily treated. Once again, the treatment of this problem goes back to the time of Hippocrates, and Lewis and Clark were probably familiar with the method for reducing the dislocation.

The explorers saw wildlife on a scale that we cannot now imagine: herds of bison numbering in the thousands, bears, wolves, and rattlesnakes (which was one problem the Arctic explorers did not have to face!). Frémont described the wild excitement of a bison hunt on horseback—the hectic chase, the thundering hooves, the snorting bison, and the danger of riding into the middle of a galloping, panic-stricken herd. Although bears were a common threat to Lewis and Clark, Frémont, Pike, and the explorers in the north, no one was mauled or killed. While they were a danger, they were also a valuable source of meat and fat. The fat could be used for cooking or for smearing on the skin to keep the mosquitoes from biting. The journals indicate that mosquitoes were a greater nuisance than bears. They attacked all the explorers in insatiable hordes, by day and night, filling the men's nostrils and irritating their eyes, making sleep impossible. On one occasion, the clouds of mosquitoes were so dense that Clark could not aim his gun. The men used sleeping nets that gave them some relief at night, but they did not have the face nets available nowadays. They did not know that insects could transmit disease. That understanding did not come until late in the nineteenth century, first with the discovery of the part played by insects in the transmission of cattle fever in the Southwest, then with the discoveries of the part played by mosquitoes in spreading malaria and yellow fever. Although malaria was common in the eastern and southern states, it did not reach the Missouri Valley until 1805 and was never a threat to the Arctic explorers.

The explorers along the southern routes encountered many rattlesnakes, but only two bites were recorded, neither serious.

Frostbite was a greater danger than snakebite. The bitter cold of the Mandan winter and the Arctic north, when temperatures dropped well below zero degrees, were the ideal conditions for frostbite. But the explorers who built winter quarters and limited their movements to the summer months greatly reduced their chances of frostbite. Pike, however, who intended to travel during the summer but disobeyed his orders and continued on into the winter months, paid a heavy price. At one time, nine of his fifteen men had frostbite. Some, who could travel no farther and were temporarily left behind on the Plains of Colorado, sent Pike some gangrenous toe bones as a bitter reminder that they needed help, and needed it soon. John Rae's companion John Beads had severe frostbite and lost part of one toe. But he was a stalwart man who refused to be carried on a sled and, despite severe pain and gangrenous feet, kept going.

The only severe frostbite the men of Lewis and Clark expedition had to deal with was in an Indian boy who lost some toes. Lewis, playing the part of surgeon, amputated the gangrenous digits after they had become black and painfree. Rae had a "cure" for frostbite, a poultice of alpine larch. But none of the explorers used the disastrous methods devised by the Baron Dominique-Jean Larrey during Napoleon's retreat from Moscow. He advised rubbing the frozen part with soft snow, a method that remained the standard therapy until the World War II. Many digits and limbs must have been lost because of Larrey's faulty reasoning, but the method had not yet filtered down to the isolated forts of the Hudson's Bay Company.

Hypothermia was a danger of exposure in the Arctic or of a dunking in the cold rivers coming off the Rockies. During Franklin's first catastrophic venture into the Canadian north, one of his men fell out of a canoe into a freezing river. He was pulled, unconscious, from the river, immediately stripped of his wet clothes, and placed between the bodies of two warm men and wrapped in blankets. This was a classic method for rewarming a victim of hypothermia, and was well known to Dr. Richardson, who presumably directed the resuscitation. It took several hours, but the man recovered. This method is still used, although scientific research has shown that it is of limited benefit.

Accidents, battle wounds, animal attacks, and environmental hazards were not the only dangers the explorers faced. Diseases could have easily brought their explorations to a halt. Perhaps one of the redeeming features that saved them from disease was that they never traveled through large cities. Cities were hotbeds of infection and disease. The Corps of Discovery traveled for weeks after leaving the Mandan village without seeing another person. When they finally met with the Shoshone, they encountered a tribe that had been isolated from exposure to the many diseases that Europeans had introduced to the continent.

The tribes along the Missouri had suffered from devastating epidemics of smallpox, and the Clatsop and Chinook Indians were similarly decimated. The Corps of Discovery was extremely fortunate not to arrive while one of these epidemics was in full swing. If that had occurred, many of the men would have caught the disease and the expedition would have come to an end.

Smallpox reached as far north as the Hudson Bay, and the Chipewyan Indians were almost wiped out by an epidemic in 1783. The result was calamitous, with dead bodies "lying about the Barren Ground like rotting sheep." Many of the Indians struck by the high fever rushed into rivers and drowned. Farther south, along the Missouri, the afflicted villagers left their homes, burned their lodges, and abandoned those who were sick. President Jefferson sent a sample of cowpox to Lewis, hoping he could vaccinate the Indians, but the sample was too small, dried up, and became ineffective.

Smallpox was a threat; venereal disease was a reality. The Corps of Discovery enjoyed the charms of the local women whenever the opportunity arose, especially during their stays at the Mandan and Clatsop Forts. The tradition among many Indian tribes was to offer their women to visiting men. The Indian women were frequently carriers of venereal diseases and the soldiers were also probably carriers. Venereal diseases were common in the U. S. Army, as they have been in all armies since syphilis became a scourge in Europe in 1495. The exchange of infections was probably mutual.

Two years after Christopher Columbus returned from America in 1493, a French army invaded Italy and a death-dealing epidemic of syphilis broke out in Naples. The strain of syphilis that struck the armies and spread to the population was particularly virulent. Perhaps the population had no

Introduced Diseases

The diseases introduced into America make a long and tragic list: smallpox, diphtheria, mumps, tuberculosis, leprosy, typhus and typhoid, chicken pox, and scarlet fever. Yellow fever and malaria came with the slaves that white men brought to work the plantations. The Indians had been isolated from all these diseases for thousands of years and were immunologically unprepared to resist them. The results were catastrophic. Nearly half the Indian population the Spanish encountered died. Smallpox spread throughout the continent, leaving a trail of rotting bodies and disfigured, terrified survivors. Mumps and other diseases took longer to exact their toll, but in localized areas were equally destructive. When the traders sold alcohol to the tribes, the results were as bad, but longer lasting. Ornamental blue beads, metal tools, and guns could not compensate for the diseases that the white man brought unwittingly.

resistance. Whatever the reason, syphilis spread through Europe like an out-of-control bushfire, and eventually reached as far as Japan. The disease was quickly associated with sex. Ulcers on the penis, swollen glands in the groin, rashes, loss of hair, changes in the face and the ultimate collapse of the nose, and, above all, the excruciating pain throughout the body caused a terror as bad as that after the Black Death. Moralists and clerics claimed that the epidemic was a judgment from God, a punishment for immoral behavior, although many clerics caught the disease. The judgment in no way reduced the spread of the disease.

Arguments over the origin of the disease continue to modern times. On which side of the Atlantic did it arise? Bones have been the most important sources of evidence. Syphilis produces thickening of the shinbones and changes in the teeth that are discernible centuries after the victims have died. But a closely associated disease, yaws, produces similar changes, clouding the anthropological evidence.

Some medical historians believe that sailors returning with Columbus brought the disease from America to Europe. The massive outbreak in Italy within two years of Columbus returning to Europe adds weight to this argument. Other historians believe that syphilis was already present in Europe and, for some reason, mutated into a virulent form, starting the epidemic in Naples. Bones with suggestive changes have been found in Hispaniola (Haiti), but similar changes have been found in bones in the north of England that predate Columbus by three centuries. Perhaps we will never know where the disease originated, but its enormous effect on history is beyond doubt, affecting kings, bishops, musicians, artists, and unknown paupers with equal impunity.

Syphilis was often confused with gonorrhea. Some victims probably suffered from both the clap and the pox. Mercury, already used as a treatment for many infections and diseases, was quickly tried against syphilis, and it worked. Mercury, as an ointment or taken by mouth, was used in massive doses until it poisoned the victims. Syphilis was the perfect disease for quacks and charlatans. The victims often wanted to keep their affliction secret, and sometimes the potion given out by a charlatan contained a small dose of mercury and suppressed the disease without causing harm. For many, the physician's "cure," a combination of sweat baths, mercury, powdered guaiac wood, and potassium iodide given over weeks and months, was a torture almost as bad as the disease. As the years passed, many physicians realized that syphilis was a cyclical disease and would improve without treatment. This observation made some doctors decide not to give mercury, but to wait for the disease to pass from one stage to the next, the final stage being insanity.

The medical kit of the Corps of Discovery was amply filled with drugs for the treatment of venereal diseases, such as mercurous chloride, either to be given by mouth as calomel, or to be used as an ointment on the primary lesions. Recent research at Traveler's Rest, one of the 600 campsites used by the Corps of Discovery, has found mercury in the residual layers of the latrines, but this finding does not prove that the men were being treated for venereal diseases while staying at the camp because the most potent laxative—Rush's Thunderbolts—also contained calomel. It would be impossible to distinguish between the mercury used for the treatment of venereal diseases and that contained in the laxative.

It is difficult to diagnose from the journals whether the men had syphilis or gonorrhea, and it was equally difficult for Lewis to make that diagnosis because the distinction between the two diseases was not always recognized. Regardless of diagnostic difficulties, venereal diseases were both a medical and a disciplinary problem. At the end of the corps' stay at Fort Clatsop, Lewis had to make an appeal to his men to refrain from associating with the young women who were brought to the camp. He did not want to be treating venereal diseases while they were struggling back through the mountains. Venereal diseases had debilitating local and systemic effects, due both to the diseases and the treatment with mercury. Lewis knew he could do without that trouble while traversing the Rockies.

The most intriguing medical problem affecting the men of the expeditions was the fate of the men of Sir John Franklin's final expedition. Their first winter, 1845–1846, during which three men died, was spent in a camp on Beechey Island, and the graves of three men who died there were found in 1850 by one of the rescue expeditions. One hundred and thirty-eight years later, in 1987, Owen Beattie and John Geiger from the University of Alberta presented a detailed study of the bodies in *Frozen in Time*. Beattie and his colleagues exhumed the bodies, X-rayed them, and took tissue specimens for analysis. Chemical analysis of the tissues revealed a surprising finding.

One specimen of hair from John Torrington, a stoker aboard HMS *Terror*, contained 413 to 657 parts per million of lead, a level greatly in excess of normal. The specimens, ten-centimeter strands of hair, were analyzed along their length. The greatest concentration of lead was found at the tip of the hair, indicating that Torrington had been absorbing lead for some time. Specimens from the two other bodies contained 138 to 313 and 145 to 280 parts per million, levels at least twenty times normal. Similarly high levels of lead were found in bone fragments recovered from King William Island.

Where had the lead come from? The expedition took preserved meat in cans made from strips of tin bent into a circle and held together with lead solder. When the bodies were first discovered in 1850, questions were raised about the purity of the canned meat, as it had been supplied at the last minute to the Admiralty by the lowest bidder. Beattie found hundreds of rusty cans in a midden some distance from the camp. The lead solder had been applied to the junction both outside and inside the cans. The food within the cans was, therefore, directly exposed to lead in a way that would not have happened if the solder had been applied only to the outside of the can.

Had the lead come from the solder of the tins, or could it have come from prolonged exposure to industrial lead before the men ever started on the expedition? The crew members were children of the beginning industrial age and from the poorest areas of large cities, where they were exposed to high levels of environmental lead. It is impossible to say how their childhood exposure contributed to lead levels found many years later. The evidence from the hair samples indicated that the poisoning occurred after the expedition had left England, but high lead levels in the bones could have been due to early ingestion.

The effects of lead poisoning are many and complex, affecting general body strength, neurologic, and cognitive functions. The symptoms include abdominal pain and colic, kidney failure, weakness, headache, and memory loss. The ability of the officers and men to make rational decisions could have been affected. And perhaps the officer's decisions might have been affected more than those of the men because it is likely that they ate more of the canned meat than the men. If the three men buried on Beechey Island were suffering from lead poisoning (in addition to the pneumonia and tuberculosis), what were the levels in the other men and how could the lead have affected them? The answer to that comes, in part, from the bones found on King William Island, which also had abnormally high levels of lead.

The influence of lead poisoning in affecting the outcome of the expedition can never be known. The samples studied were few and many other factors may have been equally important. The impossibility of the white sailors to adapt to Eskimo ways (their numbers were far too great to adapt to small-group life), starvation due to lack of game, and scurvy from insufficient vitamin C may have played equal parts with lead poisoning in deciding the outcomes of the expeditions.

The canned meat probably contained another, even more lethal danger than lead: botulism. *Clostridium botulinum* produces the most deadly bacterial toxin known and is notorious for growing in improperly preserved canned food. The Franklin expedition of 1845 carried 8,000 cans of preserved food. Scott Cookman has produced a compelling theory that botulism was the villain that killed many of the men. His evidence is circumstantial, but convincing. The maker of the canned goods, Stephan Goldner, was a crook who produced cheap and almost certainly contaminated cans of meat and vegetables. The Admiralty asked him in April 1845 to produce a prodigious number of cans, knowing that the expedition was to leave in July. Goldner offered the lowest bid. Considering the primitive methods for hand making each can and the lack of quality control, it is not surprising that an unscrupulous dealer would cut every corner imaginable. The cans taken by Beattie from Beechey Island were poorly made, with small holes at the top and bottom of the seals that would easily have allowed contaminants to enter.

Nicholas Appert, the founder of preserved foods in 1810, found that immersing the glass bottles that he used in boiling water before sealing them resulted in long-term preservation. He did not understand that he was sterilizing the food and sealing it before contamination occurred. Cans were substituted later for bottles, and Goldner had a patent for a speedy heating method that would have appealed to the Admiralty. He finished the order with great speed and probably did not care how the work was done, so long as it was done on time and allowed him to make a handsome profit. Some of the cans may never have been heated, just filled and sealed. If that occurred, the growth of *Clostridium botulinum* in the cans was almost certain.

We know nothing of the symptoms the men experienced in the months before they died when they were cooped up in the ships for a miserable winter. We know that the mortality rate was surprisingly high, especially among the officers. But as no written records remain telling of the modes of death, the speed of the fatal illnesses, the signs and symptoms, we can only speculate on what happened. The bodies exhumed on Beechey Island showed evidence of tuberculosis, pneumonia, anthracosis, and emphysema, in addition to lead poisoning. A strain of *Clostridium* was cultured from the bowel of one of the men. Two of the men died within three days of each other, but autopsies could not determine if they died from the same cause.

Botulism is a disease of the nervous system that starts with symptoms related to the cranial nerves—double vision, difficulty swallowing—and develops rapidly into a descending paralysis affecting the whole body. The incubation period varies from eight to thirty-six hours, but the patient may die within twenty-four hours. Fortunately, the toxin can be inactivated by exposure to only 100° F for only ten minutes, a temperature that the food would almost certainly have reached during cooking on board the ships. On board, the men may have been relatively protected when eating cooked food, but those desperately hauling boats across the ice to reach the Great Fish River would have eaten straight from the can and could have died within a day of eating a contaminated meal. When Francis McClintock searched King William Island, he found the skeleton of a steward lying face down, arms outstretched, as though he had fallen forward, dead in his tracks (just as the Eskimos had described to Rae). He could well have died from botulism, added to scurvy, malnutrition, and exhaustion.

The Franklin expedition was the first to rely on canned food, and possibly the only one to be seriously exposed to the risk of botulism, while other expeditions were exposed to other forms of poisoning. Lewis intentionally ate minerals and tasted the water of the Missouri, which may have contained dangerous chemicals. On August 22, 1804, Clark wrote: "Capt Lewis in proveing the quality of those minerals was Near poisoning himself by the fumes & taste of the Cobalt & alum is very pisen ... Capt Lewis took a Dost of Salts to work of the effects of the Arsenic."

The men frequently had diarrhea, which Lewis ascribed to the minerals in the water. Bacterial infections due to a lack of understanding of sterility and the passage of bacteria from one person to another obviously contributed to most of the intestinal problems. But when the entire expedition became sick with abdominal cramps after meeting the Nez Perce Indians for the first time, another type of poisoning may have added to their problems.

Dr. Elaine McIntosh, a nutritional expert, has suggested that confusion between two types of camas plant may have poisoned the men. They ate bread made from camas plant roots, but there are two types of camas plant: blue camas, which is edible and safe, and white camas, known as death camas. It is not clear if the men ate bread that had been made for them by the Indians, or if they dug up the bulbs themselves. It is easy to distinguish between the harmless and the dangerous varieties when the plants are in flower, but the expedition arrived after the flowers had long since dropped off. As the plants live side by side, it is possible that they accidentally received bread that included the roots of death camas, which would have made them sick, even in small quantities.

Many wonderful things have been claimed for Sacagawea, but one way in which she may have saved the men from poisoning themselves was to show them which plants were safe to eat and which were dangerous. We know that she collected plants to add to the cooking pot and she may well have stopped them from eating inviting, but poisonous, berries.

The men of William Bligh's group were not so lucky. When they reached the safety of the islands of the Great Barrier Reef, they found abundant berries. The botanist, David Nelson, was already very sick and may have become annoyed with constant questions about the safety of the various plants. The men became violently sick after eating some berries he had told them were safe. Nelson himself "was taken very ill with a violent heat in his bowels, a loss of sight, great thirst and an inability to walk," symptoms of a powerful neurologic toxin.

Even greater direct evidence of poisoning occurred after they caught and ate a "dolphin fish." Within a few hours, Bligh and others were dry heaving over the side of the boat in an agony of bowel cramps and nausea.

Poisonous fish are common, especially in Pacific waters. Some fish of the shark family, of which the "dolphin fish" was almost certainly a member, have livers that contain toxins, scombroids, causing nausea, vomiting, abdominal pain, sweating, and many other symptoms that would have caused Bligh to say that he had never felt worse in his life. And Bligh, under the "who shall eat this?" system, happened to receive the liver; poisoning from shark liver can be fatal.

Scombroid poisoning is the most common cause of abdominal complications after eating fish. The symptoms are much the same as those from eating shark liver, but not quite so severe and rarely fatal. Eating Hawaiian dolphin can bring about poisoning rapidly, and the fish that caused the problems was described as a "dolphin." Whatever the cause—whichever kind of fish they ate—the results showed that desperate men will eat whatever looks like salvation, regardless of the consequences.

Would these expeditions have been healthier if a physician had been part of the group? Probably not. Lewis and Clark knew about as much medicine as many physicians of the day, and the only man who died could not have been saved under any circumstances. Dr. Richardson provided supportive care and comfort to the dying, starving men, but he did not save any lives. Rae was a doctor, but he made journeys in such isolated places and with such few resources that his skills were limited by the conditions. He only lost one man, to drowning. His companions knew how to look after themselves in the bitter cold and only one of his men developed crippling frostbite of the toes.

The surgeons on Franklin's ships were well supplied with the medicines available at the time, but most of their medical ideas were still from the Middle Ages. The on-board sick bay was perhaps the worst place for an ill man to be: deep in the lower decks, badly ventilated, cramped, and with every chance for cross-infection from other patients. If a sailor was seriously injured, the surgeons knew nothing about chloroform, which was introduced by Sir James Simpson in 1848, nor about antiseptic surgery. They were aware of the importance of giving lemon juice to prevent scurvy and of keeping the ship clean, but the bleeding and purging that they probably used may well have made their patients sicker, rather than better.

It is easy to look back and pass judgment. Frémont could have listened to the advice of the locals and saved lives by not venturing into the San Juan Mountains in the middle of winter. The disasters on the *Terror* and the *Erebus* were beyond current medical understanding, but could have been partially avoided had not a crook been responsible for providing poisoned food. But regardless of the possibility of botulism or lead poisoning, the survivors, weakened by a winter of starvation, scurvy, and other diseases, still had to drag themselves and their supplies an impossible 1,000 miles to safety. Bligh, in contrast, brought his men, without loss of life, nearly 4,000 miles to safety only to have them die from diseases caught on land.

Perhaps the final conclusion should be that it is amazing that so many men survived.

13

Dealing with the Neighbors

Contacts with Indigenous People

*These are the vilest miscreants of the savage race, and must ever
remain pirates of the Missouri until such measures are pursued,
by our government, as will make them feel a dependence
on its will for their supply of merchandise.*

—William Clark, describing the Teton Sioux

*I think we can justly affirm to the honor of these people that they are the
most hospitable, honest, and sincere people we have met on our voyage.*

—Meriwether Lewis, describing the Wallawalla tribe

William Bligh and his desperate crew had only been at sea for a few days and
already knew that they would soon run out of food and water if they could
not land at Tofua, and get coconuts and water. They did not know if the
natives were friendly or aggressive. They had just come from Tahiti, where
the natives had welcomed them and where they had been able to get everything they needed. They patrolled up and down the coast for a couple of
days, looking for a good landing place. Natives waved to them from the shore
in a friendly way. They pulled into the beach and told the natives, whose
reactions were neither friendly nor aggressive, that their ship had sunk.
Some of Bligh's men were suspicious and worried, but the weather became
bad and they had to stay. Bligh thought he saw signs of an impending attack
and told his men to be prepared to leave. Suddenly, the crowd became
angry, knocking stones together, a sign they were about to attack; Bligh had
been present when Captain James Cook was killed and remembered the
ominous clacking of stones. The natives tried to persuade Bligh and his men
to spend the night onshore, so Bligh grabbed one of the chiefs by the hand
and walked with him through the menacing crowd to his boat. The chief
escaped and seized one of Bligh's men, John Norton. As Bligh and his men
pulled away from the shore, the natives beat Norton to death by smashing
his head with stones. Bligh and his men did not land on another inhabited
island until they reached Timor.

All of the explorers in the eighteenth and ninteenth centuries dealt
with indigenous tribes that had been living on the land for thousands of
years. They had developed cultures, modes of survival, social systems of
varying complexity and sophistication—a sophistication that was frequently
misunderstood and underestimated by the explorers. Language was almost

always a barrier. The Indians, such as those along the Missouri, who had been meeting and trading with white men for many years had developed a sign language familiar to both sides. But remote Eskimo groups that had never seen white men knew neither sign language nor, sometimes, the language of nearby tribes. Communication was difficult, at best, and frequently tinged—on both sides—by suspicion and fear.

First encounters with unknown tribes were often a lottery. Even within a short distance of each other, one group might be friendly and another group aggressive. When Alexander Mackenzie was near the coast, he met a very friendly, helpful group of natives that carried him downriver in their canoes. But the Indians at the mouth of the river objected to the intruders. Macubah—the natives' name for Captain George Vancouver—and his ships had visited them a short time before and one of the ship's officers had been cruel to the Indians. They were not pleased to see more white men. Mackenzie did not understand the cause of their anger. Fortunately, he was able to get back upstream to his friends before anyone was hurt.

Eskimos who had never seen white men usually fled in terror, but if they were in sufficient numbers, they sometimes threatened a small group of white men and stole whatever they could grab. If they were familiar with guns, a few shots scattered them, but if they had never seen guns, they would advance fearlessly until the first shot was fired or one of their number killed.

There was frequently ongoing warfare between neighboring groups. Powerful nomadic tribes, such as the Teton Sioux, were in constant battles with the more settled, agriculturally based tribes. Horses and guns, both introduced by the Spanish, had added speed and power to those that possessed them. Tribes without guns or horses lived in poverty and fear. The Blackfoot had both, and the Shoshone, who did not have guns, hunted on the Plains afraid for their safety. A well-armed war party of Hidatsa from the Missouri valley captured Sacagawea from her defenseless family and took her east. Not only did tribes such as the Shoshone fear other tribes, but they feared all strangers. The first Shoshone scout that Meriwether Lewis saw galloped away to warn his village. The next day, the women that Lewis met cowered in fear, certain that they were going to be killed.

The relations between the white explorers and indigenous people depended on the attitude of the white toward the natives and the perception of the natives of the intruders—had they come to trade, to kill men and steal women, or to conquer territory? Were they well known or as strange as foreign gods?

The ultimate objective of the interaction between European nations and indigenous people on every continent was to acquire riches. The acquisition of land and the control of nations increased trade—and profits followed. The first contact might seem to be based on friendly trade, but it was not long before indigenous people were seen to be in the way of colonization. The reaction of indigenous people was to fight back as soon as they realized that the white men were after their land as well as their furs, jewels, or minerals.

The attitude toward the Indians (in itself a strange term, based on Columbus's misunderstanding of where he had landed) during the early English occupation of Virginia were made clear by Governor Sir Francis Wyatt: "Our first work is the expulsion of the Savages to gaine the free range of the countrey for the encrease of cattle, swine ,&c ... for it is infinitely better to have no heathen amongst us." But these views were not without their critics. The Reverend Robert Gray, at the same time, asked, "By what right or warrant can we enter into the land of these Savages, take away their rightful heritage from them, and plant ourselves in their place, being unwronged or unprovoked by them?"

President Thomas Jefferson gave explicit instructions to Lewis and Clark about dealing with the Indians. The purpose of the expedition was not only to explore the land, but also to meet as many tribes as possible, make friends, and persuade them to live peacefully with their neighbors. "In all your intercourse with the natives, treat them in the most friendly & conciliatory manner their own conduct will admit. ... It is impossible for us to foresee in what manner you will be received, whether with hospitality or hostility, so it is impossible to prescribe the exact degree or perseverance with which you are to pursue your journey. We value too much the lives of our citizens to offer them to probable destruction."

In light of these orders, Lewis's dealings with Indians were as well controlled and friendly as he could contrive, but they were not always based on a full understanding of local politics. An important meeting was with the most powerful tribe along the Missouri, the Teton Sioux, who were in the habit of collecting tribute from passing traders. The Corps of Discovery was the most powerful group they had ever seen and their meeting became a

Plantation

When the English first colonized Ireland in the reign of Elizabeth the First, the English regarded themselves as "corn" and the native Irish were thought of as "weeds." During this time, the word plantation was coined to describe the developments started by the English. The implication of the word is obvious: the first meaning of the word was to describe the implantation of a small group of one nation within another for the purposes of control.

contest of wills rather than arms. Lewis did not understand that one of their leaders, The Partisan (Tortohongar), was a rival of Chief Black Buffalo. Black Buffalo was more powerful and proved to be a conciliator. The Partisan was hoping to usurp power from Black Buffalo and, in an attempt to impress his followers by bluffing and posturing, tried to show himself as the strong man, standing up against the powerful white men. Lewis put on an elaborate show: he raised a canvas awning and hoisted a flag, the soldiers paraded and fancy gifts and food were exchanged. But his efforts were crippled by the lack of a good interpreter, which was essential. Lewis could make a compelling speech about the change of power, the need for trade and peace, and Black Buffalo could follow up with fine oratory, but neither side understood the other. They might as well have addressed the prairie winds.

Lewis, unaware of the rivalry between the chiefs, was unable to interpret their behavior. When meeting a new tribe, Lewis always picked a "chief" and was sometimes wrong in his choice. On several occasions, he misunderstood the hierarchies of the Plains, choosing the person he thought most chieflike and presenting him with a large medal. A smaller, less significant medal was then given to a man perceived to be less important. This person might regard himself as just as important as the recipient of the larger medal. Several of the Teton Sioux thought they had been slighted and demanded more gifts, especially tobacco, a gift that had symbolic as well as practical value.

The three days spent with the Teton Sioux were a roller-coaster of anger and friendliness. One moment, the Indians were grabbing the hawsers of the boats to prevent them from proceeding upriver. The next day, the men were being entertained to a feast of roast buffalo and tender dog and being offered young women as companions for the night. Protestant morals encountered Indian custom and politics. The refusals of Lewis and Clark to accept the attentions of the women was regarded, at the very least, as an impolite action and, at worst, an insult. Fortunately, the corps was moving on and an impolitic action had no permanent effect.

These mistakes are easy enough to understand. Lewis, an army officer, coming from a society with clearly defined leaders, officers, and officials, could hardly be expected to understand the nuances of Indian society, tribe by tribe. The Corps of Discovery encountered fifty tribes and the White House had not given Lewis a position paper describing the politics of each tribe.

Lewis's main concern was to stay out of trouble, reward those who seemed worthy, and, overall, be as tactful a possible. That objective did not alter his stump speech, which began with "Children!" and proceeded to tell the Indians that they had a new Great White Chief in a place called Washington. This new chief was backed by great power but wanted to see peace between the whites and the Indians and among the Indian tribes. The Great Chief promised to send traders and supplies if this happy state of affairs could be achieved. Jefferson knew that trade would be much greater in a peaceful environment than among warring tribes. He also envisioned the land west of the Mississippi as a home for the Indians, while whites would occupy the territory east of the river. He did not foresee the flood of western emigration, pushing aside the Indian tribes.

Much of Lewis's message must have been mystifying to the Indians. Washington, Paris, Chihuahua (the current capital of Spanish America)—what was the difference? Few of these foreigners spoke tribal languages and sign language, useful for trading, was inadequate for interpreting the subtleties of tribal politics or for explaining why there was a new Great White Chief. The Louisiana Purchase would have been a mystery to the Teton Sioux or any of the other tribes that did not "own" their territory. They could not understand why a small party of white men that had not conquered their braves in battle could march in saying that they "owned" the land. Their braves numbered in the hundreds. This visiting group contained fewer than forty soldiers. The balance of power was clear to the chiefs—but it would not stay that way for long.

Lewis's attitude toward the Indians changed during the return journey from the West Coast. The Indians along the Columbia laid their hands on anything of value that was lying loose around camp. The thievery provoked Lewis to fits of anger. The coastal tribes, such as the Chinook and the Clatsop, believed in communal ownership and thought it perfectly reasonable to pick up something that "belonged" to another member of the group. This may have been the reasoning behind some of their sticky-fingered behavior. But the more likely explanation is that they looked at the Americans as wealthy people with many valuable articles, such as pots, axes, nails, and blankets. They knew the Americans were passing through their land and might not be back again. They did not seem to be interested in trading for furs, so why not steal whatever was available?

When the Indians along the Columbia River stole Lewis's dog Seaman, the reaction was immediate and threatening. Men were summoned to chase the Indians and ordered to shoot if there was any resistance or reluctance to return the dog. This was the first time Lewis ordered violence against the Indians. The theft of his dog changed the rules of engagement.

At about the same time, Lewis caught an Indian stealing a saddle and a blanket. Lewis threw a tantrum and told the Indians that if the articles were not returned, he would "birn their houses. They have vexed me in such a manner by such acts of repeated villainy that I am quite disposed to treat them with every severity." He did not like the Indians along the Columbia and seems to have looked down on them. He had been brought up in a family that owned slaves, and perhaps when he was angry, he looked at the western Indians in the same light as the slaves back home: people who were expected to obey orders and who could be beaten if they did not do as they were told. Yet a short time later, Lewis and his men had to linger for several weeks with the Nez Perce, waiting for the high winter snows to clear. Relations with the tribe were cordial and Lewis recorded, "These are a race of hardy strong athletic active men." After two young Nez Perce braves had guided the corps through the mountains along a shorter and easier route than they had traversed while going west, Lewis parted from them with regret, admiration, and affection. Lewis's greatest misapprehension about Indian intentions may have occurred a few days later during the meeting with the Blackfoot youths. If he had realized that he was dealing with a horse-stealing escapade rather than a war party led by a chief, he might have dealt with them differently, avoiding the conflict the next morning and changing the Blackfoot's subsequent antagonism toward the Americans, at least for a few years.

After the expedition ended, some of the men, such as John Colter and George Drouillard, returned to the wilderness and had much bloodier encounters with Indians than those they had had while with Lewis.

A significant difference between Canadian and American traders was that the French and British were not (at least around 1800) thinking in terms of colonizing a continent. The French lost control of Eastern Canada to the British after the end of the Seven Years War in 1763. The British claimed a trading monopoly to the vastness of Prince Rupert Land west of the Hudson Bay but did not regard themselves as imperial occupiers of the land. In fact, their few trading posts clung to power precariously along the western shore of the bay. Until the aggressive trading tactics of the North West Company forced them to establish trading posts in the center of the country, they were content to sit and wait for the Indians to bring the furs to them. Their control was based on trade, though not necessarily fair trade—a rich nation supplying goods that the poor natives needed, but also forcing the natives to pay high prices for low-quality guns and diluted liquor. The Americans, on the other hand, had purchased the land from France. In their view, it was their's to control and exploit. They felt they had every right to the furs and, later, to the minerals. The Indians were an obstruction to white expansion.

The political scene changed between the times of Lewis and Clark and John Charles Frémont and Kit Carson. A steady, bloody war had been fought for many years between the Indians and the white trappers. Frémont chose Carson as his guide in part because he was a renowned Indian fighter. He had killed his first Apache at the age of fifteen and many more by the time Frémont recruited him. He was a formidable man, tough, ruthless, and willing to kill Indians on sight. (Later in his life, having married an Indian woman, he changed his mind. But he remained a paradox because he took part in the final, brutal roundup of the Navajo. His supporters claim that the treatment of the Navajo would have been much harsher had it not been for Carson.) Jefferson's injunction to Lewis to avoid conflict had long been forgotten.

Frémont regularly took Indian hunters and guides with him. When other Indians killed one of them, they were allowed a free hand to seek revenge. Sometimes the Indians on whom revenge was wrecked were not necessarily those who had committed the offence in the first place.

Without doubt, Frémont's most egregious attack on Indians was that near Lassens's Ranch in northern California. He did not take part in it himself but tacitly approved and helped. When the local settlers came asking for help, claiming that the Indians were planning a major assault, Frémont allowed some of his soldiers to disband temporarily from the expedition and join the settlers and participate in what Carson described as "butchery" of at least 175 Indians, mostly women and children.

Not long after this disgraceful event, Frémont and his men were attacked in the middle of the night and Basil Lajeunesse, one of Frémont's favorite guides, was killed in his sleep by a smashing blow to his head with a battle axe. The Tlamath chief who had led the attack was killed and Frémont praised the chief's heroism in defending himself. Enmity and admiration went hand in hand.

It is easy to condemn men such as Frémont and Carson for their beliefs and actions. They were a small group, isolated from help, in a land where they were treading on the toes of Spanish sovereignty. They were a law unto themselves and came from a society that, with few exceptions, condoned and even encouraged violence against "unruly" Indians. Many of the Indians, too, acting in accordance with their traditions of self-defense and honor, regarded attacks on white men as legitimate responses to aggressive, land-grabbing, fur-stealing invaders.

Perhaps the differences in the actions between Lewis and Clark and Frémont can be explained by the changes over the half-century that separated their expeditions. Lewis and Clark ventured into lands where no white men had been before and they realized that they were totally reliant on help from the Indians if they were to achieve their objectives. Also, their commander in chief had given them strict orders about how to deal with the Indians.

Frémont worked in a different time. Much of the country had been explored and men had hauled their wagons to the far corners of the land, fighting Indians, killing, and being killed. The prairies had been stained with blood in a way that Lewis never anticipated. Frémont was occasionally offered help by Indians, but he often ignored it. He intended to achieve his objectives despite the Indian attacks—attacks that he fully anticipated. Lewis and Clark would certainly have defended themselves to the last man had they been attacked. During the encounter with the Blackfoot, Lewis told his three companions to expect an attack and warned them that "if they thought themselves sufficiently strong I was convinced they would attempt to rob us in which case. ... I should resist to the last extremity preferring death to that of being deprived of my papers instruments and guns and desired that they would form the same resolution and be allert and on their guard." When the Indians stole their weapons, Lewis's men responded quickly and violently. There was no pretence at negotiation, no concern about legalities. And when Lewis, Frémont, and many others returned from the wilderness and told of battles with Indians, they were praised, not condemned. There were no courts of inquiry.

John Wesley Powell had little contact with Indians, except those at Green River who told him that he was out of his mind to enter the canyons from which no man had ever emerged alive. Later, Powell visited the Shivwit village, where Oramel and Seneca Howland and Bill Dunn had been killed after they left the expedition and climbed out of the canyon. Far from wanting to extract "justice" and hang the perpetrators, Powell understood their motives and reasons. The Shivwits had been deceived into thinking that the men were enemies and killed them in self-defense. Powell was so confident in their explanation and in their friendly reception that he slept among them.

Powell met many Indians in his later explorations and had the greatest respect for their amazing ability to remember the topographic details of terrain. He thought he was good at remembering these kinds of details but was put to shame by the skill of the Indians.

Samuel Hearne, Mackenzie, and John Rae were totally reliant on friendships with the First Nations. Hearne put himself completely under their care. His first two attempts to reach the Coppermine River were foiled by being abandoned by his Cree guides. They could have killed him with ease, but probably regarded him as an obstructive nuisance, someone incapable of looking after himself. When Matonabee appeared out of the forest, rescuing him from almost certain death, his life changed. In Matonabee, he found not only a rescuer, but an instructor, guide, leader, and—above all— a loyal friend. The friendship between Hearne and Matonabee was unique. They supported each other through success, arguments, exhaustion, hunger, and, finally, tragedy and defeat. After the French captured the Prince of Wales Fort and Hearne sailed away to captivity, leaving behind Mary Norton, the wife he adored, and his indomitable friend, Hearne's life was once more changed forever. When he returned a year later, Matonabee had committed suicide in grief and Mary had died from starvation. This was a tale of loyalty and love that to some extent offsets the accounts of brutal slaughter that have been passed down as typical examples of relations between white and indigenous people.

Many of the trappers, whether employees of the big fur trading companies or individual trappers, especially in Canada, had long and happy relationships with country wives. Mackenzie, although he retired to the high life of London with his legal wife, continued to support his former country wife and children.

Sexual relations between explorers, trappers, and traders with Indians were common and expected. Many Indian tribes regarded sex as a way to pass the strength and "medicine" of one person to another. Clark's servant York, because of his color and size, was regarded by the Mandans as having special medicine and took advantage of this unique status. Visiting men were routinely, out of politeness, offered women as temporary companions. So far as can be judged, leaders such as Lewis, Clark, and Frémont refused—or kept very quiet about—any sexual contact they may have had. (It has been suggested that Lewis's later suicide was due to tertiary syphilis caught during the expedition. This is highly unlikely as the tertiary phase of syphilis takes many years to develop.) Later in life, Frémont was a notorious womanizer and it would be surprising if he did not take the occasional opportunity to have sex as it was offered. As most of what we know about these men is derived from their journals, it is not surprising that they did not mention their moments of dalliance. Frémont's letters to his wife are all we know of some of his voyages. It is inconceivable that he would have described (or even hinted at) the details of any sexual encounters in these letters.

Benjamin Rush, at President Jefferson's request, asked Lewis to find out about the habits of the Indians, including their "vices." Rush would have considered many of the sexual habits of the Indians as vices. Clark's embarrassment about the sexual ceremony at the Mandan village to entice the buffalo in which young women were presented to the old men (and to Lewis's soldiers) for sex was such that he described it in his journal in Latin. The account was only later translated into English.

Having a country wife was not the same thing as "going native" and adopting the lifestyle of the locals. The authorities of the Hudson's Bay Company did not approve of "going native." Employees were expected to stay in the forts and factories and trade with the incoming Indians. Hearne and Rae were different in part because they had no alternative. Both of them were ordered by the company to explore the interior and both traveled without a large retinue of white followers. Rae was critical of British naval expeditions with their attempts to bring Britain to the Arctic—wool-clad sailors hauling heavy sleds and living in canvas tents and supplied with typical British food. Officers gave orders, did not carry the loads, and relied on Indians to do the hunting, even though the soldiers and sailors were trained in the use of weapons. It is true that few of them would have been able to track and hunt the skittery caribou, but Rae had a completely different attitude. He believed that he was a better hunter than most of the Indians; with the exception of hunting for seals, this was probably true. As a boy in the Orkneys, he spent many days becoming an expert shot, and before he was sent on explorations, he spent ten years hunting and learning local survival skills and languages. When he went on his first long winter away from the factory, he soon became aware that Eskimo snow houses were warmer and more efficient in many ways than tents. A good-sized snow house could be built in about an hour and, once built, could be used again. Not only did he adopt their houses, but also their clothes.

There is wonderful portrait of him sitting in full Eskimo clothing: a large fur hat with long ear flaps reaching below his shoulders, tanned deerskin clothes, and a bead-embroidered pouch hanging at his waist. His left hand holds the end of a long Indian pipe and his face is adorned with lavish grey whiskers and a luxuriant handle-bar moustache. The only relic of Hearne's presence in the Arctic is his name carved into a rock up the Churchill River, "S^L. Hearne July 1 1767." (The ornate, beautifully carved letters apparently took him two years to make.) During his two-year venture up the Coppermine River, he must have gone through many changes of clothing and the women in the group would have been put to work to make the clothes for him. Hearne lived so closely with the Indians that whatever they built for shelter, he slept in, whatever they ate, he ate. European clothes and shoes would not have lasted more than few months in the rigorous environment of the Barrens.

Some of Hearne's experiences were terrible. Having to witness the massacre of the Eskimos at Bloody Falls scarred him for the rest of his life. The gap between his benevolent philosophy and the motives of Matonabee and his men in killing defenseless Eskimos was too wide to bridge.

Franklin had to deal with Indians on his two trips to the northern shore. They were his hunters and guides, and they failed him on occasion. On his first overland expedition, his life and the lives of the other white survivors were saved by the same Indians who had failed him earlier. They treated him with the greatest kindness, supporting and feeding him and his friends like sick children. On his second trip, he had an unpleasant run-in with aggressive Eskimos on the north coast. But by this time, he was a more experienced traveler than on the first expedition and avoided conflict and bloodshed.

The priests that accompanied the early Spanish and French explorers were intent on spreading Christianity and converting heathens. This was never the intent of the explorers we have been following. Some of them, especially Franklin, were intensely religious and held weekly services for their men and the voyageurs with them but never tried to proselytize the

Indians. With the exception of the missionaries, most of the explorers were interested in opening up the country and finding new routes for trapping or trade. The great trading Chouteau family of Saint Louis and Manuel Lisa were interested in making money. The explorations they promoted were to find new sources of furs. Frémont was not interested in trade but in exploring routes for a transcontinental railroad. Powell wanted to explore the Grand Canyon where no one lived, except for a scattering of Mormons. Trade was not the reason for his expedition. He was interested in filling in blanks on the map. After going down the Canyon, he cannot have ever imagined that it would be a trade route, let alone a national park with a booming business. Lewis and Clark explored trade routes but were not traveling salesmen, sometimes to the annoyance of the Indians with whom they dealt. Mackenzie was both a trader and an explorer. Hearne was sent to find the copper riches that the Hudson's Bay Company believed lay at the mouth of the river. He did not find copper but explored a huge area that, later, became a prime hunting ground for furs.

Despite the fact that some of these men were not traders per se, they always took beads and other trade items to pay the Indians for food and supplies. The largest expenditure in Lewis's and Clark's budget was for gifts for the Indians. Even so, they ran out of suitable gifts and ended up cutting buttons off their jackets and trading innocuous "eye water" for substantial supplies of food and horses.

The Indian tribes were interested in guns, metal goods, such as axes and pots, beads for decorating their clothes, and alcohol. A few tribes, such as the Arikara, scorned alcohol, questioning why anyone would drink anything that would make them stupid. Other tribes, such as the Assiniboine, were apparently addicted to alcohol, which they received in generous quantities from the British traders. Alcohol could be used to get good furs, to appease angry chiefs, or to raise morale among the explorers themselves. Lewis often recorded giving out a gill of whiskey to his men after a particularly hard day and Mackenzie had to keep his men going on several occasions with a liberal distribution of rum.

Brandy, rum, and whiskey, often well diluted, were the usual forms of liquor. Wine was taken along for medicinal purposes and probably had a fairly high alcohol content. The quantities of liquor taken seem to be large, but the Lewis and Clark group ran out of liquor by July 4, 1805, a little more than a year after they started. Mackenzie stocked up with nine gallon casks of "reduced" rum but left some for a binge when they came out of the mountains and knew they were safe.

Liquor may have been popular with both the Europeans and Indians, but so was tobacco. The Indians placed symbolic value on smoking and passing the peace pipe was an essential ritual in dealing with friends or in confirming friendship. Tobacco was both a gift and a reward. The voyageurs and the men of all the exploring parties were every bit as addicted to tobacco as the Indians. When Lewis's men dug up a cache after coming back through the mountains, the first thing they looked for was real tobacco, which they had not enjoyed for more than a year.

Disease is the ultimate connection between explorers and indigenous people. The diseases brought from Europe and Africa decimated the native populations of North America. Smallpox, tuberculosis, and measles came from Europe. Yellow fever was brought from Africa in the stinking, pest-ridden holds of the slave ships. Malaria, the ague of spring and summer, came from both Europe and Africa.

The people of the the Americas were defenseless against the microbes and viruses that had bred, mutated, and spread across Asia and Europe. Jared Diamond, writing in *Guns, Germs, and Steel*, ascribed the development of the diseases to the domestication of large mammals that acted as originators and reservoirs of germs. The crowded, unsanitary cities in Europe, where germs spread with ease, were the kitchens of disaster. Diseases spread by direct contact (smallpox), airborne contamination (diphtheria), or insect vectors (malaria and yellow fever) all thrived in the narrow streets and crowded houses of the great cities.

The American continent had no large cities—apart from the cities of the Incas and the Aztecs—and was an open book waiting for the diseases to write their terrible tales. When Cortez' men brought smallpox and other diseases to Mesoamerica, they spread like a windblown prairie fire, killing more than 18 million of the Aztec's 20 million population.

In the eighteenth century, smallpox spread inexorably through North America and took only forty years to move from Mexico to northern Canada. By the 1760s, it had reached halfway up the continent, and in 1782, three women and three children, the last survivors of a group of Cree Indians, staggered into York Factory on the Hudson Bay. The tale they told was of the total destruction of their people by a disease that made them burn with fever and brought out a terrible rash on the skin.

The Ojibwas and Crees had been infected by one of their war parties that found Mandans and Hidatsas dying from a mysterious disease, their lodges filled with rotting corpses. Twenty years later, the Corps of Discovery moved through the same area, but, fortunately, the Mandans were free of the disease—though not for long. In 1837, the tribe was almost wiped out by another epidemic.

One of the reasons that the Corps of Discovery remained remarkably healthy—apart from venereal diseases—was that they traveled through country without big cities. They met many Indians while proceeding north up the Missouri but were always on the move. During the winter of 1804–1805, while living in the Mandan Fort, several men caught—and probably gave—venereal diseases. As they moved west in the summer of 1805, weeks passed without them meeting a single Indian. The Shoshone were free of serious diseases and the men did not stay with them for long. During their stay at Fort Clatsop, they purposely separated themselves from the Chinook and Clatsop tribes, locking the gate of the fort every evening. They were not trying to avoid diseases (except just before they departed for home), but they did not want the Indians to spend the night in the fort. Once again, venereal diseases were their main health problem. The Chinook and Clatsops would later be destroyed by malaria and smallpox.

Hearne, Rae, and Mackenzie moved through a land without towns. The Indians and Eskimos were nomadic, following the caribou and seeking furs. Few white men had visited them and they had no strange diseases of their own to give to the visitors.

Bligh's men survived the starvation and storms of the ocean voyage to die from malaria and other tropical, insect-borne diseases as soon as they landed in Timor and Batavia. In 1804, insect-borne diseases had not yet invaded the center of the American continent. Malaria, a common disease along the East Coast and the Mississippi valley, did not reach the Missouri valley until 1805, after the Lewis and Clark expedition had passed through. The accounts in the journals of various fevers and agues do not resemble the course of malaria and seemed to be cured by laxatives, not Peruvian bark.

The expeditions of Pike, Frémont, and Powell neither carried nor caught any fatal diseases. They may have opened the door to a flood of emigrants, but fatal microbes were not among the gifts they gave the Indians.

14

Leadership
What Made Them Tick?

*Courage and willpower
can make miracles.*

—*Roald Amundsen, Arctic and Antarctic explorer*

*Leadership: the act of getting someone else
to do something that you want done because he wants to do it.*

—*General Dwight D. Eisenhower*

A famous judge said of pornography, "I can't define it, but I know it when I see it." The same could be said of leadership. It is as ephemeral and hard to grasp as a cloud: constantly changing, sometimes bright and gleaming, sometimes dark and threatening, filling the whole sky or suddenly appearing as a small puff on the horizon, growing as a storm approaches.

Social scientists and historians have tried to categorize leadership with a confusing galaxy of terms: transactional, transformational, authoritative, autocratic, consensual, charismatic, heroic, participative, military, intellectual, moral, opportunistic—and in many other ways. It is not difficult to find leaders that fit each description, but trying to squeeze a leader into an appropriate pigeonhole is not as easy. A leader may be autocratic at one moment and consensual at another, heroic or quiet, artistic or a sports icon, a general or a private. There are no limits.

William Bligh was autocratic, but was also participative, sharing the same hardships and miserable scraps of food with his men. He could not avoid the hardships and was meticulous in making sure that the food was shared equally between everyone. Some of the men accused him of cheating and wanted him blown out of a cannon when they returned to England, but his parsimony brought them all safely to land.

Different leaders require different qualities. Alexander the Great needed reckless courage in battle and theatrical charisma to lead a huge army from the front. Bill Gates, of Microsoft, does not ride into his office every day on a prancing horse, prepared to risk his life in face-to-face combat. Yet the leadership qualities of Alexander the Great and Gates are similar in several important ways: foresight, attention to detail, a willingness to take risks, and an ability to choose the right associates.

Most descriptions of leadership concentrate on the qualities of the leader, but this may sometimes put the cart before the horse. Gary Wills in *Certain Trumpets* had a wider definition: "The leader is one who mobilizes others toward a goal shared by leader and followers." This emphasizes the importance of goals and followers as well as the talents of the leader, the concept of a three-legged stool: each leg is important, though one leg may be more important than another for a particular endeavor.

Goals

Unworthy goals attracts few followers and weak leaders. A strong leader may be unable to blow fire into a poor goal and dynamic followers with great goals may choose the wrong leaders. In the Russian revolution, the people were powerful, their goals honorable, but their leaders led them down the path to Communism and, ultimately, Stalin. The American revolution had good goals, strong followers, and wise leaders.

Sometimes the goal is defined before a leader arises, and sometimes the leader chooses the goal. And after the goal has been chosen, an opportunity must occur for it to be achieved. The goal of reaching the West Coast preceded the choice of Meriwether Lewis as leader. President Thomas Jefferson had long dreamed of finding an all-water route to the coast. The opportunity came after Jefferson had been elected president and the Congress had agreed to provide money to support the expedition. Then Lewis was chosen. Jefferson may already have had Lewis in mind, but until the opportunity arose to put the plan into action, there was no need for a leader. Jefferson had choices. He had previously tried to persuade three different leaders—George Rogers Clark, John Ledyard, and André Michaux—to lead similar expeditions. All attempts failed for different reasons. Only when the stars came into line was it possible for the plan to go forward.

No expedition ever received more explicit goals than those given to Lewis by President Jefferson. "The object of your mission is to explore the Missouri River & such principal stream of it, as by it's course & communication with the waters of the Pacific Ocean, whether the Columbia, Oregon, Colorado or and other river may offer the most direct & practicable communication across this continent, for purposes of commerce." The goal was clear, exciting, honorable, and, Jefferson hoped, attainable. It was a goal to inspire, for its attainment would enlarge a nation and bring fame to the participants. An ideal goal.

Each of our explorers had different goals. After the mutiny, Bligh had two goals: the first was to save his life and the lives of those set adrift with him, the second was to reach England and make sure that the mutineers were caught and hanged. He reached England, although some of his men died before returning home. Some of the mutineers were caught and punished, but the main party reached Pitcairn Island and were not discovered for many years.

Zebulon Montgomery Pike was first assigned by General James Wilkinson to explore the source of the Mississippi and then, on a second voyage to survey the Arkansas, Red, and Rio Grande Rivers. His personal goal was to complete his assignment, hoping to achieve fame, promotion, and, perhaps, wealth. General Wilkinson had his own goals that led to Pike being chosen as the leader.

Goals can be stacked one upon another, like a pile of coins of differing values. Dwight Eisenhower's goal on D-day in 1944 was to recapture Europe. General Omar Bradley's goal was to capture Omaha Beach. The goal of a company commander was to capture his appointed objective. The goal of the soldier jumping off the landing craft was to stay alive.

Samuel Hearne's goals were strictly exploratory on behalf of the Hudson's Bay Company. The company set his goals, then chose him because of his skills and experience. Without the company decisions, he might have spent all his years trading in the forts and would never have opened up the vastness of the Canadian north. But when the opportunity arose, his drive and skills made him the man who fit the job. John Rae set out to explore the Arctic shore, but was also asked to find Sir John Franklin's expedition. Paradoxically, he found out about Franklin's fate when he was on a purely exploratory expedition.

Alexander Mackenzie's goals were mixed. He was intent on finding new hunting grounds for the North West Company but, at the same time, set himself the goal of crossing the continent and expanding British dominion. He wrote in his journal, "By unfolding countries hitherto unexplored, and which, I presume, by now be considered part of the British dominions, it will be received as a faithful tribute to the prosperity of my country."

The government did not send John Wesley Powell; he was a self-starter. He chose his own objectives, recruited his own men, and headed downstream. He was a leader who made his own goals and set about achieving them.

Senator Thomas Hart Benton was the real driving force behind John Charles Frémont. It was his determination to establish railroad routes to the west and his dream of making the West Coast the far limit of the United States that inspired and directed Frémont. If Frémont had not been Benton's son-in-law, he might never have been chosen to the lead the expeditions to the Wind River Mountains, the San Juans, and California. Without the right backing and influence, he might have remained a frustrated army topographer, dreaming of what might have been.

The goals behind Franklin's voyages to the far northwest of Canada were clear. The Northwest Passage sea route had not been found. Fragments of coastline had been mapped from both ends of the north shore of the continent, but there were long, unexplored stretches and delineating those gaps might lead to the discovery of the sea route. His last voyage in 1845, which ended so disastrously, was specifically launched as a final, triumphant attempt by the Royal Navy to sail through the passage.

Followers

After a leader has been chosen, "followers" must be found. The leader may already know who the followers are, or the followers may even have chosen the leader. But with most expeditions, a goal has been set, a leader chosen, and then the followers are picked.

The number and type of followers—soldiers, voyageurs, mountain men, or trappers—depends on the type of expedition, the organizing authority, and the source of money. For Lewis and William Clark, the choices were easy. The expedition was military, so the participants were soldiers with a few interpreters. The men came under the laws of the army and the government paid for the supplies.

Taking Sacagawea and a newborn baby was an unusual but important afterthought. Lewis knew he would have to get horses from the Shoshone, and having a young woman in the group who could speak both Shoshone and Hidatsa increased the chances of success. That the young woman had an infant strapped to her back does not seem to have concerned Lewis. He had probably seen many young Indian women doing hard manual labor in the fields with babies on their backs and was well aware of their strength and endurance.

Lewis had little to do with the recruitment of his men. Clark chose most of them while Lewis was sailing down the Ohio River. Lewis recruited a few critical men, including John Colter and George Drouillard, but told Clark that everything "depended on a judicious selection of our men; their qualifications should be such as perfectly fit them for the service, otherwise they will rather clog than further the objects in view." Clark avoided choosing gentlemen as he did not think they could withstand the hardships of the voyage. Instead, he found seven young men from Kentucky, "the best young woodsmen and hunters in this part of the countrey," unmarried, and "used to hardships of a remarkable degree." The time spent in the camp at Wood River distinguished the Lewis and Clark expedition from many of the others. This was an opportunity for Clark to train the men, establish standards of discipline, improve the men's marksmanship, and develop an ésprit de corps among those who would travel 8,000 miles with him on the greatest adventure of their lives.

Neither Pike nor Frémont had this advantage. They set off at short notice, sometimes picking up their men with limited knowledge of their experiences. Frémont chose Kit Carson after a short visit with him on a boat. He turned out to be a wonderful choice, but Frémont did not know him as intimately as Lewis knew Clark. In Frémont's later expeditions, he usually took along five or six men who had been with him before, providing at least a core of experienced men he could trust.

Pike also had to choose his men quickly. General Wilkinson ordered him to start at very short notice. As an army officer, he presumably picked the best men he could find in his unit, but they were not chosen as carefully as the men of Corps of Discovery. He called them a bunch of "damned rascals"—and some of them were. On Pike's second voyage, he even took along the former Sergeant Henry Kennerman who had been reduced in rank to private on the first expedition. This was a bad choice, for he deserted soon after the expedition started.

Followers have to be nurtured to stay in tune with the goals of their leader. All the followers in these expeditions experienced great hardships. Pike was not indifferent to their hardships. While they were struggling in the forests around the upper reaches of the Mississippi, he wrote in his diary, "These circumstances convinced me that if I had no regard for my own health and constitution, I should have for these poor fellows who, to obey my orders, were killing themselves." His remarks might have been more truthful if he had written, "These poor fellows who, *to fulfill my ambitions. …*" By disobeying the orders Wilkinson had given him to return to Saint Louis before the river froze, he exposed his men to a severe winter only because he wanted to be the first man to discover the origin of the Mississippi. When his men were frostbitten in Colorado, he wrote, "Thus these poor fellows are to be invalids for life, made infirm at the commencement of manhood and in the prime of their course … for what is the pension? Not sufficient to buy a man his victuals! What man would even lose the smallest joints for such a pittance?"

Pike's compassion was in stark contrast to the indifference Frémont showed toward his men when conditions in the San Juan Mountains were deteriorating catastrophically. "The courage of the men failed fast; in fact, I have never seen men so discouraged by misfortune as they were on that occasion; but as you know, *the party was not constituted like the former ones*" (emphasis added). To Frémont, they were not "the right stuff."

Frémont's men were despairing of their lives, and for good reasons. They were engulfed in a blizzard at 12,000 feet, far from help, with exhausted, starving mules dying every day. One-third of the men were frostbitten. It was not surprising that when Ben Kern awoke one morning to find himself covered by eight inches of snow, he thought "the whole expedition was destroyed and if we all get to some settlement with our lives we would be doing well." Later, after the expedition had broken up into small, undisciplined groups struggling for their lives, Frémont wrote to his wife, "My presence kept them together and quiet, my absence may have had a bad effect." He did not suggest he should have stayed with them.

Position endows a leader with power over his followers. The nature of that power depends on how he was chosen, the resources at his command, and his ability to inspire his followers with the same enthusiasm as his own for the common goals. In response, the followers, to the extent that they believe the goals to be desirable and achievable and their leaders to be compassionate, will endure whatever trials fate throws across their path. As soon as the relationship begins to fray—as it did with Frémont in the winter of 1849—the outcome of the expedition is already sealed. Even Frémont, as determined, persistent, and single-minded a leader as one could imagine, realized when the point of defeat had been reached. He wrote to his wife, "The trail showed as though a defeated party had passed by; packsaddles, scattered articles of clothing and dead mules strewed along." Abandonment of equipment and dead and dying mules were, indeed, the signs of defeat.

Frémont did nothing to boost the morale of his men. When he finally left the disintegrating group, ostensibly to seek help, his remark, later recalled by Micajah McGehee, "If we wished to see him we must be in a hurry because he was going on to California," must have cut whatever threads of trust still remained between him and his men. He accepted no blame and never once wrote, "if only ... " All he wrote was, "I wish for a time to shut out these things from my mind, to leave this country, and all thoughts and all things connected with recent events." Amazingly, after the briefest of rests, twenty survivors continued on with him to California.

Followers must trust their leaders. Edward Kern wrote that Frémont's greatest fear was that the truth of the disaster would be told. But Alexis Godey, who, above all others, might have condemned Frémont for callous abandonment of his men, wrote, "Frémont, more than any other man I ever knew, possessed the respect and affection of his men ... and unhesitatingly exposed himself to every danger and privation." The ten men who starved and froze to death never had a chance to express their opinions. They might have differed from Godey's.

It would be unfair to defame Frémont's entire reputation on the basis of the disastrous ending of one expedition. If a single failure were the criterion for permanent condemnation, Franklin's career would have ended after his first overland expedition, which ended with death and cannibalism. He was inexperienced in land travel, let alone in travel in the far north. He miscalculated time and distances and pushed ahead when he knew that his food supplies would be inadequate. Had not George Back, like Godey, made a heroic search for help and brought the Indians, everyone would have died. Franklin, unlike Frémont, did acknowledge the help he received and the loyalty of his men.

The Lewis and Clark expedition, on the other hand, was an amazing example of prolonged trust and loyalty. For 863 days, while traveling more than 8,000 miles, the cracks in discipline and morale were trivial and probably less than might be expected over a similar period of regular military service.

As the expedition set off from the Mandan village, Sergeant Joseph Whitehouse expressed the feelings of the men when he wrote in his diary that they were "trusting to providence & the conduct of our officers in all our difficulties." And Lewis wrote at the same time to his mother, "With such men I have everything to hope, but little to fear." He was not just trying to calm the natural fears of his anxious mother, he was expressing genuine feelings about his men. A bond of trust and loyalty had been forged between the leaders and the men during the journey up the Missouri.

The men had seen justice fairly and appropriately meted out. They had watched the firmness of their officers when they faced threatening Sioux. They had been well fed and rewarded with an occasional shot of whiskey and some merry evenings around the campfire, drinking and dancing to the wild fiddle playing of Pierre Cruzatte. They had spent a relatively warm and peaceful winter in the Mandan Fort, enjoying the favors of the local women. And they knew that they were embarking on a journey of national importance with the promise of good pay and a gift of land at the end. Life in a fort in Kentucky or Ohio, taking occasional revenge on marauding Indians, was never that good.

Rae and his men were the first whites to spend a winter on the Arctic tundra camped in snow houses and tents. Before making their camp, Rae asked his men if they were willing to spend a long, dark, freezing winter at risk of frostbite and starvation. The men believed in their leader and survived because of careful planning and confidence in themselves.

Leaders

The right stuff. Of all the legs of the three-legged leadership stool—goals, followers, and leaders—the one labeled "leader" is, ultimately, the most important. Good followers with a good goal but without a leader get nowhere. Having a good leader does not guarantee success. Many a well-led mountaineering expedition has ended in death and disaster because of storms, avalanches, and rockfalls beyond the control of the leader. Good, courageous military leaders do not always win battles. They may die in a blaze of glory while leading their men into an unpredictable ambush. But successful or not, good military or expedition leaders are imbued with certain essential characteristics.

No single word can describe all the qualities of good leadership. A cluster of words is needed: determination, persistence, single-mindedness, obstinacy, resolution, tenacity, steadfastness, courage, ruthlessness, and the will to win. But these words describe only one part of leadership and others are needed to highlight more qualities: compassion, justice, flexibility, teamwork, foresight, professional skill, the ability to chose the right men, self-discipline, risk-taking, and charisma. All of these qualities were found at different times and under different circumstances in our heroes.

Courage was never in short supply: Hearne, thwarted twice in trying to reach the Coppermine River, turned around and started on a third attempt within ten days; Lewis stood alone to face sixty Shoshone braves; Mackenzie and his men huddled all night on an island in the Bella Coola anticipating an attack at any moment; Pike built a fragile fort, surrounded by a little moat, and believed he could hold off the Spanish dragoons; Frémont defiantly raised an American flag in California on top of a hill and waited for the Mexicans to attack; Bligh refused the pleadings of his men for more food, knowing that they might kill him if they didn't get it; Rae, newly arrived in the Hudson Bay and shipwrecked, rescued his fellow passengers and organized a camp for the winter; Powell, day by day, lined the boats down the tumultuous rapids. The choices, whether for one man facing Indians or a group facing a river, were the same: success or death.

Napoleon thought that determination was the one essential characteristic of a general and the theme of determination echoes through the thoughts of all great generals. But the determination of a field marshal is not the same as that of a company commander.

Field Marshal Earl Haig, commander of the British forces in France during World War I, was a man of steely determination—determination to the point of madness, backed by a belief that he was guided by a voice from above. John Keegan wrote that he was "a man with no concerns for human suffering." During the first day of the Battle of the Somme, in 1916, 20,000 British troops were killed and another 25,000 seriously wounded. Haig's determination to capture 200 yards of mud and shell holes drove him to order another attack on the following day. Once again, thousands of men died for little gain.

The drive and determination of a company commander, sergeant, or even a private is much closer to that of an expedition leader than to that of a commander in chief. In the same battle of the Somme, a British officer noted in his diary, "No single officer got through untouched. The men did grandly—going on without officers and reaching all their objectives." Even though the appointed leaders were killed, others arose from the ranks to take command and achieve the goals of the unit.

An expedition needs a small unit leader, not a field marshal. The determination of the explorer is a combination of courage, the ability to "withstand hardship to a remarkable degree," and obstinacy to continue when the outlook seems hopeless.

Bligh, stepping into a twenty-three-foot open boat with his seventeen involuntary companions, was not discouraged. His diary contained this entry, "In the midst of all I felt an inward happiness which prevented any depression of my spirits." His courage and determination to succeed were buoyed by an indomitable hope that he would be able "to account to my King and Country for my misfortune." Like Frémont, his obstinacy prevented him from seeing that his misfortune was caused by his own conduct or mistakes. But unlike Frémont, he was determined, although faced by seemingly impossible odds, to bring his men to safety.

Sir Raymond Priestley, a member of the 1907 to 1909 Nimrod Antarctic Expedition, described his hero, Ernest Shackleton, as the "greatest leader that ever came on God's earth, bar none." Faced with the loss of his ship the *Endurance* in 1914, crushed by the Antarctic ice, he mobilized his men and supplies, lived out the winter months on the ice, and, when summer came, made an open boat voyage to Elephant Island. There he left his men and with five others sailed more than 800 miles to the rocky shore of South Georgia. They then climbed over snow-covered mountains to a whaling station on the north shore. As quickly as he could, he mustered a ship and crew, returned to Elephant Island, and rescued all his men. They reached the safety of the Chilean port Punta Arenas two years after they had set sail from England. No one had died. Their incredible achievement received almost no attention. The slaughter on the Western Front drew more attention than the rescue of a small group of men from a distant continent.

Choosing a Leader

It has been said that the door to fame is marked "push" on one side and "pull" on the other. Both these influences played their parts in the choices of these leaders. When the British Admiralty was seeking a leader to find the Northwest Passage in 1845, Franklin was not the first choice. He was, in reality, far down the line. He was a month short of sixty, overweight, and in poor physical shape and his record of success was poor: one disastrous expedition, one successful, and a controversial term of office as governor of Tasmania ending in his recall to London. His influential, pushy wife got him the job. Whether anyone else could have done any better than he did is an open question, because the catastrophic end to the expedition was probably out of his control. He may have made a poor navigational choice in trying to go down a channel that we now know is never open. But the ice that trapped his ships and the diseases that killed his men were not due to his poor leadership. Fate can destroy expeditions with both good and bad leaders.

The Royal Navy chose Bligh to go to Tahiti and return to the West Indies with breadfruit as cheap food for the slaves. He had served with distinction under James Cook and was a skillful navigator who had already been to the South Pacific. The Admiralty saw the commission as a routine supply trip, not as an exploration. The navy's choice was, perhaps, influenced by Bligh's friendship with Sir Joseph Banks, one of the most important men in London.

President Jefferson pushed Lewis, but it was Lewis's position as secretary to the president that gave him the pull. Jefferson chose Lewis based on an intimate knowledge of the man, his abilities and temperament, record in the army, and family background. Lewis chose Clark after Jefferson told him to find a second in command. That choice was based on the friendship and respect that had grown between them while they served together in the army. Clark was then Lewis's commanding officer and Lewis could hardly have done anything less than offer him the same rank as his, captain. It was not Lewis's fault that the army bureaucracy, to Lewis's anger, frustration, and embarrassment, chose to give him the rank of a second lieutenant.

Pike and Frémont, both soldiers, were chosen through totally different channels. Pike, the blue-eyed protégé of General Wilkinson was chosen seemingly without Jefferson's approval (although he later approved the expeditions). He was not an experienced expeditionary leader but hero-worshipped Wilkinson and was a conscientious, self-reliant officer.

Frémont also had influential friends, especially his father-in-law, Senator Benton. He had already proved himself on expeditions with the famous surveyor Joseph Nicollet, and as his job was to conduct more of a survey than an exploration, he was a suitable choice.

The Hudson's Bay Company had for many years confined their interests to the shores of the bay, but when they learned that there could be a copper mine at the mouth of a great river that ran northward into the ocean, they appointed Hearne, who had already shown his skill in wilderness exploration to find the mine and assess its future value. Later, when the North West Company began to outsmart them and steal their business by intercepting the Indians before they reached the company forts, it became necessary for them to expand their sphere of influence. Once again, they turned to Hearne, already tested and tried, to set up their first central outpost. He was the obvious choice.

Mackenzie worked his way rapidly up the North West Company hierarchy, always willing to go farther and deeper into the hinterland, although Peter Pond had explored much of the country before him. He had an adventurous spirit and hoped to find the elusive northwest river to the Pacific Ocean. His first attempt took him to the Arctic Ocean, but this experience only whetted his appetite for further exploration. In many ways, he chose himself. He was not directed by the board of the company to go to the

Pacific. He was first introduced to the idea by Pond. He followed the star that Pond had shown him.

Origins

To follow the threads of war, bloodshed, and adventure that ran through the lives of these explorers helps us to understand how they achieved what they did.

Hearne, Bligh, and Franklin were all hardened in the crucible of war, serving king and country. All joined the Royal Navy at an early age and took part in the death and destruction of close-quarter naval combat at an age when modern boys would be in high school, more concerned about football and girls than about the possibility of being blown to bits by a cannon ball. Hearne joined his first ship in Portsmouth harbor as a "young gentleman" at the age of twelve. His commander, Captain Samuel Hood, was strict but fair, and thought highly enough of his young protégé to accelerate his promotion based on talent and not on family connections. Within two months of joining the ship, Hearne saw his captain returning from the execution of Admiral John Byng for supposed cowardice—an execution that Hearne came to consider totally unjustified. Within four months, his ship was fighting the French, closing against an enemy ship, and blasting it at point-blank range. During his seven years of service in which he sailed on five ships with Captain Samuel Hood and was promoted at a very early age to quartermaster's mate, he became used to the blast of cannons, the screams of wounded men, and decks flowing with blood. He saw floggings and men hanged from the yard arm; so-called justice meted out without the benefits of courts or laws. After he was honorably discharged from the navy, he sailed for a few years on merchant ships and then joined the Hudson's Bay Company, where he found the conditions of life, the pay, and the mild discipline a blessed relief. He joined the navy as a callow boy and left it as a man, tough, self-reliant, hardened by war, and obsessed with a desire to learn.

Similar beginnings marked the careers of Bligh and Franklin. Both joined the navy as "young gentlemen" and both stayed in the navy. Bligh came from a family with strong naval traditions and never thought seriously of another career. He was only seven when he signed on but probably never set foot on a ship until he was about sixteen. He did not see as much fighting as either Hearne or Franklin (much of his service took place in the gap between the Seven Years and Napoleonic wars), but he must have been well thought of because, after only seven years, he was posted to Captain Cook's ship HMS *Endeavour* for its third voyage of exploration to the South Pacific. His association with Cook was the turning point of his life. The voyage of the *Endeavour* was Cook's last and Bligh was present when Cook was killed in Hawaii. Cook's death had a profound effect on his life, his standards of leadership, and—contrary to popular belief—his concern for the care of the crew, their health, and welfare. The discipline he enforced was not unduly harsh by naval standards and his every action was taken out of loyalty to king and country.

Franklin, too, grew up within the tough and bloody embrace of the Royal Navy. He, like Bligh, devoted his whole life to the service. He joined up at age fourteen and within a year narrowly escaped death at the Battle of Copenhagen. He was then assigned to the command of his cousin, Matthew Flinders, and, in one of the greatest naval explorations of all time sailed around Australia, was shipwrecked, saved, and returned to England. In October 1805, as a midshipman in charge of signals, he took part in England's most famous naval battle, Trafalgar, and must have seen the signal flags fluttering on the mast of HMS *Victory*, carrying Lord Horatio Nelson's message to the fleet that "England expects every man to do is duty." The message was his mantra for the rest of his life.

Mackenzie and Rae grew up with equally strong loyalties to their country's flag. Both were born and raised on bleak, wind-swept, almost tree-less islands off the coast of Scotland, Mackenzie in the Hebrides and Rae in that nursery of Hudson Bay employees, the Orkney Islands. Both had fathers who were important in their lives and communities. Mackenzie's father was a member of the local militia and Rae's responsible for managing the largest estate on the island. They were both used to a cold, wet land, surrounded by rough seas. Mackenzie went with his family to the American colonies at an early age, then moved to Canada. His father died from disease while fighting for the Loyalist troops. Rae had a wonderfully free boyhood, hunting, fishing, sailing small boats, and climbing cliffs, growing strong and oblivious to cold and wet.

The same crucible of war that produced the determination and tough-ness of Hearne, Bligh, and Franklin forged the manhood of Powell. Powell came from a religious family with an itinerant preacher for a father. When he was only twelve, he was put in charge of the family farm as his father pursued a higher calling. As his family moved from home to home, he educated himself, became a teacher, and described himself as a "naturalist." He was always inquisitive and daring, but the Civil War turned him from an adventurous young man into a one of steely resolve. He led his battery into the Battle of Shiloh, when no one was giving orders. He saw hundreds of dead and wounded on the battlefield and was severely wounded, losing his right arm. His commanding officer, General William Wallace, gave up his horse to Powell so that he could ride to safety. Wallace was killed minutes later.

Lewis and Clark both grew up in prominent Virginian families where service to one's country was an unspoken, guiding life force. Lewis's father died during the Revolutionary War and Clark's oldest brother, George

Rogers Clark, was a national hero. Lewis joined the army during the Whiskey Revolution and stayed on after the nonwar had finished, becoming a captain in the regular army, traveling up and down the Old Northwest as a regimental paymaster before being called to serve in the White House as secretary to Jefferson.

Clark grew up in the shadow of his famous brother, George. When he was still young, the family moved from Virginia to Kentucky, where he acquired many of the wilderness skills he would need later, becoming a crack shot and skilled hunter. He joined the militia in 1789, age nineteen, and witnessed the indiscriminate killing of Indians, women, children, and braves alike. They pushed through pristine wilderness, forded rivers, plunged through swamps, and endured the vicissitudes of unpredictable weather. He was said to be "as brave as Caesar."

When General Anthony Wayne was appointed as commander in chief, Clark signed on as a regular officer in the 5,000 strong continental army. His next years were spent in the dangerous job of moving supplies between isolated forts in Ohio and Kentucky. He frequently came under fire and followed a scorched earth policy, destroying Indian farms and houses. The culmination of Clark's military career came during the Battle of Fallen Timbers when a large Indian force was definitively defeated and forced to sign the Treaty of Greenville. The formal, ritualistic negotiations between General Wayne and the Indians were a lesson in Indian-White diplomacy that was not lost on Clark.

Clark was more experienced than Lewis in warfare, wilderness travel, and negotiations with Indians. The expedition from 1804 to 1806 was, therefore, an extension of the adventurous life he had already been living for fifteen years.

The noise, smoke, confusion, and terror of war were not hardening forces in the early career of Frémont. Born the illegitimate son of a charming French dancing instructor who had eloped with a married socialite from Richmond, Virginia, his early career started—and continued—because he knew the right people. He had an abundance of talent, courage, and determination, but perhaps the relative ease with which he began his career, first due to the influence of Joel Poinsett and then because of his marriage to the daughter of Senator Benton, accounts for the arrogant side of his character that, if anything, increased his desire to become a leader.

A theme common to the lives of all these men was their love of country. When Franklin was starving and dying in the Canadian Barrens in 1821, he still behaved as a naval officer, planning how best to save his men but still maintaining a separation between "officers" and "other ranks." Despite the ghastly outcome of the expedition, he was received as a national hero when he returned to London. The British always look kindly on heroic failures.

Bligh never concealed that it was his sense of duty to the navy that compelled him to drive and discipline his men. He did not order floggings or have his men thrown into irons out of intentional cruelty, although one midshipman was kept in irons for eleven weeks just to uphold the laws and traditions of the navy. John Barrow, the second secretary of the Admiralty, wrote an account of the mutiny on the *Bounty*. He said of Bligh, "He was a man of coarse habits, and entertained very mistaken notions with regard to discipline, yet he had many redeeming qualities." His terrible temper was not one of his redeeming characteristics. On one occasion, when his men refused to eat rotten pumpkin, he flew into a rage, screaming "you damned infernal scoundrels, I'll make you eat grass or anything you can catch, before I have done with you." His men followed him out of both fear and respect.

Loyalty to President Jefferson, although of a different quality, pushed Lewis and Clark across the snow-filled Bitterroot Mountains. A group of trappers, under similar circumstances, might have turned back and sought shelter for the upcoming winter.

A higher cause, whether loyalty to country, a religion, or even a political party, can empower people to reach achievement and survival. Religion often emboldens both individuals and armies, but it was not the prime motivating force for any of the leaders discussed here, although it played an important part in the lives of some. Sir John Franklin was very religious and conducted a divine service every Sunday, during calm or a storm, even when many in his congregation had no idea what he was praying about. Before Franklin started on his catastrophic journey up the Coppermine, he called the men to prayer and Dr. John Richardson was greatly moved by the simplicity of Franklin's trust in God.

In contrast, religion played little or no part in the lives of Lewis, Clark, or their men. Before setting out from Saint Charles, some of the French voyageurs attended mass, but after that religion seems to have been forgotten. Lewis, in a self-critical entry in his journal on his thirty-second birthday, wrote of feeling inadequate about his achievements and regretting the hours he had not spent acquiring more knowledge, but did not refer to God. He was too much a man of the Enlightenment, bound to reason rather than religion, to confess to a deep religious feeling. Not only did he come from the age of reason, but also from a nation that in its Constitution had explicitly defined the limits between church and state.

Franklin and Bligh both came from a nation and a service—the Royal Navy—with an established religion, the Episcopal Church. They had been brought up on land and sea to the regular ritual of divine service on Sunday. Bligh did not hesitate to ask for divine aid or to give thanks. On May 21, 1789, after surviving a tremendous storm, Bligh wrote a prayer in his journal in which he said, "Thou has showed us the wonders of the deep, that we might see how powerfull gracious a God thou art; how able and ready to help those that trust in thee. ... We promise to renew our unfeigned thanks at thy Divine Altar & mend our lives according to thy Holy word." Of their landing on a sliver of beach on the Barrier Reef, Barrow wrote, "They now returned thanks to God for his generous protection, and with much content took their miserable allowance of one twenty-fifth of a pound of bread, and a quarter of a pint of water, for dinner."

Before he left the navy, while still only eighteen years old, Hearne became intrigued with the writings of Voltaire and was always tolerant of the religious beliefs of the Indians. His friend and mentor Matonabee tried to understand Christianity but could never bring himself to accept its teachings. Rae was equally tolerant of the beliefs of the Indians and Eskimos.

Powell, named after the founder of the Wesleyan Church and brought up in a religious family, lost his faith when he studied science, and by the time of his voyage down the Grand Canyon believed more in science and geology than in God.

Belief in a higher force can underpin resolution and strength, but also provides the sense of superiority and optimism so necessary in a leader. If a leader does not feel himself superior to his enemy or stronger than the hazards that face him, he is not likely to succeed. A leader must be able to convey his sense of power to his followers, whether his power is based on superior forces or greater experience and skills. The troops that landed on D-day saw a fleet of ships stretching from horizon to horizon and a sky filled with their own planes. They were overwhelmed by the magnitude of the power behind them. They knew they were unbeatable.

Power may also be based on skill. Bligh knew that he was a superb navigator and did not believe that anyone else on the boat was capable of taking over any navigational duties. Pike was a crack shot and hunter and provided much of the meat for his men. The same was true of Rae. He had such faith in his own skills that he did not hesitate to embark on long voyages without another hunter. Great climbers may be awed by the size and beauty of the mountain they are about to assault, but if they are to succeed they must believe that they can "make it go."

Crises

The bonds between an expedition leader and his men are never tested more than during a crisis or in making a critical decision. During his voyage to the Pacific, Mackenzie chose to go down the Fraser River, which turned out to be impassable. Friendly natives he had spoken with advised him that the nations between them and the ocean were very fierce. He could try to push on but would probably not get back to Athabaska before the winter. Or he could turn back and go overland to another river that flowed to the coast. Mackenzie thought hard about his choices. "The discouraging circumstances of my situation ... were now heightened by the discontents of my people. ... It was absolutely necessary that I should come to a final determination which route to take: and no long interval of reflection was employed before I preferred to go overland."

As a good leader, he called his men together and explained the situation and his thoughts. "I declared my resolution not to attempt it unless they would fully engage. ... This proposition was met with the most zealous return, and they unanimously assured me that they were as willing now as they had ever been to abide by my resolutions ... and to follow me wherever I should go." There would be no turning back. The men would stick with Mackenzie, whatever the outcome.

In June 1805, Lewis and Clark had a similar decision to make when they reached the junction of two large rivers. "An interesting question was now to be determined. Which of the rivers was the Missouri?" wrote Lewis. He remembered his orders from Jefferson were to explore the Missouri and not be diverted by some tempting tributary. Sergeant Nathaniel Pryor was sent up the right-hand fork and Sergeant Patrick Gass up the left. Pryor reported that his fork turned north, while Gass found that his continued south and west. Lewis made a critical observation: the right-hand fork contained muddy water, exactly the same as the Missouri; the left-hand branch was crystal clear, with a bottom covered with smooth river stones. The men argued to follow the muddy river, but Lewis and Clark concluded that the clear stream came from the mountains.

Lewis, carrying a backpack (apparently for the first time in his life!), with six men walked more than sixty miles up the northern branch in two days. He observed that the river took too direct a northerly course. To his mind, it was not the Missouri. Clark, who had gone up the clear stream, agreed with him. The men still disagreed but willingly followed their leaders. The decision proved to be correct when Lewis found the Great Falls.

In a smaller crisis, Lewis showed his mettle in a different way. Private Richard Windsor fell and became panic-stricken while crossing a slippery cliff face. Lewis calmly directed him to dig a foothold with his knife and he crossed safely but shaken.

It is not always possible for a leader to persuade his followers of the correctness of a decision. Near the end of their wild and dangerous voyage down the Grand Canyon, three of the men—Oramel and Seneca Howland and Bill Dunn, who had been in a state of near mutiny for several days—said that they were going to climb out of the canyon. Try as he might, Powell could not persuade them to change their minds. They were at the head of a ferocious rapid that the three men did not think they could survive. They had lost all confidence in their leader. Breakfast the next day was as "solemn as a funeral" before the men took their sad departure. After Powell and the remaining men had successfully run the rapid, they fired their guns to indicate to the departing men, who could not have been far up the cliffs, that all was well. The invitation to return was ignored. The men were never seen again, and those who stayed on the river ran one last terrifying rapid and emerged from the canyon one day later safe and triumphant.

Powell had constant struggles with his men. His military attitude did not sit well with his laid-back, freewheeling companions. The group never knit and was constrained by geography rather than by loyalty. An embittered Jack Sumner felt he was never paid appropriately and the others went their separate ways. There were no happy reunions.

When disaster strikes, a leader's determination to continue is even more important. In 1953, 9,000 feet above base camp on K2, the second highest mountain in the world, one man lay desperately ill in his tent, but the others still had the resolve to reach the summit. The two strongest climbers set out to try to conquer the last pitches of the peak. As Charles Houston wrote in *K2: The Savage Mountain*, "After two hours they returned, having climbed perhaps 400 feet. They were still far from the summit cone. But their gesture underlined our spirit. We were not beaten."

Failure to achieve a long sought goal can prick the balloon of confidence and start a nagging suspicion of doubt. When Roald Amundsen beat Robert Falcon Scott in his attempt to reach the South Pole, Scott's diary contained two interesting entries. When Scott realized that Amundsen had reached the Pole first, he wrote, "The Norwegians have forestalled us and are first at the Pole. It is a terrible disappointment, and I am very sorry for my loyal companions." He wrote "the Norwegians," not "Amundsen." To Scott, this defeat was a national as well as a personal defeat. They turned for home and his diary gave hints of despair. "Great God! This is an awful place and terrible enough for us to have labored to it without the reward of priority. ... Now for the run home and a desperate struggle. I wonder if we can make it." His confidence in his skills and strength had been threatened. The tone of his writing echoed that of Frémont after leaving the San Juans. "I wish for a time to shut out these things from my mind, to leave this country, and all thoughts and all things connected with recent events."

Care and Compassion

Although a leader needs demonstrable power, the quality of his leadership depends on how he treats his followers. When Pike and Frémont, exerting reckless, egotistical power, led their men unnecessarily into terrible situations, the men responded with anger. Private John Brown turned on Pike and said to him, "It is more than human nature could bear, to march three days without sustenance through snow three feet deep, to carry burdens only fit for horses." Ben Kern, waking with eight inches of new San Juan snow on his blanket, wrote in his diary, "The whole expedition was destroyed." Pike waited a couple of days before haranguing Brown, complaining that he personally had withstood the same privations as the men and, "I believe my natural strength is less able to bear than any man's in the party (which was not true) ... your ready compliance and firm perseverance I had reason to expect as the leader of men and my companions in misery and danger. ... But I assure you should it ever be repeated, by instant death I will revenge your ingratitude and punish your disobedience." Pike had supplied meat for his men after the hunters became incapacitated with frostbite and could not hunt. His rage at Brown's outburst is understandable. And Frémont whined to his wife, "I have never seen men so discouraged by misfortune." Both leaders thought they had been doing their best in the face of terrible misfortune and blamed fate for being unfair. But neither Pike nor Frémont should have found themselves in these predicaments in the first place.

Justice

Discipline is essential for the achievement of an expedition's goals. If the expedition is military, the laws of the army or navy apply. If the group is a mixture of civilians and military, as was the case with Franklin's overland expeditions to the north of Canada, a conflict between one set of laws and another may be a problem for the leader. Franklin had trouble reconciling the casual ways of the Indians on whom he relied with the stricter discipline he could impose on the naval men who accompanied him. He never resorted to flogging, as did Lewis and Bligh, because flogging had almost disappeared from the British navy and the middle of the Canadian wilderness in winter was not the place to hold a court-martial and inflict severe bodily punishment. As no records exist, we know nothing about disciplinary problems on Franklin's last expedition. Franklin was well liked as a commanding officer and was never known as a fierce disciplinarian. Initially, until widespread sickness struck, morale should have been high and disciplinary problems few.

Lewis had five men flogged for insolence, drunkenness, stealing whiskey, and falling asleep while on sentry duty and desertion. Two of those offenses, falling asleep and desertion, were punishable with death. But the expedition would have been weakened by the loss of men and the effect on the others of having to execute one of their own would have destroyed morale. Lewis was wise to include men of the corps in the juries—this was perfectly legal under the code of military justice—and the resulting punishments were seen to be just and fair. Two men were discharged from the corps and returned to Saint Louis after the winter at the Mandan Fort. This by itself was a severe punishment for men who had hoped to gain financially and with a grant of land from their service, apart from the glory of being one of the few to journey to the Pacific Coast.

While Lewis and Clark were exploring the west, Pike was looking for the source of the Mississippi. He had one major disciplinary problem: when he returned to his base camp, he found that Sergeant Henry Kennerman, who had been left in charge, had consumed all the meat and given away or stolen most of the gifts for the Indians. Pike could have ordered Kennerman flogged, or even executed, but only reduced him to private. Once again, the remoteness of the place where the crime was committed and the fact that Pike was the only officer in the group may have influenced his decision to be lenient. Why he took Kennerman on the second expedition so soon after his disgrace is hard to understand. Perhaps he was a silver-tongued barrack lawyer who promised never to offend again. The next time, he deserted and disappeared. Pike was not about to search for him as Lewis had done for Moses Reed and probably thought, "Good riddance."

Many historians have regarded Bligh as a sadistic fiend. But as Caroline Alexander has pointed out in her book *The Bounty*, Bligh did not order flogging as frequently as the average naval captain of his day. He had a terrible temper and punished some men out of proportion to the crimes they committed. If there had never been a mutiny with the subsequent courts-martial, his punishments would have been accepted as part of the harshness of service.

There must have been moments on Powell's expedition when he would gladly have imposed military discipline on his men, especially toward the end when guns were drawn and his life was threatened. But he had no legal powers and had to use persuasion rather than violence to maintain the integrity of the group.

Man Management

Leadership has a softer, practical side: food, shelter, clothing, and entertainment. A good leader makes sure his men are fed and, if possible, well clothed and sheltered. Most of the expeditions started out with plenty of food, but when winter came early, game disappeared, or there was no game (as at the bottom of the Grand Canyon), it did not take long before starvation or severe hunger stalked the groups and ruined morale.

Clothing was always a problem. Even if the men started out well clothed and shod, the wear and tear on their clothes left men in tatters. Pike did not take appropriate winter clothing on either of his expeditions. Lewis's and Clark's men made clothes from deer- and elk skin as they journeyed. They made more than 300 pairs of moccasins while at Fort Clatsop. And it was probably because Lewis was wearing filthy buckskin clothes when he went hunting with Pierre Cruzatte that his half-blind companion mistook him for an elk. Rae wore Eskimo clothing because it was warm and practical. He also greatly admired the stitch work and tailoring skills of the Indian and Eskimo women.

Lewis and Clark were smart enough not to travel during the winters. They built forts for shelter and their hunters were able to keep them adequately supplied with food. They ran very short of food while struggling through the Bitterroots but managed to survive and never got into the same situation again. The food at Fort Clatsop was not good because the climate prevented the preservation of meat. But even when the larder was almost empty, the men were not alarmed because they knew that the hunters would not fail them.

Living conditions were cramped. Washing was not a part of their daily routine. The smell of drying buckskin clothes and dirty bodies filled the small rooms. The men smoked (only seven did not smoke), coughed, and belched almost in each other's faces. Most of the men were illiterate. There were no books to read, except the reference books that Lewis had brought with him. There was no "entertainment" as we now know it. They could hunt, make friendly forays into the local Indian villages, and spend long hours mending their clothes and picking lice out of their blankets. Lewis found life at Fort Clatsop so boring that he spent most of his time writing extensive reports on the culture of the Indians and descriptions of the wildlife. Clark worked on his maps. The forty-two days of rain and only three sunny days at Fort Clatsop must have been thoroughly depressing. Yet as they prepared to leave Fort Clatsop, Lewis wrote in his journal, "We have lived quite as comfortably as we had any reason to expect we should: and have accomplished every object which induced our remaining at this place."

Of all the explorers described, Rae perhaps ate better than any other. Not only was he an excellent shot, but he traveled with, and learned from, his Indians and Eskimo friends who were superb hunters. When they knew they would spend the whole winter in isolated snow houses, they shot and stocked large quantities of food. Rae never hesitated to learn as much as he could about the hunting and survival skills of the natives and he was rewarded accordingly.

Sustaining morale is one of the most important duties of a leader. Sometimes, as on Scott's return from the Pole, weather conditions become so bad that depression is almost inevitable. But Scott praised the cheerfulness of his friends to the end.

Lewis recruited Cruzatte partly because he could play a cheerful fiddle. On many occasions when the day had been particularly hard, Lewis distributed a tot of whiskey and had Cruzatte play for wild fireside dancing.

Alcohol was often used to raise morale. Mackenzie cheered his men with drink and extra food. Franklin arranged for music, books, and theatrical performances on his last expedition. Many an Arctic explorer, living for one or two winters, trapped in the ice, mounted plays and musical shows.

Charisma

The personalities of leaders are as variable as the leaders themselves. Nowadays, a politician has little hope of being elected if he or she does not have charisma, which has come to mean a bright, extrovert personality combined with good looks. The original meaning of the word was "blessed by God," which does not automatically translate into our present meaning of the word.

Great leaders somehow command respect just by appearing on the stage. As some actors have a presence that commands attention even when they are not speaking, so do some people dominate a scene: General George Patton, Winston Churchill, General Douglas MacArthur, Princess Diana. The only way we can judge the charisma of the leaders we have been describing is by their portraits and the descriptions left by others. The portrait of Rae dressed in full Eskimo furs immediately commands attention. But the portrait of Lewis dressed in a long ermine stole does not help us to see the rugged leader who crossed the Rockies. But his men thought the world of him and followed him without questioning. Frémont was a national hero and when he was selecting the men for his second expedition, he had to escape from the crowds that had collected to volunteer for the trip. We have to assume that all these leaders had that magical quality. They could not have succeeded without it.

Results

Life for everyone is a series of choices. Leadership is a matter of choices, whether in battle, on a mountain, or in a business. Successful leaders make the right choices, but the right choice for one may be the wrong choice for another. Most leaders, however, are judged by their results. If the battle is lost, if the mountain cannot be climbed, if the company fails, the leader must face blame. So how good were the results of these expeditions?

Hearne had to make several attempts but eventually reached the mouth of the Coppermine River only to find that there was no copper, and even if there had been, the sea along the coast was too shallow for a harbor or the landing of large boats. The journey was a commercial failure, but it opened a huge swath of territory to future traders and it was not long before Pond and Mackenzie were following Hearne's tracks into the most profitable trapping area in Canada. In the long run, the fur traders won.

Finding a route across the continent to extend the fur trade from coast to coast was the dream of everyone in the fur business. Mackenzie's classic journey was also a failure in that the route he found was impossibly difficult—and still is not a major route to the coast. But the psychological triumph was enormous. He wrote a book describing the journey that reached President Jefferson and influenced the instructions and hopes for Lewis and Clark. Priority is everything in success.

Jefferson was so impressed by the ease with which Mackenzie crossed the Continental Divide that he thought it would be equally easy for Lewis and Clark to traverse the mountains. He was wrong and the route that Lewis found was as impracticable as Mackenzie's. But although the route was not the answer to the president's dreams, the scientific discoveries, the maps that Clark made, and the descriptions of the country, its people, and its wildlife stirred the soul of the American people and led, eventually, to a massive westerly migration.

Frémont's expeditions differed in goals and in achievements. His first expedition exploring the way to South Pass was a success. The route he surveyed was followed by thousands of emigrants to California and Utah. His surveys of a possible railway route across the San Juans were not successful. Men died and the route was clearly impossible for a railroad. Why he tried the second time is hard to understand. His expedition to California, which resulted in the defeat of the Mexicans, was a success on one hand, but a disaster on the other, because it led to a court-martial for Frémont and the end of his career in the army. Although he had a brief political career, his expeditions after his court-martial cannot be judged as successful.

While Lewis and Clark were exploring the west, Pike was embarking on the first of his two expeditions. He found a lake that he (and others) thought was the source of the Mississippi and, to that extent, was successful. His second expedition ended with the dissolution of his group, many of his men severely frostbitten, and his capture by the Spanish. If his hidden intent was to be captured, he was successful. The information about the Spanish he brought back would have been useful to Wilkinson had Wilkinson not been in trouble by the time that Pike returned to the United States. His discoveries clarified the courses of the Arkansas and Rio Grande Rivers, correcting the maps of the time.

The incredible voyage of Bligh across the Pacific with seventeen men in a twenty-three-foot boat, despite the disastrous reason for the voyage, was a tribute to dominating leadership. His uncompromising determination to get back to England and bring the mutineers to justice and show that he was a loyal servant of his King demanded a style of leadership that almost ended with him being killed by his men. His methods were ruthless. The result was successful.

The final end of Franklin's men will never be known, but his career was a roller-coaster of ups and downs: a successful young naval officer, the leader of a death-haunted expedition for which he was quite unsuited, another expedition in the same area that was successful, a bad governorship, and a death under unknown circumstances. At one moment, his career could be judged a success, at another, one would have to call it a failure. Rae's career was filled with success: he was the greatest snow walker and Arctic explorer of his day, the man who brought to England the first information about the end of Franklin's expedition, and the discoverer of the final link in the Northwest Passage. He set new standards for Arctic overland travel, using Eskimo methods of dress and travel. The only glitch in his career was his failure to be knighted by Queen Victoria. The reason was clear: he told England about cannibalism on the Franklin expedition. His honesty was unacceptable. Perhaps, of all our explorers, he was the most successful.

Fortune is a woman; if you lose her today,
don't expect to get her back tomorrow.

—*Napoleon Bonaparte*

Epilogue
What Happened after the Expeditions?

William Bligh

William Bligh was received in London as a hero, fêted, dined, and wined. But in accordance with naval protocol, he had to be court-martialed for losing the *Bounty* but was acquitted. His account of the voyage, based on his journals, became an immediate best seller. The men he had brought safely across 3,618 miles of open sea were also tried, but only William Purcell was reprimanded for insolence. John Fryer, Bligh's thorn in the flesh during the boat voyage, rose to be a master, never lost his hatred for Bligh, and died impoverished.

An expedition was launched under Captain Edward Edwards to find and capture the mutineers. Ten mutineers were arrested and brought back to England, but not without difficulty. The prisoners were kept locked and shackled in a cage on the upper deck in conditions that would have made Abu Ghraib look like a rest camp. The ship they were on, the *Pandora*, ran aground on the Barrier Reef and broke apart. The prisoners were released only at the last moment. Thirty-one crewmen and four prisoners drowned, one while still chained in the cage. The survivors had to make an open-boat journey to Coupang, an ironic parallel with the voyage that Bligh had made one year before.

The mutineers who survived were tried. Of the nine judges, five had been involved in mutinies on their own or other captain's ships. The ship's fiddler was exonerated. Peter Heywood was pardoned and later became a captain. His daughter married "the cruelest captain in the Navy," who gave her a venereal disease on their wedding night.

Six were found guilty and condemned to death. In four cases, the charges could not be proved and the men were freed. While the trial was proceeding, Bligh was on a second voyage to the South Seas in search of breadfruit to feed the slaves in Jamaica.

The mutineers who did not stay on Tahiti finally hid on Pitcairn Island. They were found accidentally in 1808 by a Boston whaling captain, Mayhew Folger, who was surprised to come on an island that was not marked on any of the charts.

Bligh never rid himself of the scandal of the mutiny. He was made governor of New South Wales but he was recalled home and spent two years imprisoned in a ship off the coast of Australia. He spent five years away from home, fought at the battle of Copenhagen, and was finally appointed Rear Admiral. He continued to have a reputation for a terrible temper and foul language, but his men respected his care for them and he always kept a spotlessly clean and organized ship. Tragedy marred his later life. His wife, his twins, and a mentally impaired daughter all died. He died on May 26, 1817, age sixty-three, with senile dementia, unable to remember the voyage across the Pacific in a rowboat packed with eighteen other men, most of whom came to hate him.

Samuel Hearne

After Samuel Hearne was released by the French and allowed to return to England, he survived a miraculous open-boat voyage with thirty-two of his men, then stayed in England for eight months before returning to Churchill when the war with France ended. The far north was never the same for him. His beloved Mary had died and Matonabee had committed suicide in a fit of depression over Hearne's imprisonment and departure. He spent the next four years unhappy and in poor living conditions, conducting slow, long-distance arguments with the home office over expenses and the need for more houses. He set sail from Churchill for the last time on August 16, 1787. He was forty years old.

He returned to an England that had changed dramatically since his youth. He started writing his memoirs with help from his friend William Wales, but they were not published until after his death. Hearne never received any money from his memoirs because the contract stipulated payment only after his death. He died in November 1792, age forty-seven, at the time that Alexander Mackenzie was preparing for his voyage to the Pacific.

Alexander Mackenzie

After returning from the Pacific, Alexander Mackenzie spent another burdensome winter in the West. "For I think it is unpardonable in any man to remain in this country who can afford to leave it." He handed over responsibilities to his cousin Roderick Mackenzie. He left Athabaska in 1794 and continued to work for the North West Company in Montreal and London. His voyage to the Pacific had cost the company $1,500, but the fame and information obtained far outstripped the cost. He became a leading partner in the company and one of the most influential men in the fur trade. The *Journal of the Voyage to the Pacific* was published in 1801 and was read by President Thomas Jefferson, influencing his thoughts about what Meriwether Lewis and William Clark might expect.

For several years, Mackenzie worked hard to develop British trading posts on the West Coast and to reduce the competition between the North West Company and the Hudson's Bay Company. He left Canada in 1805, never to return. When he was forty-eight, he married fourteen-year-old Geddes Mackenzie, who was from the village of Avoch in the north of Scotland. He was a rich man and he and his wife moved between London and Scotland, associating with royalty and wealthy businessmen. His wife bore him three children and brought him great contentment. He died in 1820, age fifty-six, from what in retrospect sounds like angina and congestive heart failure. His wife survived him by forty years.

Meriwether Lewis

Within hours of returning to Saint Louis, Meriwether Lewis sat down to write a letter to his commander-in-chief announcing the safe return of the expedition. His next intent was to start editing the journals of the expedition; but the intent never became reality. He was caught up in a round of parties and elaborate dinners where the toasts were flowery and the drink flowed generously. Lewis was the hero of the hour and, over the next three months, made his way slowly back to Washington, taking the journals with him.

President Jefferson was delighted to see his friend and urged him to press ahead with the publication of the journals. Lewis assured his chief that he was working on them, but in the next three years, he never edited a single word.

Jefferson had appointed him as governor of the Louisiana Territory, but he did not hurry back to take up his duties. He visited his family in Virginia and spent months in Philadelphia. The names of mysterious women appeared in his correspondence but always identified only by their initials. He became enamored of Letitia Breckenridge, who turned him down and later married a wealthy man.

To his credit, Lewis spent a long time negotiating with the Congress over the rewards for his men and the promotion of William Clark, finally coming to an agreement on generous grants of land and money.

During these months, Lewis was theoretically governor of the Louisiana Territory but was not carrying out any of the duties, although he insisted on receiving the governor's salary; his secretary, Frederick Bates, governed the territory. By the time Lewis returned to Saint Louis in March 1808, Bates was already angry with his boss. From that moment on, the relationship between the two became increasingly antagonistic and Bates eventually sent reports back to Washington accusing Lewis of financial malfeasance and neglect of his duties.

Lewis became a partner with Clark in the development of the Saint Louis Missouri River Fur Company, along with the Chouteau family and Manuel Lisa, a businessman who had helped equip the original expedition.

When Lewis returned to Washington, he had taken Sheheke-shote, a Mandan chief, with him. Jefferson was anxious that Sheheke-shote should be returned safely to his own people. The first attempt ended in disaster after a bloody battle. The Saint Louis Missouri River Fur Company was then formed as a joint military and commercial venture to return Sheheke-shote to his tribe and trap the Missouri and Yellowstone Rivers for beaver. Lewis arranged to finance this expedition with U.S. government funds, an arrangement that would nowadays be a conflict of interests.

Lewis's situation over the next year and a half became worse and worse. He was an alcoholic and probably addicted to opiates he took for malaria and other illnesses. His business affairs were unsuccessful and his arguments with the government in Washington became increasingly angry. He was challenged over amounts as small as $18.00, let alone for larger amounts to pay for the return of Sheheke-shote. His alcoholism, illnesses, and arguments with Washington, on top of a temperament that tended toward melancholia and his relationship with Secretary Bates, became intolerable. When Lewis's creditors in Saint Louis knew that the government was seeking repayment of debts, they began to call in their own debts.

Lewis did not work on the journals during this time and Jefferson, who was no longer president, became increasingly frustrated with his friend. At last, a combination of pressure from Jefferson, accusations from the Treasury about illegal financial claims, and his fights with Bates forced Lewis to return to Washington and sort out the problems. Clark was sure that Lewis would return with his problems solved.

Lewis left Saint Louis on September 4, 1808, in a state of great mental agitation. One of his hosts tried to restrict his drinking and put him under a suicide watch. When he improved, he was allowed to continue, accompanied by two servants. He stopped at Grinder's Inn, a shabby little tavern in Tennessee, on October 10. That night, he walked back and forth, talking to himself, and, in the early hours of October 11, shot himself twice: the first shot grazed his skull, then a second shot went into his chest, from which he died several hours later, a tortured man, tragically changed from a heroic leader.

William Clark

The years after the expedition were happier for William Clark than for Meriwether Lewis, but were also tinged with disappointment and sadness. One month after arriving in Saint Louis, both Clark and Lewis, with an accompanying entourage of Indians, servants, and soldiers, set out for Washington. Clark stopped at his family home and then went on to Fincastle in Virginia to visit the home of his future wife, Julia Hancock. She had only been twelve when he last saw her, but they quickly became enamored again. After spending time in Washington, Clark returned to Fincastle, became officially engaged to Julia, and married her in January 1808. Clark's bride was only sixteen years old. She died at age twenty-eight, leaving her fifty-year-old husband a widower with five children. Within a few months, his daughter Mary and his father-in-law also died. One year later, Clark married Harriet Radford, Julia's cousin. Harriet died eleven years later, having borne two children.

After Lewis's death, the responsibility for editing and publishing the journals fell on Clark. He felt unsuited for this task and contracted with Nicholas Biddle of Philadelphia to edit the journals. They were finally published in 1814 under the title *History of the Expedition under the Command of Captains Lewis and Clark in 1814*. Only 1,417 copies were printed and Clark received neither royalties nor a copy of the final result.

Clark served for seven years as the superintendent of Indian affairs for the Louisiana Territory and in 1820 ran unsuccessfully for governor of the Missouri Territory. He was later reappointed as the Indian agent for the Louisiana Territory, a job for which he was well suited. His relations with the Indians had always been good; during the expedition to the Pacific, Lewis had relied on him for providing medical care to the Indians.

In the later years of his life, Clark was torn between his admiration of and sympathy for the Indians and the policies of the U.S. government that made him sign many treaties depriving Indians of their land and forcing them to migrate west of the Mississippi. He felt particularly sad about cheating the Osage Indians out of thousands of acres of land in return for a paltry reward.

Clark's relationship with his slave York has come under much criticism. York was assigned to the boy William at an early age and served him loyally for thirty years, including the years of the expedition. Clark did not give York his freedom until about 1810 and once wrote that he had had to give York a "severe trouncing" for insubordination. As much as we may criticize Clark now, he was only acting within the mind-set of the slaveholding age.

On a happier note, he educated Baptiste Charbonneau, Sacagawea's son, and started him on a life that introduced him to European aristocracy and led him to a career as a hunting guide and gold seeker.

Clark had a distinguished career after the heady days of the expedition and may have regarded his later achievements as more important than managing the day-to-day affairs of the Corps of Discovery. But his name will always be joined with that of Lewis, so that "LewisandClark" is almost a single word.

Zebulon Montgomery Pike

After he returned to Saint Louis, Zebulon Montgomery Pike tried, unsuccessfully, to persuade the Congress to pay him for his exploratory efforts. He remained in the army, and by the time of the War of 1812, he had attained the rank of brigadier. During the assault on York—now Toronto—Pike's unit chased the fleeing Canadians up a grassy slope (now near a brewery), not knowing that he was falling into a trap. When they paused at the top of the rise, the Canadians lit a fuse connected to an arsenal buried under the slope. Pike was badly wounded by flying debris and died some hours later, on April 23, 1813, with his wife by his side, and—according to tradition—covered by an American flag. In his life, he may have been reckless and naïve, but he was brave and loyal to the army to his dying breath.

John Wesley Powell

When John Wesly Powell left the Grand Canyon, he did not realize that he was only beginning his life's work. He was back at the Grand Canyon within two years with a smaller but better equipped group, including a photographer, making a detailed survey of the area. He returned to Washington and organized the Powell Survey of a large part of the Great American Desert. He was not the only surveyor vying for federal money. Clarence King, Ferdinand Hayden, and J. K. Wheeler had all made surveys of various areas, some to find routes for future railways. Powell soon became embroiled in Washington politics. He hated Hayden but liked King. In the end, Powell agreed to restrict his studies to ethnography, leaving the land surveys to Hayden. His 1878 "Report on the Arid Region of the United States" was a seminal document influencing both geology and the laws governing the water-hungry west. His writings were the first to use the terms "runoff" and "acre foot."

He was director of the United States Geological Survey from 1881 to 1894 and director of the Smithsonian Bureau of Ethnology from 1880 to 1902. He died from a cerebral hemorrhage on September 23, 1902, and was buried in Arlington National Cemetery.

John Charles Frémont

Thirty-six years passed between the end of John Charles Frémont's last expedition and his death in 1890, thirty-six years of wealth and poverty, fame and disgrace, a presidential candidacy and a conviction for fraud, marital happiness and infidelity. At the height of his fame, Frémont was the talk of the nation, drawing cheering crowds wherever he went. When he died, he was living in a cheap boardinghouse in New York, impoverished, a continent away from his wife, who was trying to make a living by writing freelance articles for magazines.

Frémont was a man with grand ideas that never came to fruition. He hoped to make millions from gold mining. He speculated in railroads, tried to borrow millions in France, because he could not raise money in America, and spent his money on lavish houses in New York and in San Francisco. His boat was always going to come in—but never did. One by one, he had to sell his homes. His beautiful La Mariposa estate in California, to which he had hoped to retire, but which his wife did not like, was the first to go. His investments in railways were never successful; one ended in bankruptcy for the railroad and a five-year sentence for Frémont (which he did not have to serve).

But there were bright spots, although even these seemed to turn to dust. In 1855, he was chosen as the Republican candidate for the presidency. Abraham Lincoln was suggested as a vice president but was not chosen. James Buchanan defeated him. Frémont was asked to run again but declined.

During the Civil War, he was commissioned as a general, but Lincoln dismissed him because of failures. In 1878, he was appointed governor of Arizona, but, once again, he had to resign because he was accused of neglecting his duties.

How to assess the achievements of such a complex man? His explorations opened up large parts of the West and his adventures in California were important in making that territory part of the United States. He was immensely popular, regarded as a hero, met by throngs of supporters, but failed as a presidential candidate, governor, general, investor, financier, and husband. His death in a poor boardinghouse, tragically, speaks for itself.

Sir John Franklin

Sir John Franklin died on June 11, 1847, on board either the *Erebus* or the *Terror* while they were still locked in the ice. The cause of his death remains a mystery and we would not even know the date of his demise had it not been for the scribbled note found in a cairn on King William Island by William Hobson during his search for remains of the expedition.

John Rae

John Rae resigned from the Hudson's Bay Company after twenty-three years of service. He and his brothers built a specially designed schooner, the *Iceberg*, hoping to explore the northern shore and find the Northwest Passage. But the boat sank in a storm before ever reaching the Arctic.

Rae went into business with his brothers in Hamilton and later married Kate Jane Alicia Thomson, many years his junior and a beautiful, talented woman. They were married for thirty-three years, had no children, and never lived permanently in Canada. Rae did not sit back and vegetate. He made long trips across Iceland and in western Canada. They had homes in London and the Orkneys.

Lady Franklin maintained a feud with Rae and was probably responsible for blocking Rae's knighthood. Rae wrote many articles and lectured extensively about Eskimo ethnography and Arctic ecology, and was elected to the Royal Society. The greatest Arctic traveler of his day, Rae died on July 22, 1893, in his bed with his wife holding his hand.

Notes on Sources

The title of this book was inspired by a quotation in *Sea of Glory: America's Voyage of Discovery* by Nathaniel Philbrick. While sailing through hundreds of icebergs in Antarctica, Lieutenant Cadwallader Ringgold turned to his captain, Lieutenant Charles Wilkes, and remarked, "This is adventuring with boldness."

The number of resources available for anyone seeking information about the ten explorers whose exploits are described here is almost infinite. Many good, short biographies are available on the Internet and can be consulted by readers looking for rapidly accessible information.

Following is a discussion of the primary sources that were used in researching this book. They are listed by chapter so that a reader interested in only one or two of the explorers can easily find the reference material that was used. Because a number of the explorers traveled in the same areas of northwest Canada, several of the sources provide equally useful information for all of those journeys.

The second section of this book, which describes how the explorers dealt with problems common to all of them, draws on the primary resources for each exploration, as well as additional special sources specific to the individual problems.

Part One

Chapter One
William Bligh (1754–1817)—Beast or Hero?

Three books provide excellent accounts of William Bligh's voyage across the Pacific. *The Bounty: The True Story of the Mutiny on the Bounty* by Caroline Alexander is a full biography of Bligh; the mutiny and its aftermath was only one part of his life. *Captain Bligh's Portable Nightmare* by John Toohey is a more racy account of the journey across the Pacific, but it is based on hard facts and gives a graphic impression of the drama of the voyage. *The Mutiny of the Bounty:*

An Illustrated Edition of Sir John Barrow's Original Account was written in 1831 by the famous second secretary of the Admiralty, John Barrow. This is a straightforward and interesting account of the mutiny and its aftermath.

William Bligh was present when Captain James Cook was killed in Hawaii. Cook had taught Bligh to be a first-class navigator, and his standards of captainship were learned from Cook. *Blue Latitudes: Boldly Going Where Captain Cook Has Gone Before* by Tony Horwitz and *Captain James Cook: A Biography* by Richard Hough provide excellent accounts of Cook's life. To understand Cook is to understand Bligh.

Alan Moorehead's *The Fatal Impact: An Account of the Invasion of the South Pacific, 1767–1840* also explains the story of the exploration of the Pacific.

Life in the Royal Navy for a young midshipman is graphically recorded in Ken McGoogan's *Ancient Mariner: The Arctic Adventures of Samuel Hearne, the Sailor who Inspired Coleridge's Masterpiece* and Peter Steele's *The Man Who Mapped the Arctic: The Intrepid Life of George Back, Franklin's Lieutenant*.

Chapter Two
Samuel Hearne (1745–1792)—First to the Coppermine

The definitive modern work on Samuel Hearne is Ken McGoogan's excellent biography *Ancient Mariner: The Arctic Adventures of Samuel Hearne, the Sailor Who Inspired Coleridge's Masterpiece*. Hearne's work with the Hudson's Bay Company is also described in a history of the company, *Empire of the Bay: The Company of Adventurers That Seized a Continent* by Peter C. Newman, which provides the essential background for understanding the lives of Hearne, Alexander Mackenzie, and John Rae as well as the power of the company. In 1879, H. M. Robinson wrote an interesting account of traveling with the voyageurs and traders, *The Great Fur Land: Sketches of Life in the Hudson's Bay Territory*. Although the account was written some years after the explorers had died, the methods of travel and the culture of the fur trade had not changed. *The Fourth World: The Heritage of the Arctic and Its Destruction* by Sam Hall describes the lives and culture of the circumpolar populations of the Eskimos and provides a useful insight into the people that Hearne and the traders of the Hudson's Bay Company dealt with. The distinguished Canadian writer Farley Mowat wrote a trilogy about the exploration of the far north of which the third volume, *Tundra: Selections from the Great Accounts of Arctic Land*, describes the journeys of Hearne and his adventures with Matonabee.

Chapter Three
Alexander Mackenzie (1762–1820)—First to the Pacific

Alexander Mackenzie's own account of his journey across the far west to the coast was republished in recent years with a useful commentary by Walter Sheppe. *Journal of the Voyage to the Pacific* is the story in Mackenzie's own words and is obviously an essential source. *First across the Continent: Sir Alexander Mackenzie* by Barry Gough also provides valuable information and insight into Mackenzie's background and motivation. All the books referred to in chapter two that describe the fur trade, the Hudson's Bay Company, and other explorations of the far north were equally valuable resources for this chapter. An additional useful source is *Ninety Degrees North: The Quest for the North Pole* by Fergus Fleming. Although it is an account of the race to the North Pole, it is an important source of information about early Arctic exploration and the hardships endured by those who lived and traveled in the far north.

The international implications of Mackenzie's expedition are described by Bernard DeVoto in *The Course of Empire*.

Chapter 4
Meriwether Lewis (1774–1809) and William Clark (1770–1838)—First Americans across the Continent

Gary Moulton's multivolume, meticulously edited *The Journals of the Lewis and Clark Expedition* are the essential sources of information about the expedition. These volumes have been the sources of most quotations and cited dates. Other quotations, including President Thomas Jefferson's instructions to Meriwether Lewis, have been taken from Donald Jackson's *Letters of the Lewis and Clark Expedition, With Related Documents*. Stephen Ambrose's *Undaunted Courage: Meriwether Lewis, Thomas Jefferson, and the Opening of the American West* is a highly detailed, readable, and exciting account of the expedition. *Exploring Lewis and Clark: Reflections on Men and Wilderness* by Thomas P. Slaughter takes an interesting and somewhat more critical look at the expedition and the behavior of Lewis and William Clark than most adulatory books. M. R. Montgomery's fast-moving account of the intertwined histories of Lewis, Zebulon Montgomery Pike, and others, *Jefferson and the Gun-Men: How the West Was Almost Lost*, emphasizes that the expedition did not occur in a political vacuum. *The Lewis and Clark Companion: An Encyclopedic Guide to the Voyage of Discovery* by Stephanie Ambrose Tubbs and Clay Jenkinson is a very useful small encyclopedia of names, including brief biographies, of all the members of the expedition, as well as information on everything from air guns to York.

Landon Y. Jones has written a definitive biogrpahy of Clark: *William Clark and the Shaping of the West*.

The interesting story of John Ledyard is told in *Blue Latitudes: Boldly Going Where Captain Cook Has Gone Before* by Tony Horwitz.

The Louisiana Purchase is well described in Paul Johnson's *A History of the American People* and *The New Encyclopedia of the American West* edited by Howard. R. Lamar.

President Jefferson's views on imperialism and his vision for the future of America are well expounded in *Jefferson's Empire: The Language of American Nationhood* by Peter S. Onuf.

The Chouteau family played a prominent part in helping with supplies. Their story has been vividly told in *Before Lewis and Clark: The Story of the Chouteaus, the French Dynasty That Ruled America's Frontier* by Shirley Christian.

Four books have been written about the health problems of the expedition, including my own, *Lewis and Clark: Doctors in the Wilderness*, as well as *Only One Man Died: The Medical Aspects of the Lewis and Clark Expedition* by Eldon P. Chuinard, *Or Perish in the Attempt: Wilderness Medicine in the Lewis* and *Clark Expedition* by David J. Peck, and *Venereal Disease and the Lewis and Clark Expedition* by Thomas P. Lowry. The first three books deal with the medical aspects, including the preparations for the journey, the medications taken, and the problems encountered on the trail, especially the death of Sergeant Charles Floyd and the illness of Sacagawea. The fourth book deals with the specific problem of venereal diseases, including a discussion of Lewis's mental state at his death.

Dr. Elaine Nelson McIntosh has scientifically analyzed the food that the men of the corps ate in *The Lewis and Clark Expedition: Food, Nutrition, and Health* and raises the interesting possibility that the illness the men came down with when they met and ate with the Nez Perce was due to eating death camas.

The interactions between the men of the expeditions and the Indians have been described by James P. Ronda in *Lewis and Clark among the Indians*. The cultural differences between the Indians of the Plains and those on the West Coast are made clear in *Naked against the Rain: The People of the Lower Columbia River, 1770–1830* by Rick Rubin. The Blackfoot interpretation of the incident up the Mariahs River that resulted in the death of one or two Indians is told to tourists who visit the fight scene by Blackfoot guides in Montana.

The men of the expedition were often attacked by bears, and this problem and their other experiences with the teeming wildlife they met are well covered in *Lewis and Clark among the Grizzlies: Legend and Legacy in the American West* by Paul Schullery and *Our Natural History: The Lessons of Lewis and Clark* by Daniel B. Botkin.

Dr. Susan Solomon has analyzed the weather encountered on the expedition in the *Bulletin of the American Meteorological Society*.

Chapter Five
Zebulon Montgomery Pike (1779–1813)—Explorer or Spy?

Donald Jackson edited Zebulon Montgomery Pike's original accounts of his journeys, *The Journals of Zebulon Montgomery Pike, With Letters and Related Documents*. Volumes one and two are invaluable sources of material. Another version of Pike's own writings, *Exploratory Travels through the Western States of North America: Comprising a Voyage from Saint Louis, on the Mississippi, to the Source of That River and a Journey through the Interior of Louisiana and the North-Eastern Provinces of New Spain* was published in 1811 and may be difficult to find, but it is a very valuable source of information. *The Lost Pathfinder: Zebulon Montgomery Pike* by William E. Hollon is a comprehensive biography and the source of the quotations from Pike in this chapter. M. R. Montgomery's book *Jefferson and the Gun-Men: How the West Was Almost Lost* interweaves the stories of Pike, Meriwether Lewis, William Clark, James Wilkinson, and Aaron Burr in an interesting manner and explores the possibility that Pike was a spy for General Wilkinson. Theodore Roosevelt in *The Winning of the West: From the Alleghenies to the Mississippi, 1769–1776* discusses Wilkinson's crimes in critical detail.

Frostbite that so incapacitated Pike's men is discussed in my own book *Lewis and Clark: Doctors in the Wilderness*.

Pike's dealings with the Indians were similar to those of Lewis and Clark and James P. Ronda's book applies to the chapter on Pike as well as to the one on Lewis.

Chapter Six
John Wesley Powell (1834–1902)—First Down the Grand Canyon

John Wesley Powell's diary was published with commentary and photographs by Eliot Porter as *Down the Colorado: Diary of the First Trip through the Grand Canyon, 1869*. This is the most available source for reading Powell's own descriptions of their trials. *Beyond the Hundredth Meridian: John Wesley Powell and the Second Opening of the West* by Wallace Stegner is the most elegantly written account of the journey. Donald Worster's account of Powell, *A River Running West: The Life of John Wesley Powell*, is a longer work that describes Powell's life in great detail. For those interested in the geology of the Grand Canyon, *The River That Flows Uphill: A Journey from the Big Bang to the Big Brain* by William H. Calvin is an erudite discussion of the topic.

Howard R. Lamar's *The New Encyclopedia of the American West* contains a detailed biography of Powell's life both as an adventurer and afterward, as a politician.

Chapter Seven
John Charles Frémont (1813–1890)—The Pathfinder

As a general introduction to the opening of the West, William H. Goetzmann's *New Lands, New Men: America and the Second Age of Discovery* is an invaluable source of information.

The information about John Charles Frémont's voyages comes from his two official reports and from letters to his wife, *The Expeditions of John Charles Frémont*, in three volumes, edited by Mary Lee Spence and Donald Jackson. Two books published in the 1850s, *Life, Explorations, and Public Services of John Charles Frémont* by Charles Wentworth Upham and *Memoir on the Life and Public Services of John Charles Frémont* by John Bigelow, both quote extensively from the letters Frémont wrote to his wife about the disaster in the San Juan Mountains.

The opening of South Pass is well told in *The Big Divide* by David Lavender. This book also tells the sad story of Frémont's journey into the San Juans. Another classic source of information about Frémont is Irving Stone's *Men to Match My Mountains: The Opening of the Far West, 1840–1900*. Frémont and his men suffered from altitude sickness while climbing in the Wind River Mountains. The causes and symptoms of this condition and the history of mountaineering are fully described in Charles Houston's *Going Higher: Oxygen, Man, and Mountains, Fifth Edition*.

The history of the overland trails, a good map, and a detailed account of Frémont's part in opening the Oregon Trail are found in *The Overland Trail* by Jay Monaghan and in *The Oregon Trail: An American Saga* by David Dary. David Lavender's *Land of Giants: The Drive to the Pacific Northwest, 1750–1950* is another valuable source of information about the exploration of the American Northwest.

The story of Frémont's most disastrous journey is graphically described in David Robert's *A Newer World: Kit Carson, John C. Frémont, and the Claiming of the American West*. While living in a small town in Colorado near the scene of the fourth expedition's disaster, Patricia Joy Richmond spent years following their trail and has provided more details about camping sites and the expedition's route through the mountains than any other author. Her book *Trail to Disaster: The Route of John Charles Frémont's Fourth Expedition from Big Timbers, Colorado, through the San Luis Valley to Taos, New Mexico* is a mine of useful information.

"The Crossing of the Sierra Nevada in the Winter of 1843–44" in Charles Neider's anthology *The Great West: A Treasury of Firsthand Accounts* is another first-person account of Frémont's winter crossing of the Sierra. *Bent's Fort* by the western historian David Lavender is a historical description of the fort where Frémont stopped on several occasions. Frémont twice crossed the desert between Utah and California and Jedediah Smith's journal, *The Travels of Jedediah Smith: A Documentary Outline Including the Journal of the Great American Pathfinder*, edited by Maurice S. Sullivan, is a graphic description of a similarly arduous trip that nearly ended in disaster.

Solomon Nunes Carvalho's account of the last journey, *Incidents and Travel and Adventure in the Far West with Colonel Frémont's Last Expedition*, provides fascinating insight into Frémont's character as well as a description of the conditions under which they struggled through the mountains.

Frémont used Sutter's Fort on several occasions and usurped Johann August Sutter's authority. The incidents involving Sutter are written in his diary, *The Diary of John Sutter*, which is also found in *The Great West*.

It is impossible to research the life of Frémont without at the same time examining the life of Kit Carson. *Kit Carson's Autobiography*, edited in modern times by Milo Milton Quaife, is an abbreviated account of his life. He was a man of few words during his life, and his autobiography is in character, but it is useful for confirming some of the incidents Frémont described. *A Newer World: Kit Carson, John C. Frémont, and the Claiming of the American West* by David Roberts is a highly readable account of the events that joined the lives of these two remarkable men that does not hesitate to condemn their sometimes egregious behavior.

Chapter Eight
Sir John Franklin (1786–1847)—The Man Who Attracted Disaster

Many aspects of Sir John Franklin's life, including an account of his first disastrous expedition, are covered in *Barrow's Boys: A Stirring Story of Daring, Fortitude, and Outright Lunacy* by Fergus Fleming, which also puts Franklin's expeditions into a historical context. The early circumnavigation of Australia is detailed in Alan Moorehead's *The Fatal Impact: An Account of the Invasion of the South Pacific, 1767–1840*. The battle of Trafalgar, in which Franklin was a young midshipman, has been described in detail by Roy Adkins in *Nelson's Trafalgar: The Battle That Changed the World*.

An account of the terrible first overland voyage is told in *Arctic Ordeal: The Journal of John Richardson, Surgeon-Naturalist, With Franklin, 1820–1822* by John Richardson.

Volumes one and three in the Mowat trilogy, *Ordeal by Ice* and *Tundra: Selections from the Great Accounts of Arctic Land Voyages*, provide good accounts of the disastrous voyage and the many attempts to find an answer to the disappearance of the ships and men. *The Arctic Grail: The Quest for the Northwest Passage and the North Pole, 1818–1909* by Pierre Berton is another well documented account of Franklin's voyages. *The Man who Mapped the Arctic: The Intrepid Life of George Back, Franklin's Lieutenant* by Peter Steele tells the story of Franklin's two overland voyages. *Ring of Ice: True Tales of Adventure, Exploration, and Arctic Life* by Peter Stark also provides useful background information.

Thirty years in the Arctic Regions by Sir John Franklin is a 1988 reprint of Sir John's original account of his earlier voyages and the only firsthand account of his two overland voyages. Most of the direct quotations of Franklin's thoughts come from this source.

In 1860, Captain Sir Francis Leopold McClintock, the first discoverer of direct evidence of the fate of the Franklin expedition, wrote about his expedition in *A Narrative of the Discovery of the Fate of Sir John Franklin and His Companions*. This book describes finding the lifeboat surrounded by four corpses that confirmed the story already brought to England by John Rae. Six years earlier, Charles Dickens had written a strongly worded article attacking the findings brought by John Rae, *The Lost Arctic Voyagers*.

Many people of the day did not believe that Eskimo informers could provide accurate information. *Unraveling the Franklin Mystery: Inuit Testimony* by David C. Woodman lays this myth to rest and presents convincing evidence of the route taken by the survivors and their last days based on testimony from the Eskimos.

The possibility of lead poisoning is discussed in *Frozen in Time: Unlocking the Secrets of the Franklin Expedition* by Owen Beattie and John Geiger, who exhumed the corpses on Beechey Island. Another possible cause of death, botulism, was more recently proposed in *Ice Blink: The Tragic Fate of Sir John Franklin's Lost Polar Expedition* by Scott Cookman. Details of the history of canned foods are available in several articles on the Internet, all of which provide the same essential details. Historical details on canning are available in Earl Chapin May's book *The Canning Clan: A Pageant of Pioneering Americans*.

Chapter Nine
John Rae (1813–1893)—The Man Who Walked on Snowshoes

Ken McGoogan has written the most informative biography of John Rae, *Fatal Passage: The Story of John Rae, the Actic Hero Time Forgot*. This biography is well researched and well written. R. L. Richard's *Dr. John Rae* is also a source of good information, but is not readily available. The Scottish National Museum's catalog of its 1993 exhibit on Rae, *No Ordinary Journey: John Rae, Arctic Explorer, 1813–1893* edited by Ian Bunyan, is a useful source of information and is beautifully illustrated.

Life for the men of the Hudson's Bay Company is well described by Peter C. Newman in *Empire of the Bay: The Company of Adventurers That Seized a*

Continent and H. M. Robinson in *The Great Fur Land: Sketches of Life in the Hudson's Bay Territory*.

George Back journeyed twice with Franklin. Two sources of information illuminate Back's explorations, "Narrative of the Arctic Land Expedition to the Mouth of the Great Fish River in the Years 1834, 1835, and 1836" by George Back in *Arctic* and *The Man Who Mapped the Arctic: The Intrepid Life of George Back, Franklin's Lieutenant* by Peter Steele. Volume one of Farley Mowat's trilogy about the Arctic, *Ordeal by Ice*, and Pierre Berton's *The Arctic Grail: The Quest for the Northwest Passage and the North Pole, 1818–1909* are both excellent references to the many explorers who ventured north during this era.

Charles Dickens's refutation of the information that Rae brought home about the fate of the Franklin expedition is available on the Internet at www. victorianweb.org/authors/dickens/arctic/pva342.html.

The quotations from Rae's writings about the Franklin expedition come from McGoogan's *Fatal Passage: The Story of John Rae, The Arctic Hero Time Forgot*, Steele's *The Man Who Mapped the Arctic: The Intrepid Life of George Back, Franklin's Lieutenant*, and David C. Woodman's book *Unraveling the Franklin Mystery: Inuit Testimony*, which confirms Rae's belief that Ekimo testimony was reliable.

Rae's interactions with the Eskimo were important. The *Book of the Eskimos* by the famous Arctic explorer Peter Freuchen and *The Fourth World: The Heritage of the Arctic and its Destruction* both provide important insights into Eskimo culture.

Part Two

The last five chapters of the book describe problems that were faced by all the explorers. These chapters were based on the previous accounts of their expeditions as well as specific sources dealing with the problems the explorers encountered.

Chapter Ten
Survival—Who Lives, Who Dies, and Why

Five books were used as references to discuss theories and practices of survival: *Deep Survival: Who Lives, Who Dies, and Why* by Laurence Gonzales, *Survival Psychology* by John Leach, *Life at the Extremes: The Science of Survival* by Frances Ashcroft, *How to Survive on Land and Sea, Fourth Edition* by Frank C. Craighead and John J. Craighead, and *NOLS Wilderness First Aid* by Tod Schimelpfening and Linda Lindsey. *In the Heart of the Sea: The Tragedy of the Whaleship Essex* by Nathaniel Philbrick was used as an example of desperate survival. *Shackleton's Way: Leadership Lessons from the Great Antarctic Explorer* by Margot Morrell and Stephanie Capparell demonstrates how good leadership enhances the chances of survival.

The importance of weather in survival is the subject of *The Coldest March: Scott's Fatal Antarctic Expedition* by Susan Solomon, an account of Captain Robert Scott's final expedition to the South Pole. Solomon also wrote an important paper analyzing the weather during the Meriwether Lewis and William Clark expedition. That the environment is not an active participant in survival is brought out in Spencer F. Chapman's *The Jungle Is Neutral: A Soldier's Two-Year Escape from the Japanese Army*.

Chapter Eleven
Marching on Their Stomachs—Food, Famine, and Cannibalism

Most accounts of the explorations contained details of the food eaten. One aspect, however, needed special attention: starvation. All the expeditions experienced periods of severe hunger, and some of them went through times of genuine starvation and even cannibalism. *The Medical History of the Bengal Famine, 1943–44* by K. S. Fitch describes a famine that occurred in India in the middle of World War II in which 2 to 3 million people died. Cannibalism was not noted during that famine, but it was described in *The 900 Days: The Siege of Leningrad* by Harrison E. Salisbury. *In the Heart of the Sea: The Tragedy of the Whaleship Essex* by Nathaniel Philbrick tells a harrowing tale of survival and cannibalism after the sinking of a whaling ship in the Pacific Ocean. "The Donner Party" is another historic example of survival through cannibalism and is described in *Men to Match My Mountains: The Opening of the Far West, 1840–1900* by Irving Stone.

Volumes one and two of *The Biology of Human Starvation* edited by Ancel Keys, et al., are accounts of classic experiments conducted on volunteers at the University of Minnesota during World War II to determine the physiologic effects of starvation. The quotation by G. B. Leyton comes from volume two in a chapter on the history of starvation. The details of starvation in concentration camps during World War II come from two books, *Courage under Siege: Starvation, Disease, and Death in the Warsaw Ghetto* by Charles G. Roland and *Factories of Death: Japanese Biological Warfare, 1932–45, and the American Cover-up* by Sheldon H. Harris. *The Lewis and Clark Expedition: Food, Nutrition, and Health* by Dr. Elaine Nelson McIntosh is a small, but detailed, analysis of the diet eaten during the expedition.

Chapter Twelve
Pox and Poisons—Disease, Injuries, Medicine, and Morale

A History of Medicine by Douglas Guthrie, *Blood and Guts: A Short History of Medicine* by Roy Porter, *The Cambridge Illustrated History of Medicine* by Roy Porter, and *American Indian Medicine* by Virgil J. Vogel all provided the basic background information on the state of medical knowledge at the time of these expeditions. Smallpox was a deadly threat throughout this period and decimated the American Indian population. *Pox Americana: The Great Smallpox Epidemic of 1775–82* by Elizabeth A. Fenn is a carefully researched account of the spread of smallpox throughout North America.

Thomas Jefferson's views on doctors were written in a letter from the president to Dr. Caspar Wistar, quoted in *Only One Man Died: The Medical Aspects of the Lewis and Clark Expedition* by Eldon P. Chuinard.

Venereal diseases were a serious problem on the Meriwether Lewis and William Clark and William Bligh expeditions. *The History of Syphilis* by Claude

Quétel, *Pox, Genius, Madness, and the Mysteries of Syphilis* by Deborah Hayden, and *Plagues and Poxes: The Impact of Human History on Epidemic Disease* by Alfred J. Bollet cover the broader aspects of these diseases. *Venereal Disease and the Lewis and Clark Expedition* by Thomas P. Lowry deals specifically with the problems on the Lewis and Clark expedition, but also discusses the broader, controversial origins of syphilis.

Only *One Man Died: The Medical Aspects of the Lewis and Clark Expedition* by Eldon P. Chuinard, my own *Lewis and Clark: Doctors in the Wilderness*, and *Or Perish in the Attempt: Wilderness Medicine in the Lewis and Clark Expedition* by David J. Peck describe all the medical problems on the Lewis and Clark expedition and cover the wider aspects of disease and trauma in the wilderness. These books also describe the medical kits and medications taken on the expedition. Frostbite and hypothermia, problems on several expeditions, are described in detail in my book *Lewis and Clark: Doctors in the Wilderness*.

The possibility of severe arrow wounds was a constant threat on many expeditions. The severity of arrow wounds is described in the "Report on Surgical Cases Treated in the Army of the United States 1865–1871" written in 1871 by George Otis and republished in 1974.

Malaria may have affected some of the expeditions in which "ague" was described as an *illness*. *Mosquito: A Natural History of Our Most Persistent and Deadly Foe* by Andrew Spielman and Michael D'Antonio not only covers malaria, but also describes the general biology of mosquitoes that plagued every expedition.

The special medical problems of Sir John Franklin's expedition are discussed in Scott Cookman's *Ice Blink: The Tragic Fate of Sir John Franklin's Lost Polar Expedition* and *Frozen in Time: Unlocking the Secrets of the Franklin Expedition* by Owen Beattie and John Geiger.

Chapter Thirteen
Dealing with the Neighbors—Contacts with Indigenous People
Lewis and Clark among the Indians by James P. Ronda explains the complicated dealings between the Indians and the leaders and men of the expedition. *Naked against the Rain: The People of the Lower Columbia, 1770–1830* by Rick Rubin explains the great cultural differences between the Plains Indians and those around Fort Clatsop. *The Character of Meriwether Lewis: "Completely Metamorphosed" in the American West* by the Meriwether Lewis and William Clark scholar Clay Straus Jenkinson sheds light on the reasons behind Lewis's reactions to the Indians' behavior.

John Colter: His Years in the Rockies by Burton Harris, *The Mountain Men: The Dramatic History and Lore of the First Frontiersmen* by George Laycock, *Jedediah Smith and the Mountain Men of the West* by John Logan Allen, and *Across the Wide Missouri* by Bernard de Voto explain not only the history of the mountain men, but also how their exploits affected the opening of the West and the warfare with the Indians that followed the Lewis and Clark expedition. *Overland with Kit Carson: A Narrative of the Old Spanish Trail in '48* by George Douglas Brewerton deals specifically with John Charles Frémont's great guide, Kit Carson, who was both an Indian fighter and Indian protector.

The interactions that Samuel Hearne, Alexander Mackenzie, Sir John Franklin, and John Rae had with the First Nations and Eskimos of Canada are described in the books listed above in each expeditions' particular chapter.

Chapter Fourteen
Leadership—What Made Them Tick?

The general qualities and classifications of leadership are covered in *Leadership* by James Macgregor Burns and *Certain Trumpets: The Nature of Leadership* by Gary Wills.

Military leadership, which is very similar to the leadership required on these expeditions, has been written about in *The Mask of Command* by John Keegan, *On War and Leadership: The Words of Combat Commanders from Frederick the Great to Norman Schwarzkopf* by Owen Connelly, and *On Point: The United States Army in Operation Iraqi Freedom* by Colonel Gregory Fontenot, Lieutenant Cololnel E. J. Degen, and Lieutenant Colonel David Tohn.

Earl Haig's sometimes disastrous leadership is described in *The First World War: A Complete History* by Martin Gilbert.

Stephen Ambrose praised the leadership of Meriwether Lewis and William Clark in *Undaunted Courage: Meriwether Lewis, Thomas Jefferson, and the Opening of the American West* and Jack Uldrich has examined the leadership of the same expedition in *Into the Unknown: Leadership Lessons from the Lewis and Clark's Daring Westward Expedition*. Another example of superb leadership is found in *Shackleton's Way: Leadership Lessons from the Great Antarctic Explorer* by Margot Morell and Stephanie Caparell. This book relates Shackleton's success to examples of modern business success, a theme also covered in Bob Baron's book *Pioneers and Plodders: The American Entrepreneurial Spirit*.

Courage, an essential ingredient for all leaders, is well covered in Ian William Miller's *The Mystery of Courage*.

Sources

Adkins, Roy. *Nelson's Trafalgar: The Battle That Changed the World*. New York: Viking Press, 2005.

Alexander, Caroline. *The Bounty: The True Story of the Mutiny on the Bounty*. New York: Viking Press, 2003.

Allen, John Logan. *Jedediah Smith and the Mountain Men of the American West*. New York: Chelsea House Publishers, 1991.

Ambrose, Stephen. *Undaunted Courage: Meriwether Lewis, Thomas Jefferson, and the Opening of the American West*. New York: Simon & Schuster, Inc., 1996.

Ashcroft, Frances. *Life at the Extremes: The Science of Survival*. London: Flamingo Press, 2001.

Back, George. "Narrative of the Arctic Land Expedition to the Mouth of the Great Fish River in the Years 1834, 1835, and 1836." *Arctic* 53, no. 2 (June 1, 2000): 199–200.

Baron, Robert C. *Pioneers and Plodders: The American Entrepreneurial Spirit*. Golden, Colo.: Fulcrum Publishing, 2004.

Beattie, Owen and John Geiger. *Frozen in Time: Unlocking the Secrets of the Franklin Expedition*. New York: E. P. Dutton, 1988.

Berton, Pierre. *The Arctic Grail: The Quest for the Northwest Passage and the North Pole, 1818–1909*. New York: Viking Press, 1988.

Bigelow, John. *Memoir on the Life and Public Services of John Charles Frémont*. New York: H. W. Derby and Co., 1856.

Bollet, Alfred J. *Plagues and Poxes: The Impact of Human History on Epidemic Disease*. New York: Demos Medical Publishing, 2004.

Botkin, Daniel B. *Our Natural History: The Lessons of Lewis and Clark*. New York: Penguin Putnam, 1995.

Brewerton, George Douglas. *Overland with Kit Carson: A Narrative of the Old Spanish Trail in '48*. Lincoln: University of Nebraska Press, 1993.

Bunyan, Ian, et. al. *No Ordinary Journey: John Rae, Arctic Explorer, 1813–1893*. Montreal: McGill-Queen's University Press, 1993.

Burns, James Macgregor. *Leadership*. New York: Harper & Row, 1978.

Calvin, William H. *The River That Flows Uphill: A Journey from the Big Bang to the Big Brain*. San Francisco: Sierra Club, 1986.

Carpenter, Kenneth J. *The History of Scurvy and Vitamin C*. Cambridge: Cambridge University Press, 1986.

Carson, Kit. *Kit Carson's Autobiography*, ed. Milo Milton Quaiffe. Lincoln: University of Nebraska Press, 1967.

Carvalho, Solomon Nunes. *Incidents and Travel and Adventure in the Far West: With Colonel Frémont's Last Expedition*. Lincoln: University of Nebraska Press, 2004.

Chaffin, Tom. *Pathfinder: John Charles Frémont and the Course of American Empire*. New York: Hill and Wang, 2002.

Chapman, F. Spencer. *The Jungle Is Neutral: A Soldier's Two-Year Escape from the Japanese Army*. New York: W. W. Norton & Company, 1949.

Christian, Shirley. *Before Lewis and Clark: The Story of the Chouteaus, the French Dynasty That Ruled America's Frontier*. New York: Farrar, Straus and Giroux, 2004.

Chuinard, Eldon P. *Only One Man Died: The Medical Aspects of the Lewis and Clark Expedition*. Fairfield, Wash.: Ye Galleon Press, 1999.

Connelly, Owen. *On War and Leadership: The Words of Combat Commanders from Frederick the Great to Norman Schwarzkopf*. Princeton: Princeton University Press, 2002.

Cookman, Scott. *Ice Blink: The Tragic Fate of Sir John Franklin's Lost Polar Expedition*. New York: John Wiley and Sons, Inc., 2000.

Craighead, Frank C., Jr., and John J. Craighead. *How to Survive on Land and Sea, Fourth Edition*. Annapolis, Md.: Naval Institute Press, 1984.

Dary, David. *The Oregon Trail: An American Saga*. New York: Alfred A. Knopf, 2004.

DeVoto, Bernard. *Across the Wide Missouri*. Boston: Houghton Mifflin Company, 1947.

———. *The Course of Empire*. Boston: Houghton Mifflin Company, 1952.

Dickens, Charles. "The Lost Arctic Voyagers." 1854. www.victorianweb.org/authors/dickens/arctic/pva342.html

Dolnick, Edward. *Down the Great Unknown: John Wesley Powell's Journey of Discovery and Tragedy through the Great Canyon*. New York: HarperCollins, 2001.

Fenn, Elizabeth A. *Pox Americana: The Great Smallpox Epidemic of 1775–82*. New York: Hill and Wang, 2001.

Fitch, K. S. *Medical History of the Bengal Famine, 1943–44*. Calcutta: Government of India Press, 1946.

Fleming, Fergus. *Barrow's Boys: A Stirring Story of Daring, Fortitude, and Outright Lunacy*. London: Granta Books, 1998.

———. *Ninety Degrees North: The Quest for the North Pole*. New York: Grove Press, 2001.

Fontenot, Colonel Gregory, Lieutenant Colonel E. J. Degen, and Lieutenant Colonel David Tohn. *On Point: The United States Army in Operation Iraqi Freedom*. Annapolis, Md.: Naval Institute Press, 2005.

Franklin, Sir John. *Thirty Years in the Arctic Regions*. Lincoln: University of Nebraska Press, 1988.

Frémont, John Charles. "The Crossing of the Sierra Nevada in the Winter of 1843–44." In *The Great West: A Treasury of Firsthand Accounts*, ed. Charles Neider. New York: Bonanza Books, 1958.

Freuchen, Peter. *Book of the Eskimos*. New York: Fawcett Premier, 1961.

Gilbert, Martin. *The First World War: A Complete History*. New York: Henry Holt and Company, 1994.

Goetzmann, William H. *New Lands, New Men: America and the Second Great Age of Discovery*. Austin, Tex.: Texas State Historical Association, 1995.

Gonzales, Laurence. *Deep Survival: Who Lives, Who Dies, and Why*. New York: W. W. Norton & Company, 2003.

Gough, Barry. *First across the Continent: Sir Alexander Mackenzie*. Norman: University of Oklahoma Press, 1997.

Guthrie, Douglas. *A History of Medicine*. London: Thomas Nelson and Son, 1945.

Hall, Sam. *The Fourth World: The Heritage of the Arctic and Its Destruction*. New York: Alfred A. Knopf, 1987.

Harris, Burton. *John Colter: His Years in the Rockies*. Lincoln: University of Nebraska Press, 1993.

Harris, Sheldon H. *Factories of Death: Japanese Biological Warfare, 1932–45, and the American Cover-Up*. London: Routledge, 1994.

Hayden, Deborah. *Pox, Genius, Madness, and the Mysteries of Syphilis*. New York: Basic Books, 2003.

Hollon, William E. *The Lost Pathfinder: Zebulon Montgomery Pike*. Norman: University of Oklahoma Press, 1949.

Horwitz, Tony. *Blue Latitudes: Boldly Going Where Captain Cook Has Gone Before*. New York: Henry Holt and Company, 2002.

Hough, Richard. *Captain James Cook: A Biography*. New York: W. W. Norton & Company, 1994.

Houston, Charles S., M.D., David Harris, and Ellen Zeman. *Going Higher: Oxygen, Man, and Mountains, Fifth Edition*. Seattle: Wash.: The Mountaineers Books, 2005.

———— and Robert H. Bates. *K2: The Savage Mountain*. New York: McGraw Hill, 1954.

Jackson, Donald, ed. *Letters of the Lewis and Clark Expedition, With Related Documents, 1783–1854*. Urbana: University of Illinois Press, 1962.

Jenkinson, Clay Straus. *The Character of Meriwether Lewis: "Completely Metamorphosed in the American West."* Reno, Nev.: Marmath Press, 2000.

Johnson, Paul. *A History of the American People*. New York: HarperCollins, 1998.

Jones, Landon Y. *William Clark and the Shaping of the West*. New York: Hill and Wang, 2004.

Keegan, John. *The Mask of Command*. New York: Viking Press, 1987.

Keithley, George. *The Donner Party*. New York: George Braziller, 1972.

Kennedy, Gavin, ed. *The Mutiny of the Bounty: An Illustrated Edition of Sir John Barrow's Original Account*. Boston: David R. Godine, 1980.

Keys, Ancel, et. al., eds. *The Biology of Human Starvation, vols. I and II*. Minneapolis: University of Minnesota Press, 1950.

Lamar, Howard R., ed. *The New Encyclopedia of the American West*. New Haven, Conn.: Yale University Press, 1999.

Lavender, David. *Bent's Fort*. Garden City, N.Y.: Doubleday and Company, Inc., 1954.

————. *Land of Giants: The Drive to the Pacific Northwest, 1750–1950*. Garden City, N.Y.: Doubleday and Company, Inc., 1958.

————. *The Big Divide*. Edison, N.J.: Castle Books, 2001.

Laycock, George. *The Mountain Men: The Dramatic History and Lore of the First Frontiersmen*. New York: The Lyons Press, 1988.

Leach John. *Survival Psychology*. Washington Square, N.Y.: New York University Press, 1994.

Lowry, Thomas P. *Venereal Disease and the Lewis and Clark Expedition*. Lincoln: University of Nebraska Press, 2004.

Mackenzie, Alexander. *Journal of the Voyage to the Pacific*, ed. Walter Sheppe. New York: Dover Publications, 1995.

May, Earl Chapin. *The Canning Clan: A Pageant of Pioneering Americans*. New York: The Macmillan Company, 1937.

McClintock, Sir Francis Leopold. *A Narrative of the Discovery of the Fate of Sir John Franklin and His Companions*. Boston: Ticknor and Fields, 1860.

McGoogan, Ken. *Ancient Mariner: The Arctic Adventures of Samuel Hearne, the Sailor Who Inspired Coleridge's Masterpiece*. New York: Carroll and Graf, 2004.

———. *Fatal Passage: The Story of John Rae, the Arctic Hero Time Forgot*. New York: Caroll and Graf, 2001.

McIntosh, Elaine Nelson, Ph.D., R.D. *The Lewis and Clark Expedition: Food, Nutrition, and Health*. Sioux Falls, S.Dak.: The Center for Western Studies, Augustana College, 2003.

Miller, William Ian. *The Mystery of Courage*. Cambridge: Harvard University Press, 2000.

Monaghan, Jay. *The Overland Trail*. Indianapolis, Md.: Bobbs-Merrill Company, 1947.

Montgomery, M. R. *Jefferson and the Gun-Men: How the West Was Almost Lost*. New York: Crown Publishers, 2000.

Moorehead, Alan. *The Fatal Impact: An Account of the Invasion of the South Pacific, 1767–1840*. New York: Harper & Row, 1966.

Morrell, Margot and Stephanie Capparell. *Shackleton's Way: Leadership Lessons from the Great Antarctic Explorer*. London: Nicholas Brealey, 2001.

Moulton, Gary, ed. *The Journals of the Lewis and Clark Expedition, vols. 1–11*. Lincoln: University of Nebraska Press, 1986–1997.

Mowat, Farley, ed. *Ordeal by Ice: The Search for the Northwest Passage (Top of the World Trilogy), vol. 1*. Toronto: McClelland and Stewart, Ltd., 1989.

———. *Tundra: Selections from the Great Accounts of Arctic Land Voyages (Top of the World Trilogy), vol. III*. Toronto: McClelland and Stewart, Ltd., 1989.

Newman, Peter C. *Empire of the Bay: The Company of Adventurers That Seized a Continent*. New York: Penguin Books, 2000.

Onuf, Peter S. *Jefferson's Empire: The Language of American Nationhood*. Charlottesville, Va.: University Press of Virginia, 2000.

Otis, George A. "Report on Surgical Cases Treated in the Army of the United States 1865–1871," circular no. 3. New York: Sol Lewis, 1974. Reprinted from a report by the War Department, Surgeon General's Office.

Paton, Bruce C., M.D. *Lewis and Clark: Doctors in the Wilderness*. Golden, Colo.: Fulcrum Publishing, 2001.

Peck, David J., D.O. *Or Perish in the Attempt: Wilderness Medicine in the Lewis and Clark Expedition*. Helena, Mont.: Farcountry Press, 2002.

Philbrick, Nathaniel. *In the Heart of the Sea: The Tragedy of the Whaleship Essex*. New York: Viking, 2000.

———. *Sea of Glory: America's Voyage of Discovery: The U.S. Exploring Expedition 1838–1842*. New York: Viking, 2003.

Pike, Zebulon Montgomery. *Exploratory Travels through the Western Territories of North America: Comprising a Voyage from St. Louis, on the Mississippi, to the Source of That River and a Journey through the Interior of Louisiana and the North-Eastern Provinces of New Spain*. London: W. H. Lawrence & Co., 1811.

————. *The Journals of Zebulon Montgomery Pike, With Letters and Related Documents, vol II*, ed. Donald Jackson. Norman: University of Oklahoma Press, 1966.

Plutarch. *The Life of Alexander the Great*, trans. John Dryden. New York: The Modern Library, 2004.

Porter, Roy, ed. *Blood and Guts: A Short History of Medicine*. W. W. Norton & Company, 2002.

————. *The Cambridge Illustrated History of Medicine*. Cambridge: Cambridge University Press, 1996.

Powell, John Wesley. *Down the Colorado: Diary of the First Trip through the Grand Canyon, 1869*. New York: E. P. Dutton, 1969.

Quétel, Claude. *The History of Syphilis*. Baltimore, Md.: Johns Hopkins University Press, 1990.

Richards, R. L. *Dr. John Rae*. North Yorkshire, England: Caedmon of Whitby Publishers, 1985.

Richardson, John. *Arctic Ordeal: The Journal of John Richardson, Surgeon-Naturalist, With Franklin, 1820–1822*, ed. C. Stuart Houston. Montreal: McGill-Queen's University Press, 1984.

Richmond, Patricia Joy. *Trail to Disaster: The Route of John Charles Frémont's Fourth Expedition from Big Timbers, Colorado, through the San Luis Valley to Taos, New Mexico*. Denver: Colorado Historical Society, 1990.

Roberts, David. *A Newer World: Kit Carson, John C. Frémont, and the Claiming of the American West*. New York: Simon & Schuster, Inc., 2000.

Robinson, H. M. *The Great Fur Land: Sketches of Life in the Hudson's Bay Territory*. New York: G. P. Putnam's Sons, 1879.

Roland, Charles G. *Courage under Siege: Starvation, Disease, and Death in the Warsaw Ghetto*. New York: Oxford University Press, 1992.

Ronda, James P. *Lewis and Clark among the Indians*. Lincoln: University of Nebraska Press, 1984.

Roosevelt, Theodore. *The Winning of the West: From the Alleghenies to the Mississippi, 1769–1776, a modern abridgement with introduction by Christopher Lasch*. New York: Hastings House, 1963.

Ross, W. Gillies. "The Type and Number of Expeditions in the Franklin Search 1847–1859." *Arctic* 55, no. 1 (March 1, 2002): 57.

Rubin, Rick. *Naked against the Rain: The People of the Lower Columbia River, 1770–1830*. Portland, Ore.: Far Shore Press, 1999.

Salisbury, Harrison E. *The 900 Days: The Siege of Leningrad*. New York: Harper & Row, 1969.

Schimelpfenig, Tod and Linda Lindsey. *NOLS Wilderness First Aid, Third Edition*. Mechanicsburg, Pa.: Stackpole Books, 2000.

Schullery, Paul. *Lewis and Clark among the Grizzlies: Legend and Legacy in the American West*. Guilford, Conn.: Falcon, 2002.

Slaughter, Thomas P. *Exploring Lewis and Clark: Reflections on Men and Wilderness*. New York: Alfred A. Knopf, 2003.

Smith, Jedediah. *The Travels of Jedediah Smith: A Documentary Outline Including the Journal of the Great American Pathfinder*, ed. Maurice S. Sullivan. Lincoln: University of Nebraska Press, 1992.

Solomon, Susan. *The Coldest March: Scott's Fatal Antarctic Expedition*. New Haven, Conn.: Yale University Press, 2001.

———— and John S. Daniel. "Lewis and Clark: Pioneering Meteorological Observers in the American West," from the *Bulletin of the American Meteorological*

Society 85, no. 9 (2004): 1273–1288.

Spence, Mary Lee and Donald Jackson, eds. *The Expeditions of John Charles Frémont, vols. 1–3*. Urbana: University of Illinois Press, 1970–1980.

Spielman, Andrew and Michael D'Antonio. *Mosquito: A Natural History of our Most Persistent and Deadly Foe*. New York: Hyperion, 2001.

Stark, Peter, ed. *Ring of Ice: True Tales of Adventure, Exploration, and Arctic Life*. New York: The Lyons Press, 2000.

Steele, Peter. *The Man Who Mapped the Arctic: The Intrepid Life of George Back, Franklin's Lieutenant*. Vancouver: Raincoast Books, 2003.

Stegner, Wallace. *Beyond the Hundredth Meridian: John Wesley Powell and the Second Opening of the West*. New York: Houghton Miflin, 1954.

Stone, Irving. *Men to Match My Mountains: The Opening of the Far West, 1840–1900*. Edison, N.J.: Castle Books, 2001.

Sutter, John. "The Diary of John Sutter." In *The Great West: A Treasury of Firsthand Accounts*, ed. Charles Neider. New York: Bonanza Books, 1958.

Toohey, John. *Captain Bligh's Portable Nightmare*. London: Fourth Estate, 1999.

Tubbs, Stephanie Ambrose and Clay Jenkinson. *The Lewis and Clark Companion: An Encyclopedic Guide to the Voyage of Discovery*. New York: Henry Holt and Company, 2003.

Uldrich, Jack. *Into the Unknown: Leadership Lessons from Lewis and Clark's Daring Westward Expedition*. New York: American Management Association, 2004.

Upham, Charles Wentworth. *Life, Explorations, and Public Services of John Charles Frémont*. Boston: Ticknor and Fields, 1856.

Vogel, Virgil J. *American Indian Medicine*. Norman: University of Oklahoma Press, Norman, 1970.

Wills, Gary. *Certain Trumpets: The Nature of Leadership*. New York: Simon & Schuster, Inc., 1994.

Woodman, David C. *Unraveling the Franklin Mystery: Inuit Testimony*. Montreal and London: McGill-Queens University Press, 1991.

Worster, Donald. *A River Running West: The Life of John Wesley Powell*. New York: Oxford University Press, 2001.

Index

White, Elijah, 75
Whitehouse, Joseph, 199
Wilkinson, James, 45, 46–47, 52–53, 195
Willard, Alexander, 37
Williams, William Sherley "Old Bill Williams," 88–89, 90, 144
Windsor, Richard, 146, 208

Winning of the West, The (Roosevelt), 46
Wootton, "Uncle Dick," 88
Wyatt, Sir Francis, 182

Yellowstone River, 43
Young, Brigham, 93

Also by Bruce Paton

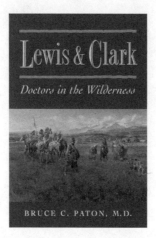

Lewis & Clark: Doctors in the Wilderness

A vivid account of the dangers, emergencies, and medical problems encountered during America's most famous expedition, *Lewis & Clark: Doctors in the Wilderness* examines early nineteenth-century medicine and offers a unique perspective on the journey that opened the American West.

" ... an interesting labor of love, a fascinating footnote to an epic journey, and worthwhile reading for the armchair traveler."
—*The Roanoke Times*